NEW E   RAPY

NEW ESSAYS
IN DRAMA THERAPY

Unfinished Business

By

ROBERT J. LANDY

Charles C Thomas
PUBLISHER • LTD.
SPRINGFIELD • ILLINOIS • U.S.A.

Published and Distributed Throughout the World by

CHARLES C THOMAS • PUBLISHER, LTD.
2600 South First Street
Springfield, Illinois 62704

© 2001 by CHARLES C THOMAS • PUBLISHER, LTD.

ISBN 0-398-07235-3 (hard)
ISBN 0-398-07236-1 (paper)

Library of Congress Catalog Card Number: 2001037599

With THOMAS BOOKS *careful attention is given to all details of manufacturing
and design. It is the Publisher's desire to present books that are satisfactory as to their
physical qualities and artistic possibilities and appropriate for their particular use.*
THOMAS BOOKS *will be true to those laws of quality that assure a good name
and good will.*

Printed in the United States of America
MM-R-3

Library of Congress Cataloging-in-Publication Data

Landy, Robert J.
    New essays in drama drama therapy : unfinished business / by Robert J. Landy
    p.cm.
    Includes bibliographical references and index.
    ISBN 0-398-07235-3 (hardback) -- ISBN 0-398-07236-1 (paper)
    1. Psydhodrama. I. Title.

RC489.P7 L345 2001
616.89'1523--dc21   2001037599

In memory of Edith and George Landy

PREFACE

In a recent drama therapy session, a client named Ray invoked a striking image. He saw himself holding onto a thick rope. The rope was attached to a sailing vessel which he identified as The Mayflower. Although he imagined that all the significant people in his life sailed on The Mayflower, he told me that the ship was empty.

"Then why are you holding onto the rope?" I asked.

"I don't know," he replied. "I just can't let go of all the ghosts."

The subtitle of this new book of essays is "Unfinished Business." As the author of the following 12 essays written over a period of five years, one of my major concerns is to examine the possibilities of letting go and the notion that by doing so, individuals like Ray move closer to an effective closure. Throughout this book, I hold the assumption that an effective closure will come as individuals attempt to complete their unfinished business. By unfinished business I mean the many unresolved, uncomfortable moments that are avoided or denied, that spring from uneasy intimacies and unsatisfactory attachments, from the failure to speak one's mind, to assert one's will, and to acknowledge and correct a real or imagined wrong.

Another more general concern is to continue my work toward the shaping of the broad parameters of drama therapy. Now in its third decade of life as an established profession, the field of drama therapy is still a bit sketchy in terms of clear self-identity, clinical efficacy, means of assessment and evaluation and effective research protocols. The several pioneers in Britain and America have collectively created a substantial body of work, each one defining his/her territory so well that the field can now point to recognizable models. I think first of the early work of Peter Slade in England who conceived of the spontaneous dramatic activity of children as an art form and a therapy. Significantly, Slade created a developmental model that spoke to the emerging dramatic forms created by children.

Marian Lindkvist founded Sesame Institute in London which spearheaded her ideas of integrating drama with movement and art. Her cross-cultural research supported her approach to training and clinical treatment. Sue Jennings, who began her creative therapeutic work with disabled individuals, offers several challenging and influential models of drama therapy, including a powerful approach to working therapeutically with dramatic texts. Perhaps her most influential model is that of embodiment-projection-role (EPR), which conceives of human development in terms of movement from the body to the developing ability to take on and play out roles.

Alida Gersie's work in England and Holland has also been pioneering in presenting a model of therapeutic storymaking based upon a cross-cultural understanding of stories and their medicines. And Ann Catternach contributes a model of play therapy based upon a deep understanding of the stories and enactments of abused children.

In the United States, the two major academic training programs in Drama Therapy offer two separate models. Renée Emunah at the California Institute for Integral Studies works from an eclectic five-phase model of dramatic play, scenework, role play, culminating enactment and dramatic ritual. And I work from a role perspective in theory and practice, an approach which will be amply explored in this book.

David Read Johnson continues to be one of the leading American drama therapists whose model of developmental transformations, an improvisationally-based approach of "playing the unplayable," has strongly influenced many practitioners and researchers. Other American pioneers include Eleanor Irwin who works from a psychoanalytic model, Pat Sternberg and Nina Garcia, who work from a sociodramatic model, and Pam Dunne, who has developed a narrative approach to drama therapy. Among the newer generations of practitioners, there are even more approaches to drama therapy and more ways to conceive its theoretical framework and its application to mental health and community life. In a recent anthology (Lewis and Johnson, 2000), 16 American approaches are highlighted. The field has also developed internationally, in countries including Israel, Greece, Italy and Germany. With such a cornucopia of figures, where is the ground?

This volume attempts to lay more of the groundwork within a consistent framework of theory and practice. Rather than an anthology of many voices, it offers a single voice intoned in many keys. It is not at all accurate to say that I am attempting to finish the business that has been pioneered for the past several decades. Rather, I am taking a next step, extending the work that Peter Slade envisioned in the 1950s, that Sue Jennings envisioned in the 1960s and that several other pioneers pursued through the end of the millenium. And I am taking another step beyond my first volume of essays (Landy, 1996), whose theme was the double life and whose concern was primarily theoretical.

This book focuses upon theory and practice, as did its predecessor. But it moves into new territory by addressing issues of assessment, supervision and termination. And it does so in a style that becomes increasingly personal, measuring the meaning of the process of drama therapy against my awakening as a teacher, healer, scholar, father and son.

Notable in this volume is attention to cultural and spiritual issues, the former represented by an essay concerning my dialogue with Chinese culture in Taiwan. The latter is explored in "How Children See God," where I offer some thoughts on ways to access and assess the spiritual lives of children. This work has since been expanded into two books: *How We See God and Why It Matters* (Landy, 2001) and *God Lives in Glass* (Landy, 2001).

In the two essays, "Fathers and Sons" and "Open Cabinets," I attempt to integrate most fully the theoretical and the personal in wrestling with issues of intimacy and responsibility.

Throughout this book I play with some of the intricacies of a model that springs from my earlier work, that of role, counterrole and guide (R-CR-G). It is not only the center of my approach to drama therapy, but also my essential way of seeing the interplay of shadow and light, evil and good, death and life, adult and child. This model is similar to the Western philosophical notion of thesis, antithesis, synthesis, the Chinese divination system of trigrams found in the *I-Ching*, the Christian holy trinity of Father, Son and Holy Spirit, and the Hindu holy trinity of Rama, Vishnu and Shiva—the Creator, Preserver and Destroyer. It mimics the primary biological reality of Mother, Father, Child.

The role trinity moves beyond the notion of polarity, of either/or, into the more complex territory of the continuum, of both/and. It implies an acceptance of metaphor and paradox as essential aspects of the human condition. Like the aesthetic experience itself, this model of healing is based upon an openness to parts of the psyche and of the world that are irrational, intuitive, unseen and mysterious. It is a scheme that attempts to hold together pieces of existence that are perpetually in motion.

In the clinical vignette I mentioned earlier, there are three roles present: a man named Ray holds onto an empty boat called The Mayflower by means of a rope. "Why not let go?" I ask. He does not know the answer, responding only: "I just can't let go of all the ghosts." And suddenly the role of the boat expands. The empty Mayflower is full of ghosts. Although this striking image might be a guiding one, it also might be a counterpart of Ray, who needs to discover a way to release the vessel that hold his fears.

Ray comes to therapy hoping that I can help him to let go and complete his unfinished business. I am his guide. But I cannot cut the rope for him. I can only play the witness. As such, I stand by him, waiting for him to transform the role of the one who holds onto the ghost vessel to that of the one who lets go. I am there to witness his discovery of a guide figure within himself, a vessel that can carry him and hold him safely on dry land, a surgeon that can cut the umbilicus that has bound him to his traumatic past. I am there with him to watch The Mayflower sail out to sea and drop off the edge of the earth.

To complete unfinished business, I suggest in this book, individuals need to invoke imagery rich enough in paradox, in role and counterrole, and work with it as long as it takes to cut loose from the ghosts, those frightening figures from the past that sail into the unconscious at will. And because this task is a dangerous one, they need effective guides. The first one, the drama therapist, is a stand-in. The true guide is an inner figure brave enough to recognize and confront the ferocity of the ghosts, wise enough to understand their illusory substance, and practical enough to drop the rope and move onto dry land.

I write this book with the thought that to complete unfinished business and to live safely on the dry land of consciousness, one needs to have sailed out on dark unconscious seas again and again.

R.J.L.

ACKNOWLEDGMENTS

During my years as Editor-in-Chief of *The Arts in Psychotherapy*, I took great pleasure in my dialogue and friendship with Sylvia Halpern, the managing editor. Sylvia was instrumental in encouraging me to keep writing about drama therapy and the creative arts therapies at an early point in my career. With her guidance I persisted, one result of which is this collection of essays. Sylvia passed away in 2001 at age 90. I will sorely miss her.

A number of articles were first published in *The Arts in Psychotherapy*: "Drama Therapy–The State of the Art," Volume 24, pages 5–15, 1997; "Establishing a Model of Communication between Artists and Creative Arts Therapists," Volume 25, pages 299–302, 1998; "Drama Therapy and Distancing: Reflections on Theory and Clinical Application," Volume 23, pages 367–373, 1996; and "Drama Therapy in Taiwan," Volume 24, pages 159–173, 1997. They are reprinted here with permission from Elsevier Science.

The article, "Role Theory and the Role Method of Drama Therapy," was first published in *Current Approaches in Drama Therapy*, Charles C Thomas, 2000, edited by Penny Lewis and David Read Johnson. It is reprinted here with permission from Charles C Thomas, Publisher.

"The Role Model of Supervision" was first published in *Supervision and Dramatherapy*, Jessica Kingsley, 1999, edited by Elektra Tselikis-Portmann. It is reprinted here with permission from Jessica Kingsley.

I am very grateful to my students who continue to guide me deeper and deeper into an understanding of the power and gentleness of drama therapy. I especially wish to acknowledge Erin Conner who has helped me with the assessment research. And I also want to express my appreciation to the New York University class that includes Susan Clayton, Erin Conner, Dana Greco, Young-Ah Kang, Elyssa Kaplan, Amal Kouttab, Lisa Merrell, Junko Muraki, Alan Pottinger and Jim Tranchida.

I want to acknowledge my clients whom over the years continue to be a source of enlightenment and inspiration. Their courage and their fear, their need to open and to close keep me on a path of many wonders.

I wish to also acknowledge the beautiful work of many hundreds of children from many faiths and countries who openly expressed their images of God.

Michael Thomas of Charles C Thomas continues to be a loyal and generous supporter. I am most grateful for his active support not only of my work, but of the entire field of creative arts therapy.

CONTENTS

FIGURES

NEW ESSAYS IN DRAMA THERAPY

Part One

THEORY

Chapter 1

DRAMA THERAPY–THE STATE OF THE ART

I've been told that just below the ruins of the ancient Theatre of Dionysus in Epidauros, Greece, lie the remains of an equally ancient hospital. On one crumbling pillar is a plaque which informs the tourist that patients of this hospital were cured by performing in the Greek chorus. Historians of the theatre (see Brockett, 1992) frequently tell us that the art form originated in religious rituals and rites or in shamanic healing ceremonies (see Kirby, 1975). Aristotle's mention of the cathartic effects of tragedy on an audience in the third century B.C. further attests to the healing function of early theatre. The origins of healing through the dramatic art form are very deeply set in history. To this day, the female shamans of Korea, the Taoist priests of China, the masked dancers at Owuru Festivals in Nigeria, and the celebrants at Mardi Gras in Louisiana and Carnival in Brazil, all enact a form of cathartic healing through assuming archetypal roles and working their magic.

To truly appreciate the therapeutic values of dramatic activity of all sorts, including ritual, play, improvisation, storytelling, mask, puppetry, festivals and theatre performances, one would need to carefully study the cultural systems of prayer and medical care, of art and philosophy. Even then, we would only get a snapshot of a single culture that dramatizes its existence in particular ways. It is possible to find in-depth studies of culture from the point of view of those who see experience filtered through the lens of the drama as therapy. See, for example, Sue Jennings' (1995a) study of the Temiar of Malaysia and Richard Courtney's (1986) study of the Amerindian experience.

Culture is on my mind because I have recently spent a considerable amount of time traveling to other cultures to present my sense of drama therapy. Not surprisingly, when in a foreign culture, far away from home, I not only try to make sense of the drama of Taiwan or Israel or Greece, but also of my own form, home grown. As I move out in the world, I am transported back inside, to the vessel which has brought me there. That form, that vessel is drama therapy. This paper is an attempt to give my sense of its status as a

healing form in the present, with some reference to its history and some speculation as to its destiny.

A BRIEF HISTORY

Phil Jones (1996) traces the early twentieth century development of drama
therapy in part to two contemporaries of Stanislavski, Evreinov and Iljine.
The former, a theatre director, examined the process of enactment as an
instinctual means of making meaning for actor and audience, alike. Evreinov
(1927) conceptualized two realities, that of the person and that of the persona,
which he called "another ego." This other ego functioned to enter the imagi-
nal realm and create a sense of alternative ways of being by ". . .
transform[ing] the life that was into a life that is different." Through taking on
and playing out fictional roles, the actor is able to overcome a number of psychological and physical ailments, according to Evreinov.

Vladimir Iljine developed a notion of therapeutic theatre based upon
improvisation training. His technique was delineated through the following
stages: theme identification, reflection on themes, scenario design, scenario
realisation, and reflection/feedback (see Petzold, 1973 and Jones, 1996).
During the last stage, actors were given the opportunity to reflect upon their
dramatizations and relate the fictional elements to their everyday lives. Jones
(1996) tells us that the work of Iljine is most influential in the development of
drama therapy in Germany and the Netherlands where it is published in
German. To my knowledge, Iljine's work has not been translated into English.
Evreinov's work, however, is available in English as *The Theatre in Life* (1927).

The major European figure in the history of drama therapy is J.L.
Moreno, a contemporary of Freud whose early work in psychiatry and theatre occurred in Vienna in the early 1920s. Moreno's notions of psychodrama and sociodrama have been well documented in literally thousands of pub-
lications by Moreno and countless scholars and practitioners throughout the
world. His early work in Vienna and the United States included experiments
in improvisational enactment with dispossessed people—prostitutes, homeless
children, and prisoners, among others. His aim, often stated in grandiose
terms, was nothing short of transforming the psyche, the polis, the cosmos
into a more spontaneous state of being. Moreno's most lasting legacy is the
invention of the forms of psychodrama and sociometry which provide a
means of therapy through enactment and the rudiments of a theory of catharsis and role, intended to explain how and why the dramatization of experience leads to an amelioration of distress.

A recent study (see Shieffele, 1995) examines Moreno's contributions to the art form of theatre. This is significant because it bases Moreno's work more directly in the art form of theatre and thus brings him closer to the tradition of drama therapy. In specifying the differences between psychodrama and drama therapy, one often states that the former is less based in the art form. But if Scheiffele's thesis is true, then that distinction becomes less credible and the two fields move closer together in principle, if not practice. For a clear discussion of Moreno's work and its effects, see Blatner (1997) and Hug (1997).

The most comprehensive histories of drama therapy, as such, are to be found in England and the United States. The Netherlands also has a rich history of drama therapy practice, and recent developments are underway in Greece, Italy, Portugal and Israel. With few exceptions, practitioners in these countries have published little concerning their work.

In England, the term dramatherapy (one word) was coined by Peter Slade, who became well known for his notion that the dramatic play of children is a natural form of learning and healing (see Slade, 1954). His ideas of drama as a therapeutic modality for people of all ages would provide impetus to all who came after (see Slade, 1959). Marian Lindkvist, another British pioneer, became instrumental in the field by developing the Sesame training program in 1964 aiming at training practitioners to work through drama and movement in therapy (see Pearson, 1966). Lindkvist in her own research traveled frequently to other cultures where she studied the movement, rituals, and dramatizations that others used as means of defining their existence.

The major figure in British dramatherapy, Sue Emmy Jennings, began her work in the early 1960s and became most influential early on with the publication of *Remedial Drama* (1973), setting forth her approach to working with various groups of children with special needs through drama and play. Jennings would go on to found many of the major university-based and training institutes in the U.K., and many of the training centers throughout Europe and the Middle East. During the past 20 years, she has stretched the borders of the profession by engaging in research in social anthropology, in collaborating with actors and directors, in expanding the metaphorical bars in the lives of prisoners, psychiatric patients, infertile couples, among many others, through exposure to the healing potential of dramatherapy.

New generations of dramatherapists in the U.K., influenced and educated by Peter Slade, Marian Lindkvist, and Sue Jennings are moving the field in new directions. These include the very poetic and precise work of Alida Gersie (1991, 1997; Gersie and King, 1990) in storymaking, the groundbreaking work in drama and play therapy with abused children of Ann Cattanach (1993, 1994), the theoretical and practical work with emotionally disturbed children of Phil Jones (1996), the psychodramatic work of Dorothy Langley (1989), the paratheatrical work of Steve Mitchell (1996), the study of dramatherapy and spiritual life (Grainger, 1995), the work with eating disordered individuals of Ditty Dokter (1994), among many others.

In the United States, the emergence of drama therapy (two words) stemmed from the work of several practitioners. The reigning American dramatic approaches to therapy through the 1970s included psychodrama and several existential, humanistic and primal modalities, e.g., Gestalt therapy, psychosynthesis, transactional analysis, re-evaluation counseling, and primal therapy. Further, within the experimental theatre and performance art communities, actors, directors, and writers like Joe Chaikin and Jean Claude van-Itallie, Julian Beck and Judith Malina, Jeff Weiss and Karen Finley were challenging forms and aims of theatre, moving into notions of transforming the actor and audience's states of consciousness.

In the late 1970s, a number of people working in hospitals, clinics and schools through drama began to meet to share some of their common interests. The series of meetings centered around the diminutive but charismatic figure of Gertrud Schattner, who was then practicing drama therapy at Bellevue Psychiatric Hospital in New York City. From a loose organization of educators, social activists and therapists came the idea to form an association which became the National Association for Drama Therapy, founded in 1979. One early figure, Eleanor Irwin, began her professional work as a speech therapist and creative drama specialist. Irwin was, at the time, training in psychoanalysis and has become a leading researcher in the field and practitioner of play therapy (see Irwin, 1985). Another, David Read Johnson, a clinical psychologist and drama therapist, did his early work with populations of schizophrenic adults, then specialized in the area of post-traumatic stress disorder. His years of work with psychiatric patients, Vietnam war veterans, and normal neurotics has led to the development of a specific approach to practice which he calls developmental transformations (see Johnson, 1991). Renée Emunah, trained in theatre and the drama/movement approach of the Sesame program in England, also appeared on the scene as she developed the drama therapy program at Antioch College, then California Institute for Integral Studies in San Francisco in the 1980s. Emunah's (1994) contributions in practice, research and writing extended from her pioneering work with emotionally disturbed adolescents in San Francisco.

My own ideas evolved from several sources—a study of literature and psychology, a broad experience in theatre as actor, director and writer, and most particularly, four years of work with emotionally disturbed children and adolescents in the mid-1960s in New York City. Applying my knowledge of theatre and improvisation to the special problems of neurological impairment and a wide range of conduct, anxiety, and psychotic disorders, I slowly developed approaches in and theory of drama therapy.

Many experiments in drama therapy and related disciplines appeared throughout the United States and Canada in the 1970s and 1980s. Some continue through the present. Linda Gregoric Cook of Media and the Arts for Social Services, Ramon Gordon of Cell Block Theatre and John Bergmann of Geese Theatre, among others, developed approaches to using drama therapy with prison populations. Pat Sternberg and Nina Garcia (1989) developed sociodramatic approaches to healing through the art form. Pam Dunne developed projective methods to work with children and later detailed a constructivist narrative approach to treatment. Rosalind Wilder and Naida Weisberg (1984) developed approaches to the treatment of elders through drama therapy. That rich area was also explored in the work of Susan Pearlstein in Life History Theatre and Maria Scaros-Mercado in intergenerational drama therapy.

THE PRESENT—THINGS AS THEY APPEAR TO BE

A number of challenges exist for practitioners in the field:

1. SIZE. The community of drama therapists in the United States and indeed in the world, is small. The National Association for Drama Therapy, for example, has less than 400 members. Given a climate of managed care insurance companies taking control of the health care system and calling for more and more justification for the use of particular approaches to healing, a small, non-mainstream organization is in a weak position to fight for its place among other therapeutic approaches. Further, in a time where licensure qualifies only some for insurance reimbursement and the right to practice, the small profession of drama therapy is also vulnerable. Within the last 15 years, only two fully accredited drama therapy programs have existed within the United States, those at New York University and California Institute for Integral Studies. Both are healthy and in full swing, with a sizable number of applicants each year. But sizable is a relative term. Both programs are small and can only accept a small number, approximately 15 new students each year. The challenge is to increase the base of students and trainees, teachers and trainers while retaining the quality of education and training. A larger corps would then take on the responsibility for pioneering new employment opportunities for drama therapists. Further, this larger body would then take a more active political position in the struggle to be recognized for licensure and insurance reimbursement.

2. RESEARCH. In the 30 or so years since drama therapy has been an organized profession, a literature has slowly emerged. Much of the literature is descriptive in nature, offering the history, sources, practices, populations, and theoretical underpinnings of the field (see, for example, Emunah, 1994; Jennings, 1987; Johnson, 1982; Jones, 1996; Landy, 1994). In that the field is still young, this is hardly surprising. Concurrently, writers in the field have been trying to carve out appropriate research strategies and research methodologies. Within the two American M.A. programs, all students are required to write a Master's thesis. In recent years, professors in both programs have been encouraging students to begin to move from the mere descriptive to more methodologically-based research. Throughout the 70s and 80s, there were several attempts in drama therapy to study subjects in a quantitative way, keeping within the parameters of mainstream research in the social sciences (see Irwin et al., 1972; Johnson and Quinlan, 1985; Landy, 1984). However, as we approach the new millennium, it seems clear that drama therapists, as well as other creative arts therapists, have turned to more qualitative approaches, to newer research paradigms (see Junge and Linesch, 1993) as appropriate for their search for meaning within the creative, therapeutic process. At this writing, a review of the literature indicates that the majority of work still tends to be descriptive in nature (see Grainger, 1990, Emunah, 1994; Jennings, 1995; Johnson, et. al., 1996; Jones, 1996; Mitchell, 1996). However, within that literature and alongside it, a body of case study materials is also emerging (see Cattanach, 1997; Landy, 1993; 1996; Schnee, 1996).

In preparing for M.A. research, students often find themselves at a loss. Some have never before studied research and because of their strong artistic backgrounds tend to gravitate toward developing a piece of autobiographical theatre and documenting their process. Although this approach is acceptable to both American M.A. programs, the larger question remains—but does this form of research advance the knowledge base in the field? The challenge posed by this debate is to educate students at an early point as to the research possibilities and as to their responsibilities not only to their own personal process, but also to an emerging field sorely in need of compelling research.

3. THEORY. I see the present state of theory in drama therapy as healthy. In the earlier stages, many who were writing and practicing tended to affiliate with psychological and sociological theories, so that, for example, Irwin based her work in psychoanalysis, Johnson based his work in developmental psychology and object relations theory, Landy based his work in symbolic interaction theory, and others found sustenance in the archetypal theory of Jung (see Gersie, 1991), constuctivist theory (see Dunne, 1992), and various

humanistic approaches of Rogers, Maslow, and May (see Emunah, 1995). Although some of these approaches and affiliations have remained constant, in other cases there continues to be movement from the psychological sources to more aesthetic ones. Johnson (Johnson et al., 1996) and his colleagues, for example, now see Grotowski's poor theatre approach as a theoretical model for their work in drama therapy. Preceding Johnson, Mitchell (1996) has written about his grounding in paratheatrical models created by Grotowski. Jennings has turned fully to the theatre not only as a theoretical framework, but as a profession. In recent years, she has turned to Shakespeare and other classical dramatists for their therapeutic insights. A lively addition to the theoretical discourse has been the prolific work of the British psychiatrist, Murray Cox (Cox, 1992, Cox and Theilgaard 1994), who collaborated with Jennings in bringing Shakespearian drama to prisons for violent offenders. In his landmark book, *Shakespeare Comes to Broadmoor*, Cox and others speak of the therapeutic effects of this classical theatre on distressed and dispossessed individuals.

In my own work, I have expanded upon sociological sources to move more directly into theatrical ones. In creating a taxonomy of roles (Landy, 1993), based upon an archetypal reading of plays throughout the cannon of Western drama, I have centered my work firmly in the art form. In focusing upon the concept of role, I make the assumption that drama therapy, like theatre, plays with the dual realities of person and persona and of world and stage and helps clients negotiate that paradoxical state of being and discover in the process a way to effectively live "the double life" (see Landy, 1996).

Others draw theoretical clarity from the process of storymaking, basing their ideas in the notion that human beings make sense of their lives through creating and telling stories. We see this model clearly explicated in the work of Alida Gersie (1991, 1992, 1997), in the careful discussion of the framework undergirding Playback Theatre (Fox, 1994), and in the newly developing program in story and drama in therapy at Lesley College in Israel, under the guidance of Avi Hadari.

The challenge in this arena is to keep the discourse open and allow the richness of voices to be heard. On the other side, the challenge is to avoid the dissonance created by too many voices sounding at once. In that drama therapy is an interdisciplinary field, it is by nature eclectic. But that does not mean that it is a container for every social scientific and aesthetic model in sight. Without the grounding of a finite perspective, it will lose the kind of clarity essential to maintain its inherently open nature.

4. PRACTICE. The pioneers in drama therapy came to the field with a wealth of techniques and approaches from theatre, from therapy, from vari-

ous personal growth workshops and from life experience. They were actors, dancers, directors, teachers, therapists, health care professionals of all sorts. Many in England were initially trained in the methods of Peter Slade and other mentors in the burgeoning field of drama in education. Strong influences included Gavin Bolton and Dorothy Heathcote, Brian Way and those involved in the theatre-in-education movement.

Americans, like myself, were also influenced by these British approaches. In fact, one of my primary training techniques is what I call the extended dramatization, an extensive 30-hour experience in creating and enacting a fictional role (and its counterparts), a fictional family, and a fictional community. The impetus for this approach came directly from my early work with Gavin Bolton and Dorothy Heathcote which I describe elsewhere (see Landy, 1982a). Perhaps my strongest influence, in terms of both theory and practice, has been Richard Courtney, who taught for many years at the Ontario Institute for Studies in Education and the University of Toronto. Through Courtney, I learned how to mix the stew of exercises and enactments, of stories and plays, derived from a wide range of sources. Through Courtney, I learned the difference between a dilettante and a divergent thinker and in this distinction, I learned how to accept my own mix of approaches.

In witnessing and leading drama therapy sessions over a 30-year span, I have come to appreciate the diversity of practice. Drama therapists direct plays, engage children in play therapy and sandplay, warm-up groups through Viola Spolin-influenced theatre games, create rituals derived from a variety of cultural experiences, apply aspects of psychodrama and sociodrama to the work of many groups, tell stories and help others make their own stories, lead story dramatizations and various improvisational enactments, encourage groups to write poetry, to sing, to dance, to improvise roles and themes and feelings. Drama therapists work through mask and puppetry, through make-up and video. Drama therapists dramatize dreams and fantasies and help shape autobiographical performances for many clients. And drama therapists work with culturally-specific materials to explore elements of cultural experience dramatically.

As the field establishes a history, some have developed a particular approach to treatment. Some more prominent approaches include the theatrical text-oriented approach of Sue Jennings, the play therapy approach of Ann Cattanach, the storymaking approach of Alida Gersie, the five-stage eclectic approach of Renée Emunah, the developmental transformations approach of David Johnson, and my own role method approach.

With so many bags of tricks, the challenge becomes one of deciding whether to become a generalist or specialist. This challenge is compounded by the fact that private institutes have been evolving offering specialized training. In attaching oneself to a particular approach, does one limit one's clinical abilities or expand them? Is it possible to be a generalist and specialist at the same time?

5. POPULATIONS. Here a similar question arises concerning the generalist or specialist orientation. Does one particular approach appear to be most effective with one particular population? Or does any effective means of treatment tend to work across the board, assuming it is modified to meet special needs? In reality, most clinicians in drama therapy go where the work is. Once there, they bring their training with them and attempt to modify it to suit the needs of their clients. In that all drama therapy approaches are relatively new, there is much room for experimentation. One can say, as I have done, that there are theoretical reasons to use less verbal approaches with less verbal populations and to use more structured approaches with more disorganized populations. Yet it becomes clearer to me over time that the rules and the techniques become less and less important as the human beings in the room become more visible. If technology is an extension of the human body and mind, then technique in drama therapy becomes an extension of the group's need to express and connect.

What is the group? What kind of person is best suited for drama therapy? Traditionally, I would say that drama therapists were assigned those more custodial cases whom others deemed too non-responsive to traditional psychotherapies. Drama therapists have worked with schizophrenic adults, with frail and disoriented elderly, with autistic children, with moderately to severely developmentally disabled children and adults, with violent sex offenders, among others. Over time, we find somewhat of a shift. In the British publication, *Dramatherapy—Clinical Studies* (Mitchell, 1996), reference is made to work with personality disorders, learning disabilities, depression, and eating disorders, among others. As mentioned earlier, Jennings has worked extensively with populations of infertile couples and prisoners.

In the United States, drama therapy is widely practiced in institutions with the elderly, with the mentally ill, including homeless mentally ill, with Vietnam and other war veterans, with prisoners, with those with eating disorders and substance abuse, with developmentally disabled adults, and with sexually-abused children. Within the scope of individual and group private practice, a wider range of clientele receives services, from normal neurotic to various individuals with affective and anxiety disorders, learning disabilities and attention deficit disorders.

Many raise the question whether a client in drama therapy should be skillful in acting. Although I generally answer no, it has been my experience that people who choose a drama therapist for treatment are generally open to, if not skilled in acting. There is an irony here in that the people who probably would benefit most from drama therapy are those who are not terribly spontaneous and are quite fearful of enactment and overt expression of emotion. The challenge, then, becomes trying to find a way to attract those who would be most likely to benefit by treatment through drama therapy. At some level, one could argue that all human beings would benefit by dramatizing their experience as a way to gain mastery of it. Yet again, in specifying the particular groups most likely to benefit from treatment, the field moves closer to a contained focus.

6. SPLITS AND AFFILIATIONS. Drama therapy, like other fields, is split. The splits exist in choices of mentors, educational and training institutions, theories, practices, and populations. In the most positive sense, these splits represent the healthy growth of ideas and attachments to one or the other. When dialogue between those attached to, for example, the role method, and those attached to, for example, the developmental method results, then such splits can be acknowledged and all can rest assured that diversity is tolerated. But in the heat of orthodoxy, the splits become chasms. It seems to me that it is not ideas that split a field but people who need to be correct in their assessment of their small domains within small domains. The splits within drama therapy, as I see it, are not chasms, simply the struggles of people attempting to forge an identity within a field with its own sense of insecurity within the larger fields of psychology, psychotherapy, and theatre.

The theoretical split between role method and developmental method is not very interesting on the level of power struggle between people. It is much more interesting as it furthers a discussion about the nature of drama therapy as driven by a removal of blocks, a *via negativa* in Grotowski's terms, as opposed to a recognition of the possibilities of living with contradictory tendencies as expressed in roles. In theatrical terms, this debate suggests a distinction between Grotowski's early work in poor theatre and Brecht's work in aesthetic distancing and epic theatre. The former implies a spiritual, almost Reichian notion of penetrating to the core where the essence of the actor/person lies. The latter represents a sociological and philosophical notion of a paradoxical existence between roles and their counterparts, an existence that can be most profoundly approached indirectly, through style. The drama therapy debate, as I see it, has to do with the efficacy of style, that is, if style is removed and one moves directly to the depths of the person, will that person be ultimately revealed and then healed? Or is the aim of drama therapy to proceed in an indirect fashion, unraveling layers of being by masking, penetrating surface through formalizing surface?

Students studying drama therapy want to know the truth. What is the British approach and is it better than the American? Which theoretical framework is best for working with schizophrenic adults? Should each session close with some form of verbal processing? But if it is true that the truth is only relative, then such questions can only be answered relative to specific circumstances.

This is a time in the history of drama therapy for collaboration, not only within the field, but with related disciplines. There is some strong evidence. For years, there has been a split between psychodrama and drama therapy. Now there are published debates in the journal *The Arts in Psychotherapy*, among others (see Casson, 1996; Fox and Snow, 1996; Kedem-Tahar and Kellerman, 1996), looking at the similarities and differences. There are a growing number of workshops looking at the confluence of the two disciplines. In recent years, I have collaborated with psychodramatists Peter Pitzele and Tian Dayton in examining these connections. In 1996, a major collaborative conference occurred between drama and dance therapies. And in 1997, a conference among the dramatic therapies, linking the disciplines of theatre, psychodrama, and drama therapy took place at New York University.

The challenge is to hold onto a center while spinning about in the world. The challenge is to affiliate without creating splits so big that they become chasms. In the present, drama therapy is a coherent field with a number of different perspectives as to theory, practice and populations served. It has held its own in relationship to its bigger and stronger siblings–theatre, psychodrama, and other creative arts therapies. Some in the field have made affiliations within and without the borders of drama therapy and the house still stands.

TOWARD THE MILLENNIUM–SOME SPECULATIONS ON THE FUTURE

It seems to me that drama therapists would be wise to affiliate to avoid the pitfalls of standing alone. There is some comfort in being small and contained within a vastly expanding universe of fields and disciplines and data. But in order to move forward politically, economically and intellectually, drama therapists would do well to seek out like-minded collaborators and colleagues. I have written elsewhere (Landy, 1994a) of three possible scenarios for such collaboration within the communities of theatre, psychology, and creative arts therapies. I still feel that these are likely affiliates. However, I would offer another option–for drama therapists to ally with those who practice related forms of dramatic therapy, e.g., psychodrama and sociodrama, forum theatre and rainbow of desire (see Boal, 1995), playback theatre, play therapy and sandplay, among others. Further along the line, I envision an expansion of dramatic healing to include those who apply the dramatic process to education, social activism, community and spiritual life.

It may be that all of dramatic activity, from the play of children to the ritual enactments of communities, to fully mounted theatre performances, serves, in part, a therapeutic function. That function can be conceptualized as moving people in some essential way from a position of lesser awareness, power, pleasure, challenge, hope, to the potential of discovering more of the same. In increasing its affiliations and its visibility, the field of drama therapy has the potential of moving closer to the realization of these goals. The one danger in affiliating so broadly is the loss of the field's integrity. When reaching out, then, practitioners must be secure enough in their own knowledge base to ensure that gain and loss will remain in balance.

As for research, I envision an expansion beyond description into looking at the precise ways that the dramatic experience can affect change. I envision research based firmly in theory that is, itself, dramatic in nature and applying new research paradigms such as heuristic and hermeneutic methodologies. I see drama therapy as offering significant approaches to psychological assessment and evaluation, again, by basing the work firmly within the parameters of the dramatic experience. Several assessment instruments have already been developed. These include the diagnostic role-playing test developed by Johnson (1988), the puppetry interview developed by Irwin (1985), and two applications of Landy's taxonomy of roles (see Landy, 1993), Role Profiles (Landy, 1998) and Tell-A-Story (1998a). In her doctoral dissertation, Sherrie Raz (1997) applies Landy's taxonomy of roles to an assessment of undergraduate drama students.

Theory will continue to develop in drama therapy. New models will be proposed and older ones will fade away. But even as drama therapists reach out for new understandings, I would hope that some take the existing models and apply them carefully to their research and practice. Some would argue that hard-edged theory constricts the free flow of therapeutic practice and I would agree that this can be the case. Many insist upon developing eclectic models and that, too, is a viable point of view. However, I would urge practitioners and theorists to continue raising the hard theoretical questions—How is performance healing? What is it about the dramatic experience that moves people in one direction or another? What are the essential aims of drama therapists and what are the best ways to get there? And I would urge them to look for answers in language that furthers the theoretical discourse within the field and across disciplines.

I envision a continuing application of existing practices, including projective and psychodramatic approaches. If there is a further move toward affiliation and collaboration, I would expect the mix to affect practice. I can foresee drama therapists in collaboration with music therapists, art therapists, dance and poetry therapists. For a number of years, colleagues in music, art and drama therapies at New York University have been teaching a course called Collaboration in the Creative Arts Therapies and experimenting with interrelated process groups in drama and music therapy. In a recent collaborative workshop with the dance/movement therapist, Bronwyn Warren, we led each other through an experience of working from the body to generate and explore role qualities, and from the role back into the body to discover its own polarities. Further extensions of practice can stem from work in theatre and drama therapy and in any number of collaborations with workers in related psychotherapeutic and creative fields.

Populations served by drama therapists will continue to evolve, some remaining constant, some fading, others appearing. I envision less concern with the ebb and flow of particular populations and more attention to the environments where they receive treatment. If in the climate of managed care the hospital becomes less likely to support extended treatment by drama therapists, then we might look to other environments. I would suggest that the school is an extremely rich environment to do more preventive work and offer service to a system in transition that is sorely in need of ways to conceptualize and realize an affective curriculum. Drama therapists have worked within special education classrooms and should continue to do so. In addition, I would urge a move into the mainstream where, I believe, students are in great need of expressing themselves and mastering skills beyond that which is currently offered.

I also foresee a move into the prisons where groundbreaking work in drama therapy has a history (see Landy, 1994) and conceivably a bright future. Education and crime will continue to be significant social problems as the millennium approaches. Drama therapists can and should respond to both.

As for splits, they, too, will come and go as some passionately present and defend their points of view. I do not envision a fully harmonious community of drama therapists happily improvising on the beaches of the twenty-first century. But I do see individuals respecting other's wishes to work alone or together, with others in the field or outside. My hope is for a greater acceptance of diversity and a greater opportunity for dialogue within and without. Along with this hope is a challenge to those of us who are teachers and trainers, practitioners and supervisors, to continue our search for excellence both intellectually and ethically, to be willing to address our own contradictions, self-doubts and obsessions, and to help those whom we train to do the same.

MEANWHILE, BACK IN GREECE . . .

Let me conclude by revisiting Greece, the Western source of therapeutic theatre. Recently, I led a series of workshops and one particular session comes to mind. I was halfway through a morning session on role method when a group member arrived quite late. Her arrival had a strong impact upon the process because all had agreed previously that no latecomers would be admitted. A heated discussion ensued, very much based upon issues well embedded in the group process and quite removed from the current drama therapy process. I allowed several voices to be heard, then decided to bring the issue back to the current topic—demonstrating the intricacies of the role method.

"If this late person were a persona, a role type, what might she be called?" I asked.

Several names were offered and the group decided to choose "the intruder."

"Which role might be on the counterpart of the intruder?" I asked.

The group chose "the people," a kind of choral role which seemed fitting to me in terms of the place of the Greek Chorus in classical drama.

Earlier in the workshop, I had asked each member of the group to invoke the role of guide, a figure who could lead them on an imaginative journey. Following our discussion, I asked all to conceive a story concerning the three roles of guide, intruder and the people, and to write it out from the point of view of one. One woman, whom I shall call Sofia, created this:

I live in a village bound by tall scarred rock-faces and the rim of a silent sea. The people of my village are not too many, for few can withstand the isolation and the pitiless terrain. But we who have stayed love this land with passion. We have beaten the rocks into stones and fashioned shelter with them. We have dug deep into the sinews of the earth for water and with it watered our trees, our vegetables and our fruit, and of it we have drunk.

One day, a strange plant was discovered in the village garden—perhaps the seed was brought by birds, perhaps by the wind, perhaps it had always been there, waiting. The plant had no fruit, only blossoms, of such beauty that even the tightest most wrinkled mouth smiled to see them. The fame of this flower spread and our village was known by its name, but none came to see it, for the sea was great and silent and the mountains still and high. And we agreed that our village was only for those whose hearts laugh with the sunbeams on these rocks and cry with the raindrops in this sea. And so time passed.

A morning dawned when the silence of the sea was broken by the splash of oars. We gathered to see who had traveled so far to reach us. And we saw.

It was a man with beads in his hair that tinkled down his back, knives in his belt and a song on his breath. He leaped from the boat and pulled it onto the beach.

"I have come," he said, "to know you and to look on the blossoms with you. Perhaps I will stay, if you wish it. Perhaps I will not." And fear and anger found voice in the people.

"Why have you come to know us with knives?" shouted one.

"We have labored to live, but you come with a song to live off our labor," said another.

And I shouted with them: "If you stay others will follow. There is no room for you. It has been agreed long since. Go now."

But he did not move. He did not go. He looked at us with determination and disbelief, and we looked at him with fear, fear that what had been would be no longer.

And then the wise woman came forward and stood between the determination and the fear. And she said to us: "He is already here. The pebble that breaks the surface of the lake lies even in its depths. What has been is no longer. Choose now what is to be. Hide behind your fear or walk with it."

And she said to the man: "Gifts are freely given. The blossoms were a gift to us as your coming is a gift to us. To look on the blossoms will be our gift to you. Food and rest will be our gifts to you. But to stay and know us is not a gift that can be given. It is a labor of love."

And the rock-face of the people opened and the man stepped forward, and together we walked to the garden.

After Sofia told me the story, I asked her to name the figures of the narrator (whom I assumed to represent the voice of the people) and the intruder. Sofia named the intruder Harry. Being bilingual in English and Greek, her association with the name was as a verb, to harry, as in to harass, annoy or torment. But later, the group reminded her of the Greek meaning of the name, χαρα, bright joy, and the noun form, αχρη, grace, referring to both graceful movement and the grace of God. She named the narrator the Stump.

In working through the story, I enroled Sofia as the Stump. As Stump, she said: "Things are hard. There's so much to do and not a lot of help. You have to do it yourself, pay attention to so much and it's tiring. People think what is hard is strong, but it's not. It's just hard."

Enroling as Harry, Sofia began to move in a graceful, joyful fashion, but soon separated out from Harry and transformed into a figure angry at Harry for his sense of spontaneous freedom and adventure. She named this figure Eliza. With Sofia's permission, I enroled as Harry and we began to play. At first, the play was light and joyful, but then a dialogue occurred where Eliza confronted Harry for breaking on appointment while he was on one of his spontaneous adventures. She was angry that he did not consider her feelings and he simply defended his freedom to roam. Through a series of role reversals, Sofia experienced both roles and finally began to cry. We deroled and processed the enactment.

"Who is Harry?" I asked.

"He's the part of me that is an adventurer, curious, creative, daring. He's a part of me that I've squashed into a tiny box and the more I squash him in, the more he fights to get out. Poor Harry. And without Harry, the Stump takes over."

I noted that when one is stumped, confusion, frustration and defeat take over. If the Stump is the voice of the people, then these people are cut off, fearful of Harry's energy, clueless and critical. I also referred to Eliza as a good guide, standing between Harry and the Stump. But Sofia was unsure of accepting Eliza as a guide. She did not seem as wise as the wise woman in the story who tells the people to accept the reality of Harry in their midst.

At the end of the story, there is an integration of the intruder and the people: "And the rock-face of people opened and the man stepped forward and together we walked to the garden." At the conclusion of the enactment, I asked Sofia how she might integrate her three roles of Harry, Eliza, and the Stump. Feeling a bit silly, she responded: "Bake them in a cake. The Stump would be the dough, flour and sugar, Harry would be the flavoring, and Eliza would be the leavening to make it rise. Then I'd eat it all up."

I responded: "Then you could have your cake and eat it, too." We laughed and the session ended.

Reflecting upon this experience, I became aware that I was an intruder, a foreigner, an American among Greeks, who entered a country, far away from my home, of mountains and sea. As many others, I was drawn to Greece by its indescribable beauty and ancient splendor. As is usual in a community of drama therapists, I was a man among women and I played out my rarefied role. In the end, I stay just long enough to know a few people in this country of islands and in doing so, I become a guide, offering my version of drama therapy. It could be that all groups (the people) willing to move ahead in their process need an intruder. If this intruder is successful in shaking them up, then he/she will become a guide. Without an intruder, a group will remain complacent. With an intruder in its midst, a group has the possibility to appreciate its own beauties and mysteries even more.

Harry, the harried one (or is it the one who harries?), becomes transformed into Harry, the graceful one, the shining joy. The greatest power of drama therapy exists in this kind of transformation from intruder to guide, from torment to grace. Not everyone can tell such beautiful stories or integrate a clear triumvirate of roles. Not everyone can experience the direct connection between theatre and healing or visit the mysteries of ancient civilizations where myth lies just below the surface of things. But all human beings dramatize their lives every day of their lives in ways that are limited only by the limits of the imagination. They dramatize by thinking imaginatively, by dreaming, by wishing, by being more than they appear to be. And if they are willing to look just below the surface of their dramas, they, too, might discover a myth, a story, a persona or two or three that might reveal or guide, that might help them discover within their harried minds a bright joy.

One way of describing the state of the art of drama therapy as a profession is to look at its training, practices, theories and research, its populations served and its splits and affiliations. Another way is to look to the stories, dreams, and roles created by all human beings who dramatize as a way to make sense of their lives. I have my own Harry stories as you, dear reader, have yours. In recognizing the importance of these creations in keeping us balanced, we affirm that the state of the art is healthy, indeed, and has always been so, long before the patients at the hospital below the Theatre of Dionysus practiced their lines and movements in the Greek Chorus. In acknowledging this healthy state of affairs, perhaps we who believe in the healing power of the arts can, like Sofia, have our cake and eat it, too.

Chapter 2

ESTABLISHING A MODEL OF COMMUNICATION BETWEEN ARTISTS AND CREATIVE ARTS THERAPISTS

Tens of thousands of years ago, long before the word art had entered the language system of any culture, there existed a human need for creative expression beyond that required for the completion of utilitarian tasks. That which we now call art, the making of events or objects of contemplation through an act of the imagination, displayed or performed in special environments, was then simply another aspect of everyday existence. Yet, though a natural and accepted activity, art-making was once removed from the business of hunting and gathering. Its otherness was marked by its detachment from the profane and the commercial. The adornment of the body with scars and tattoos and jewels, the painting of caves, the choreography of stone monoliths, the chanting and masquerading and dancing and telling of stories upon a feast day or during an ordinary gathering all pointed to the sense of the doubleness of human life. It was as if the human being was also another form of being–an animal or deity, a spirit or part of nature. It was as if by being human, one had the option or right or obligation to transcend the limitations of body and mind and enact a drama of super-human proportions.

In its original form, art-making was a natural human expression of transcendence, sanctioned in cultural practices and community life throughout the world. Human beings made art, paradoxically, to transcend their human limitations. Certainly there were other, more grounded functions of traditional art-making–for example, documenting an event such as a hunt or a battle, beautifying the body, and entertaining an audience gathered for the purpose of entertainment. However, from the point of view of the creator of the art object, the making endowed the maker with extraordinary powers. As cre-

---

Note: This paper was presented at the 4th European Arts Therapies Conference in London, England, September 1997.

ator, the traditional artist fashioned images of an alternative reality, that of the imagination, different from the one given by nature and taken in through the five senses.

Art objects are now regularly called works of art or art works. In former times the juxtaposition of art and work would have seemed rather strange to one who believed that movement and painting and storytelling were playful means of expression.

Like other natural human endeavors, art has become compartmentalized, split off and ultimately, commercialized. It is generally made and performed in spaces far removed from community life and accessible only to a few. Or if art is accessible to an audience, it is generally conveyed through the mass media which tend to, like Andy Warhol painting soup cans, blur the boundaries between the two realities of the everyday and the imagination. Art has been split off not only from community life, but also from the original internal impulse to create, that is, a transcendent one pointing to the doubleness and paradox of human existence. A transcendent notion of art still exists in the minds of many artists but often the transcendence of Self is onto other selves like Cindy Sherman photographing herself in endless media-inspired persona or the novelist Philip Roth (1993) creating a fictional novelist named Philip Roth in his book, *Operation Shylock*. The notion of storytelling and myth-making, of playing God or gods and creating a universe or two, is often missing in contemporary art.

There are many exceptions to this statement as some post-modern novelists and playwrights, musicians, dancers and visual artists have deconstructed conventional texts and images in an attempt to create mythic environments within communities and within the psyches of the individual spectator/participant. And as a harbinger for the future, fringe artists have attempted to do the same through focusing upon the body as if it were a canvas or stage and using and abusing it by piercing, tattooing, and in the case of filmmaker, Peter Greenaway (see *The Pillow Book*), constructing entire texts upon every crevice of the flesh.

In a most compelling way, occasionally a community will respond to a tragic event through a spontaneous outpouring of feeling through art. Two recent examples occurred in Israel and England. The former was the creation of the poetry wall in Tel-Aviv in 1996 adjacent to the spot where Yitzhak Rabin was murdered. To express their horror, despair and hope, Israelis and others from all around the world adorned the drab concrete structure that framed Rabin's place of murder with poems, songs, and drawings. These creative expressions exist as a memorial to a brave, inspirational leader and as a reminder to the bereaved that images can aid in healing.

The second example is the explosion of poems and drawings, collages, flower arrangements and personal gifts that appeared at the entrance of Buckingham Palace and Kensington Palace at the time of the death of Diana, Princess of Wales. The profundity of grief experienced by millions who participated in the symbolism of the people's princess found expression in art objects displayed publicly at the gates of power.

These examples, however, as powerful as they are, are exceptions to the trend toward the profane and commercial in art. Generally speaking, art is removed from the community and from its transcendent function within the psyche. As brilliantly demonstrated some 25 years ago by John Berger and his colleagues (1973), art has become de-contextualized, removed from a sense of place or occasion, as easily seen on a tourist hotel wall or in a print ad in a tabloid magazine as on the ceiling of a holy cathedral.

In part, the profession of creative arts therapy arose as a response to the evolution of art-making. Creative arts therapy, modeled in part on the early forms of creative expression and healing rites, is also in the tradition of twentieth century artists who conceived of their work in extra-aesthetic terms. I think of the French theatre artist, Antonin Artaud (1958), who conceived of his work in spiritual terms; the German Bertolt Brecht (see Willett, 1964) who conceived of his work in political and sociological terms, the British Peter Brook (1978), the Polish Jerzy Grotowski (1968) and the American Richard Schechner (1985), all of whom conceived of their work in anthropological terms; and I think, especially, of the Russians, Constantin Stanislavski (1936) and Nicolas Evreinov (1927), who conceived of their work in psychological terms. But it was an Austrian psychiatrist, J. L. Moreno, who ultimately provided the clear modern link between the arts and healing. In his early theatrical experiments with the dispossessed in Vienna and later with the mentally ill in the United States, Moreno (1947) offered an alternative to what he called the cultural conserves of art, that is, an art removed from an immediate connection to the lives of people. It was Moreno's wild idea that modern social and psychological illness could be counteracted by taking on dysfunctional roles and playing them out within a psychodrama theatre until people indeed become like God, that is, creator and shaper of their own destinies.

The impulse of these and other artists and performance theorists looking for ways to envision their art as an integral force in making meaning in human life was shared by an emerging group of creative arts therapists in drama and psychodrama, dance and movement, music and art and poetry throughout the second half of the twentieth century. Like their counterparts in the arts they, too, searched for ways to restore some of the essential functions of art-making. From my point of view as a drama therapist, one essential function is that of transcendence, the playing of the other, the not-me, the not-human, in order to better understand and appreciate what it means to be me, a not-god, an imperfect human being.

If it were possible for creative arts therapists to speak with the aboriginal art makers or even with the performance theorists mentioned above, all would, I think, share many common opinions. For one, they would recognize the creative expressive activity of human beings as healthy and as a means of releasing, if not unhealthy tendencies, then at least fearful ones. Further, all would probably assert the significance of the human need to impersonate the superhuman, that is, to transcend their own limitations. In doing so, they might agree that safety and boundaries are established by imagining dangers and playing at the edges of dangerous places where even angels fear to tread. And finally, all might agree that to adorn the body, the hearth, the field and the street is a means of making not only meaning but also beauty. And in making a thing beautiful, one experiences a sense of harmony and satisfaction. I suppose that in extreme cases of creating art that exemplifies the negation of beauty, as in the mutilation and defacement of persons and objects, the issue of beauty is raised by evoking its counterpart.

Such an imagined encounter between creative arts therapists, aboriginal art-makers and twentieth century performance theorists might occur in some virtual reality outpost in cyberspace. But the everyday reality of communication is more determined by the alienation of one part of human experience from the other. Many contemporary working artists are not in the business of healing or meaning making or transcendence or even beauty. Many artists are astute readers of cultural and formal trends motivated by the market place. Others are motivated more by the work itself (as opposed to the play) and risk financial hardship to realize their vision. Still others are part-time artists who attempt to balance the demanding roles of breadwinner, parent and spouse with that of artist. The latter often limit their aesthetic efforts to late nights, weekends and vacations.

Within their separate boxes, it would seem that artists and creative arts therapists have little in common. The former are workers whose art is a means of making a living, asserting a vision, gratifying the need for recognition, balancing responsibilities. They are in it for themselves, far removed from the anonymous sculptors of Stonehenge and the painters of the caves of Lascaux. The latter are healers whose art is, presumably, in the service of others. Furthermore, both artists and creative arts therapists harbor certain negative fantasies about the other which might intrude upon their ability to engage in any productive dialogue. From the point of view of certain artists, creative arts therapy might be an unknown profession or if known, a dubious one. Some artists fear the loss of their creativity through any form of therapy and will embrace their pathological tendencies at all costs. Other artists look to those who apply art to some extra-aesthetic arena as failed artists or, at best, foolish ones. From the point of view of certain creative arts therapists, the artist is an egotist, an elitist, a social misfit or, at worst, a paparazzi who feeds on celebrity.

Although these examples are stereotypical, it seems to me that communication between those in an arts-based discipline and those in its applied creative arts therapy is very difficult, indeed. I'd like to propose a model for facilitating a dialogue between two separate fields that at one time were quite naturally linked and at this time could well be again.

Let me begin with several assumptions:

1. There are many diverse philosophical notions of art to be found in the discipline of aesthetics that speak to the functions, values, and meaning of art.

2. Art exists in many forms, from the pure expression of infants smearing a wall with their feces to the sophisticated sculpting of clay and marble.

3. Art serves many purposes, both aesthetic and extra-aesthetic, e.g., art as education, art as political action, art as prayer, and art as therapy.

4. Art-making is democratic, that is, anyone can engage in expressive, creative activity; yet each art, whether dance or drama or literature or music or visual art, is also a formal discipline which requires skill and training and is, at its most sophisticated, the domain of a few. Art as process is the domain of all. Art as product is the domain of some.

Without an acceptance of these assumptions, especially the notion of the democratic nature of creative activity, dialogue between artists and creative arts therapists would be difficult at best. Given these assumptions, we can proceed to five points of the model. These points are based upon the earlier discussion of commonalities shared by creative arts therapists, performance theorists and aboriginal art-makers. Each of the following is intended to serve as an element in a dialogue around mutual concerns of creative arts therapists and artists within their related arts discipline:

1. Creative Expression: A primary need of human beings is an expressive/creative one. One measure of effective mental health is the ability to express one's feelings through movement, sound and music, visual and verbal imagery, role-playing and storymaking . When the need for creative expression is thwarted, individuals become more dehumanized and less capable of self-revelation.

2. Catharsis: Through creative expression catharsis is possible, that is, one can release a number of often painful feelings through one's movement, music, visual representation and enactment. The art-making serves as a container for the feelings and often allows the art-maker to release feelings in a safe fashion.

3. Imagination: In the creative act, one enters an alternative reality, that of the imagination, one that is qualitatively different from the reality of the everyday. This is a realm of metaphor and symbol, a language that can best be read subjectively. In dramatic terms, one takes on a role, impersonating another. As other, one transcends the reality of the everyday and is free to express oneself in new and unique ways, safely ensconced in the fictional role. The relationship between the realities of the imagination and the everyday provides a basis for understanding aesthetic distance as it relates to art-making and identity-making.

4. Beauty: The act of making art is a transformational one. A thing that was ordinary becomes a thing that is extraordinary. In the make-over of the ordinary, the artist creates an object of beauty. Sometimes the object created embodies reprehensible qualities, the shadowy sides of beauty. But in the transformation of a body, a face, a sound, in the making of photographs of torture, in the performance of acts of despair or self-mutilation, a more complex conception of beauty and transformation can be discovered.

5. Transcendence: In making art, one transcends the everyday human task of taking care of business. As creator of new forms or re-creator of older ones, one enters the sphere of the gods who created the universe. Art-making is a form of self-portraiture. By making art, one re-creates humanity in one's own image.

If we as creative arts therapists are truly ready to talk to those in our arts-based discipline (and vice-versa), we must do so as equals. We must do so as individuals who understand the original impulse of human beings, both historically and developmentally, to express themselves creatively. We must do so as artists in our own right, whether in terms of our skills and training or in terms of our search for making meaning out of our own lives through a creative process. The only reason why this dialogue should not occur is the fear of losing something precious—one's identity and one's creativity. In recognizing that we share some common assumptions about the nature of art and its concern with expression, emotional release, imagination, beauty and transcendence, the fear can diminish. The conversation can begin. The model above offers an agenda.

One final point—I have noted over the years my own reluctance to engage in an inner dialogue between the part of me that is a theatre director and the part of me that is a drama therapist. When directing a play, I have shut down the therapeutic part with the thought in mind that my work is only in the service of the play. When leading a therapeutic group, I have shut down the aesthetic, formal part to stay focused upon the needs of the clients. Having written this paper, I have become more aware of the need for intrapsychic dialogue between the artist and therapist parts of myself. It is possible to serve a text and a person at the same time. It is possible to care about the feelings of actors and those of the roles they will play. It is possible to speak about the difficulties and role confusions when trying to serve both actors and their roles, both person and persona. It is possible to be the servant of two masters and lead the double life. In recognizing this internal paradox, I am better prepared to engage in productive dialogue with another voice in a related discipline.

Once upon a time, the artist and the healer were one—both reaching for the power of the gods. Together they held a paradox—that the body and the imagination co-exist, that to be more human requires a stretch toward the transcendent. Today that paradox is still with us even as we choose to remain in our isolated boxes. But we still dream of that time once upon a time when others lived effortlessly within that paradox, and we still reach out to them and we still hope that although we cannot recapture the long ago and faraway, we can at least attempt to communicate with our counterparts, one artist to another, right now. For once we have penetrated the surface of our differences we surely have a lot to exchange.

Chapter 3

ROLE THEORY AND THE ROLE
METHOD OF DRAMA THERAPY

INTRODUCTION–THEORY AND METHOD

Role theory has a history throughout the twentieth century in the fields of psychology, sociology and anthropology. It was developed by a number of theorists and practitioners who believed that the dramatic metaphor of life as theatre and people as actors could be applied to an analysis of social and cultural life and inner psychological processes. Those most associated with its early development include William James (1890, 1950), Charles Cooley (1922), George Herbert Mead (1934) and Ralph Linton (1936).

In the 1950s, two prominent role theorists, Theodore Sarbin and Erving Goffman, further developed the metaphor and offered complex social psychological views of life as performance. Goffman's book, *The Presentation of Self in Everyday Life*, became required reading for many psychology and sociology courses since its publication in 1959. The idea of life as performance influenced many social scientists throughout the 1960s and 1970s who analyzed everything from cabdrivers and their fares to gynecological examinations from the perspective of role theory (see Brissett and Edgley, 1975).

Somewhere on the fringe of scholarly acceptability lurked another theorist with a more direct and insistent message. The theorist was Jacob Moreno (1946, 1947, 1960) and his message was that life is not *like* theatre; life *is* theatre. Moreno was less patient and precise than his fellow role theorists. Rather than refining his theoretical speculation, he worked hard to apply his almost theological beliefs to the development of whole systems of therapy, social and cultural analysis and even means of dialoguing with God.

Moreno's work is significant to drama therapists and psychodramatists alike because it is practical. He created a role method of treatment even though his intention was to create both a theory and a practice. Although there have been attempts to glean psychodramatic role theory from Moreno's voluminous and redundant opus (see Fox, 1987), it seems clear that the theory remains in the shadow of the practice.

Drama therapy as a profession developed in a way similar to psychodrama although a number of individuals are responsible for pioneering the field. Since its inception, it has been a practical approach concerned more with the playing of roles than the thinking about roles. Although a number of methods have been developed in the past 30 years, little attention has been focused upon theory. Why is this?

It could be that drama therapists, like their counterparts in other applied forms of therapy, are oriented toward practice and less concerned with cognitive issues. Some with strong backgrounds in the arts and alternative modes of healing tend to value action more than reflection. Others might simply question the value of theory or ignore it altogether, trusting in the power of the spontaneous healing moment. Many of the leaders of the field have come of age during the cultural wars of the 1960s when stogy systems of academic thought were pushed aside to yield practical ways of solving profound and frivolous problems.

I was one of the fighters pushing my way beyond the old ideas. I still consider myself a fighter although I am aware that within this small field of drama therapy, I may have become a representative of a stogy system of academic thought. In reflecting back on the 60s I realize that my goal was not Maoist in nature—attempting to destroy all traditional cultural systems—but rather an attempt to integrate ideas that were worth conserving with those that needed to be changed. Although I thought that theory had to go and direct action had to be taken, I have come to change my view and to even understand that I misunderstood my meta-cognition at the time.

And so I can unabashedly write that I believe in theory and in the traditions of role that have been established by my predecessors. And as a 1960s radical suspicious of scientific thought, I believe that role theory is not just based upon recent trends in social science, but also in ancient traditions of performance that offer explanations of the meaning and purpose of entering into the guise of the other. I have certainly been influenced by the critics and philosophers writing about theatre like Aristotle and Cicero, Goethe and Nietzsche, Walter Benjaman and Northrup Frye, Martin Buber and Victor Turner. But more so I have turned to the thoughtful theatre directors and writers for a deeper understanding of the meaning and function of role. My theatre mentors include Stanislavsky and Brecht, Gordon Craig and Peter Brook. These have been theorists for me to emulate as they have been able to do the work and to reflect upon it with an equal measure of excellence.

From these and many other sources I have learned that the act of taking on and playing a role is mysterious and complex. And I have learned that it occurs in many contexts—in everyday life, in artistic performance, in education, in therapy and in prayer, communing with one's god. In this chapter, I will try to clarify my understanding of role and to offer my version of role theory as it relates to drama therapy. And like my most respected theatre mentors, I will offer an application of my theoretical approach to drama therapy—the role method. The role method is not a theory, but a practical application of role theory. Like any other approach to drama therapy or any other healing practice, the method will be most effective if it can be understood and validated within the context of its theory. My aim in writing this chapter is to demonstrate the continuity of role theory and role method and to make a strong case for a sound intellectual foundation for the still nascent field of drama therapy.

When I speak of role theory in the following pages, I am referring to my version as it applies to drama therapy.

ROLE THEORY

There are several assumptions that lie at the heart of role theory. The first is that human beings are role-takers and role-players by nature. That is, the abilities to imagine oneself as another and to act like the other are essentially unlearned and genetically programmed. Further, human behavior is highly complex and contradictory and any one thought or action in the world can be best understood in the context of its counterpart. Human beings strive toward balance and harmony and although they never fully arrive, they have the capacity to accept the consequences of living with ambivalence and paradox. It is not ultimately the need to resolve cognitive dissonance that motivates human behavior, but the need to live with ambivalence.

A further assumption is that the personality can be conceived as an interactive system of roles. This notion is close to other models that attempt to create a taxonomy to classify personality structures. Philosophically, role theory is more akin to archetypal systems, such as that offered by Jung (1964), than to more reductive behavioral systems, such as that offered by Bloom and his colleagues (1956).

When I published my book on role theory, *Persona and Performance* (1993), I stated emphatically that there was no room for the concept of self. I argued that the Self was a problematic, tired term too easily linked to modern, humanistic models and that role theory offered a more post-modern understanding of human existence as multi-dimensional. Many of my students and colleagues have challenged me on this point and accused me of creating a reductive system, flawed largely by my rejection of some form of observing ego and some essential core construct. As I have continued to work through role theory in practice and thought, I have been able to respond to that criticism by offering a new concept, that of the guide, which I will describe below. This part of the personality, a transitional figure that stands between contradictory tendencies and leads one on a journey toward awareness, is not quite the same as the self, although it serves some similar functions.

Basic Concepts in Role Theory

Role, Counterrole and Guide

Human experience, according to role theory, can be conceptualized in terms of discreet patterns of behavior that suggest a particular way of thinking, feeling or acting. Role is one name for these patterns. Each role, although related to other roles, is unique in terms of its qualities, function and style. Role is not necessarily a fixed entity, but one that is capable of change according to the changing life circumstances of the individual role-player. However, like Jung's notion of archetype, each role is recognizable by virtue of its unique characteristics. For example, when one plays the role of mother, certain discernable qualities will be expressed, including a sense of nurturing and caretaking of another. Although the archetypal nature of the role will remain constant over time, certain specific qualities may change as, for example, one in the mother role expresses the desire to be mothered herself or to abrogate her responsibilities toward her child. Even in the extreme, as a mother engages in fantasies of infanticide, Medea-like, she still maintains the essential qualities of mother. Each role can therefore be identified by its archetypal qualities and its degree of deviation from those qualities, as long as the deviance is understood in relation to the norm.

The primary source of role is the theatre where an actor takes on a role as a means of signifying a particular character with a particular set of qualities and motivations. The metaphor of life as theatre has been so powerful throughout history because so much of human existence concerns a struggle between opposing desires and opposing levels of consciousness. The dramatic structure of antagonist vs. protagonist is played out time and again in everyday life in social interactions and in the struggle with dissonant cognitions. In fact, one way of conceptualizing thought is as an inner dialogue among discrepant points of view (see Moffett, 1968).

When a client begins drama therapy, the drama therapist working from the point of view of role theory often assumes that at least one role the client needs to play in life is either unavailable, poorly developed or inappropriately aligned with other roles or other people in their roles. The initial task of therapy, then, is to help the client access that role and identify it.

In theatrical terms, the role is the protagonist in the client's drama, even though this figure might not yet be aware of the struggles it will undergo in its search for awareness and connection. The counterrole (CR) is the figure that lurks on the other side of the role, the antagonist. It is not the opposite of the role as evil is to good, but rather other sides of the role that may be denied or avoided or ignored in the ongoing attempt to discover effective ways to play a single role. CR is not necessarily a dark or negative figure. If one plays the social role of mother, the CR might be brother or daughter or father. Or it might be something more particular to a client's issues, like helper. For such a client, mother might represent a punitive or abusive figure.

The CR has no independent existence outside of the role. Role appears to have an independent existence and many clients hope to find a way to enact a given role with a degree of competence. Yet even role seeks connection to its counterparts. To be a truly moral person demands an ability to acknowledge and make peace with the immoral or amoral qualities that lurk on the other side.

Role and CR often shift, so that role reversals occur with some regularity. In struggling with moral issues, a client can choose to work with the role of saint or sinner and allow for a shift as one role moves from foreground to background.

The guide, as mentioned above, is the final part of the role trinity. The guide is a transitional figure that stands between role and CR and is used by either one as a bridge to the other. One primary function of the guide is integration. Another is to help clients find their own way. As such, the guide is a helmsman, pilot and pathfinder, a helper who leads individuals along the paths they need to follow. In its most basic form, the guide is the therapist. One comes to therapy because there is no effective guide figure available in one's social or intrapsychic world.

The following story illustrates the notion of therapist as guide. It was October and eight baseball teams were vying for a spot in the World Series. At the beginning of one session, Joe, a man in his mid-40s whom I had been treating in drama therapy for a number of years, asked me whether I had seen the Mets game the previous night. He told me that he watched the game intently so that he would be able to talk with me about it. He knew that I was an ardent Mets fan. The game had been particularly exciting and we chatted about it for a few minutes. Then he told me, with some sadness, that his father never took him to a baseball game.

During the session, we worked on a number of issues, one concerning his relationship with his adolescent nephew, whom he treated in a fatherly way on a recent visit. He worked very deeply with material concerning his relationship to present and absent family members, especially his father who had died 20 years earlier. At the end of the session, Joe quite spontaneous took my hand and said: "Thanks for taking me to the game." He embraced me, as if to say good-bye, a usual ritual for our closure. I held him for a moment and sang:

Take me out to the ballgame,
Take me out to the crowd,
Buy me some peanuts and cracker jacks,
I don't care if I never get back....

When I reached the chorus he joined in:

For it's one, two, three strikes you're out
At the old ball game.

We looked at each other and laughed and then he left.

In that session, I became not only Joe's transferential father, but also his guide. Although his real father could not take him to a real ballgame, his guide could take him to a virtual one. Our therapy session was a ballgame in that we were able to share an intimacy painfully denied by his father. In the moment of intimacy, with the help of the guide, the past rejections of the father were corrected.

The guide figure is first visible as existing in the world outside the client. It takes many forms in everyday life including: parent, sibling, special relative or friend, teacher, coach, religious leader, media personality, criminal, demon and God. The guide can be moral, immoral or amoral.

Although drama therapy begins with the tacit understanding that the therapist will take on and play out the role of guide, the process moves toward a different aim—that clients will internalize the guide and discover, ultimately, a way to guide themselves.

Another way to look at the same internal understanding of guide is that all clients enter therapy with all kinds of potential inner guide figures. For many, these figures are hard to access. Through the process of drama therapy, clients are challenged to re-create their inner guides which, once developed, can lead them through difficult territory.

Role and CR are more clearly properties of the client. They are revealed through behavior and thought. And like the guide they too will serve as internal figures that seek balance within the psyche. Joe seeks such a balance between the part of him that is a child, longing for a father's love, and the part of him that is a grown-up, capable of fathering others even as he fathers himself.

When the three parts of the psyche are intact, the inner guide will facilitate the connection between child and father. It will allow Joe to feel loved and loving at the same time. And it will allow Joe to feel the pain of the missed moments of fathering without shame.

Role Types and the Taxonomy of Roles

For many years I asked the question—if it is true that the personality is a system of interactive roles, what are the specific roles within that system? In looking for answers, I turned to others systems. From Jung (1971) I learned about the attitudes of the extrovert and introvert and the four functions of thinking, feeling, sensing and intuiting. For a more archetypal understanding of role, I also looked toward Jung's notion of anima and animus, of shadow and persona and puer. From latter-day Jungians such as Campbell (1949) and Hillman (1983) I discovered a more contemporary way to understand role types.

I looked at less conventional systems such as the spiritual enneagram that proposes nine personality types: the reformer, the helper, the status seeker, the artist, the thinker, the loyalist, the generalist, the leader and the peacemaker (see Riso, 1987). And I also looked at a more literary system such as that offered by Carol Pearson (1989) who envisions personality structure as comprised of six types: innocent, orphan, magician, wanderer, martyr and warrior.

Although all these systems were valuable and revealing, no one led me to the essential source of all work in drama therapy—the theatre. Having realized that the one unique feature of drama therapy, distinguishing it from all other healing forms, is its theatrical underpinnings, I paused for a long drink at the well of theatre.

It occurred to me that the one indivisible element in theatre is role. Many plays have neither plot nor spectacle nor even language. But all share the basic premise that actors take on roles to create a character. Starting with this premise, I began to look at the many roles available in theatrical plays since the beginning of recorded history. I limited myself to an exploration of Western dramatic literature as I was unfamiliar with the Eastern traditions. In recent years as I became more aware of such Eastern theatrical forms as Japanese Noh theatre, Peking Opera and Indian Kathakali, I have come to realize that these traditions, free from the modern Western influence of psychological realism, lend themselves more easily to classification according to character type. But this must remain the subject of another study.

As I searched the *dramatis personae* of many hundreds of Western plays, I became aware of a repeated pattern of character types that seemed to transcend time, genre and culture. They included heroes and villains, nobility and commoners, victims and survivors, wise fools and ignorant kings, deceivers and helpers and lovers of all kinds.

The repeated role of hero, for example, from the Greek Oedipus to the British Lear to the American Willy Loman, embodied certain archetypal qualities and I began to specify them. They included a willingness to confront the unknown and to journey forth on a spiritual search for a meaning just beyond their grasp (Landy, 1993, p. 230). I also noticed that all heroes serve a common function within the drama, which I noted as taking a risky psychological and spiritual journey toward understanding and transformation (Landy, 1993, p. 230).

And finally, I noticed that each role type, consistent with its aesthetic form and genre, tended to be enacted within a particular style. I noted two primary styles, the presentational, a more abstract form removed from the trappings of real-life speech and action, and the representational, a more reality-based form. Given my understanding of aesthetic distance, I postulated that presentational styles are linked to more cognitive modes of expression, and representational styles are linked to more affective modes. In playing a role, the actor achieves the desired aesthetic effect, whether comic or tragic, whether melodramatic or farcical, by playing with the level of distance. However, the role that an actor takes on is in itself determined by its aesthetically-based stylistic tradition. While it is true that the modern Willy Loman is a kind of anti-hero popular in mid-twentieth century literature, he still is typically measured against the classical tragic hero from which he derives. And although many actors play him in a realistic manner, attempting to discover the emotional depths of his suffering, he was written by Arthur Miller within a presentational style, consistent with the traditions of the role type, hero.

Parallel to the stage actor, the client in drama therapy is led through particular levels of cognition and affect as the drama therapist introduces more or less stylized roles and activities. The drama therapist facilitates the client's play with style in order to help her discover a balance of affect and cognition so that she might be able to work through a dilemma with the capacities to feel and to reflect intact. Style is the distancer in drama therapy, a way to move a client closer or further away from a role that she needs to play in order to discover balance.[1]

---

1. For a full discussion of distancing in drama therapy, see Landy, 1983.

In completing the taxonomy of roles, I listed 84 role types and a number of subtypes. My main criterion for choosing a role type was its appearance in at least three historical periods, e.g., classical, renaissance and neoclassical, or repeated use throughout one particular period and/or genre. In recent years I have refined the taxonomy, eliminating redundancy, especially for the purpose of developing an assessment instrument, to be discussed below.

It should be noted that all roles in the taxonomy work within the triadic system of role, counterrole and guide. Any one role type, such as the Child, can serve as protagonist (role), antagonist (CR) and/or guide within an individual's therapeutic drama.

Role System

In developing the taxonomy of roles, I made the assumption that all human beings have the potential to take on and play out all the identified roles plus others not specified. The quantity of roles available will be based upon many factors including biological predisposition, social modeling, psychological motivation, environmental circumstance, and moral judgment, as well as such secondary factors as readiness and will. The totality of roles available at any one moment is known as the role system. Role system is another way of thinking about personality structure. It is the container of all the intrapsychic roles. Within the role system are those roles that are available to consciousness and that can be played out competently. But there are also dormant roles within the role system that have faded from consciousness because of neglect or abuse or lack of need. Roles that are not called out will not be played out, even though they may exist within. They will be activated when given the proper social or environmental circumstance.

As an example, Jill was repeatedly told by her family that she was dull and unimaginative. She was discouraged from continuing her education beyond the age of 16. After her minimal schooling, she took on a series of menial and unfulfilling jobs. After a brief time in drama therapy, she enrolled in a continuing education course in art history. She recalled that her hand shook as she filled out the registration form. During the first class, when slides were shown of classical paintings, she was overcome with emotion and had to leave the room. She secluded herself in the bathroom and sobbed. The next class, for the first time in her life, she discovered that she had something to say about the paintings. She dared to speak up and was acknowledged for her insightful comments.

With my encouragement, Jill began to do her own drawings, very intimate images concerning her abusive past. Although the creation and dialogue with the images was very painful, she took great pride in discovering that a whole new role–that of artist–was suddenly available. During one session she exclaimed: "I think the artist has been there all the time. It was just asleep."

The structure of the role system is dynamic. When one role is called into the foreground, others fade into the background. One way of viewing the structure is as a staged scene in a play. When one actor speaks, the others on stage need to listen and react appropriately. Some remain silent and unseen, playing out their roles as extras.

Within the structure of the role system, roles tend to seek balance with their counterparts. This is especially true in a healthy, integrated personality. Such a personality would also be one where a variety of roles from a variety of domains would be prepared to, if called, take a leading part in an individual's life drama.

View of Health and Illness

The healthy person, from the point of view of role theory, is noted by an ability to live with ambivalence, contradictory tendencies and paradox. In a previous book of essays (Landy, 1996), I refer to this person as one who is effectively able to live a double life. The image does not refer to schizoid splits but to an acknowledgement that the human condition is in part one of living simultaneously within paradoxical realms of mind and body, thought and action, subject and object, actor and observer, one role and its counterpart. The healthy adult person who functions responsibly has found a way to live with her contradictory tendencies to act up like a child and to act out like an adolescent. The role and CR are in balance and when the need arises to play the child or adolescent, the individual can do so without the fear of losing all sense of maturity and judgment.

When out of balance, that is, when too much the child or too much the adolescent, the healthy person is able to draw upon the wisdom of a guide figure to help move back toward the center. The guide might be a friend or a therapist or it might be an inner figure that signals a time for reflection and a time for a shift of behavior.

The healthy person is also noted by her ability to take on many, if not most, of the roles in the taxonomy and to play them out in everyday life with some degree of proficiency. Very few people, the best character actors notwithstanding, are able to enact all 84 roles with a full measure of competency. Proficiency and competency are often hard to measure. However, these traits are generally present when one is able to behave in role and reflect upon that behavior in a balanced way, that is, with feeling and with understanding. Also the competent role player is one who is able to articulate in words and/or action the appropriate qualities, function and style of any given role.

Health, then, is a measure of both the quantity of roles one internalizes and plays out and the quality of the role enactment.

The unhealthy person, from a role perspective, is one who has given up the struggle to live with ambivalence and has, instead, embraced one role or a cluster of related ones, at the exclusion of all others. Feeling overwhelmed by complexity, the unhealthy person finds ways to limit the quantity and quality of roles within his inner and outer world. This is the domain of the fundamentalist who worships one belief system as he rejects all other forms of belief or ways of seeing the world. And this is the domain of the autistic whose world is limited to a very small private set of thoughts and behaviors. In most forms of extreme mental illness marked by obsessional or delusional thinking, the role system is severely limited.

From a social point of view, the unhealthy person is marked by an inability to take on the role of the other and thus to empathize with another. We find that narcissistic individuals, for example, live in a very narrow universe of roles. Each social encounter which offers a possible means of taking on a new role becomes a distorted mirror. Instead of looking at the other and seeing a reflection of what she might become, the narcissist looks at the other and sees a reflection of how she is. For the narcissist, the other cannot mediate or represent any new ways of being. In offering a fixed mirror, the other becomes the pool of water that ultimately drowns the mythological Narcissus.

The unhealthy person is also marked by his inability to internalize and enact a number of roles competently. In the extreme, this person would find many of the roles listed in the taxonomy foreign and distant. Further, he would find it difficult to attribute qualities, functions and styles to those roles with which he identifies.

Assessment

In applying the taxonomy of roles to clinical work in drama therapy, I have developed two assessment instruments. The first, called Role Profiles (see Chapter 9), is a simple pencil and paper test which offers a modified list of the roles within the taxonomy and asks the subject to rate each one on a Likert-type scale from 0-4 according to two measures: how much one acts like the role in one's everyday life and how much one plays out the role in one's imagination. Role Profiles is currently undergoing revisions. It is evolving into a card sort test and will soon be subjected to measures of reliability and validity. However, a number of studies have already been done (see Raz, 1997, Tangorra, 1997, Rosenberg, 1999,) attempting to establish these and other benchmarks of research. Once the appropriate research and clinical protocols have been established, this instrument should serve as an effective means of viewing an individual's role system in terms of quantity and quality of roles taken and played. With further research, a clinical drama therapist should be able to apply this data directly toward treatment.

The second instrument developed from role theory is called Tell-A-Story (see Chapter 10). Its aim is to assess an individual's ability to invoke a role, CR and guide and to move toward some integration and connection among the roles. Through Tell-A-Story, the subject is given the following task: *I would like you to tell me a story. The story can be based upon something that happened to you or to somebody else in real life or it can be completely made-up. The story must have at least one character.*

The tester is instructed to provide any prompts necessary to help the subject tell the story. The tester encourages those who are not very verbal to tell the story through miniature objects or puppets. Following the story, the subject is asked to specify the characters in the story, limited to three, and answer a number of questions concerning their qualities, function and style of presentation. The subject is also asked to specify the theme of the story and comment on the connection between the fictional roles and their everyday life.

This assessment instrument is still in its formative stages and needs further research and refinement before it is applied to a broad clinical spectrum.

In evaluating change, the therapist looks for a shift in the quantity and quality of roles taken and enacted, as well as an ability of the client to identify and work through role, CR and guide figures. To determine the effectiveness of the treatment the therapist asks several questions:

1. Is the client able to identify a problematic role(s) and to take it on and enact it with a degree of competency? By competency I mean an awareness of the qualities, function and style of role presentation and an application of that awareness to effective social interactions in role.
2. Is the client able to identify a CR and take it on and enact it with a degree of competency?
3. Is the client able to identify a guide figure and use it as an aid in moving through a crisis?
4. Is the client able to live among contradictory roles?
5. Is the client able to take on and play out a range of roles throughout the six domains of the taxonomy of roles?

The therapist can evaluate a client's progress at the end of each session, at the conclusion of a given number of sessions or at the termination of the treatment. At any juncture, having made the evaluation, the therapist can share her observations and offer suggestions to the client. She can also help the client evaluate his own progress by sharpening his ability to identify roles, counterroles and guide figures.

The Role Method

Role theory is applied to treatment by means of the role method (RM). In *Persona and Performance* (1993), I specified the method as proceeded through eight steps:
1. Invoking the role.
2. Naming the role.
3. Playing out/working through the role.
4. Exploring alternative qualities in subroles.
5. Reflecting upon the role play: discovering role qualities, functions and styles inherent in the role.
6. Relating the fictional role to everyday life.
7. Integrating roles to create a functional role system.
8. Social modeling: discovering ways that clients' behavior in role affects others in their social environments.

The model still holds although I have revised step four to accommodate my understanding of CR and guide. During the working through stage, the client is presumably working with a single role that he has identified and named. For example, George, a visual artist in his late 50s, came to therapy because he felt like a professional failure. I pointed out that failure was more of a quality than a role and helped George discover that the failed role was that of artist. We worked with the artist role through stories and dreamwork and role play. Soon we discovered that it wasn't the artist part of George that felt like a failure, but its counterpart whom George first named the bank and then the businessman.

In identifying his problematic role as the businessman, George did not appear to me to be exploring a subrole of the artist but in fact discovering a counterrole. When George acknowledged his feelings of incompetence concerning the sale of art, he was able to reclaim the artist on the other side of the businessman and work toward ways of integrating the two with the help of several guide figures whom he identified and named.

There is an intermediary step between three and four This is the step of de-roling which generally applies to a shift in realities from the dramatic to that of everyday life. In this first instance of de-roling, however, the client distances himself from one role, enters for a moment into a neutral position associated with everyday life, and then prepares to take on the CR.

De-roling also occurs between steps four and five as the client moves fully out of the imaginary realm, leaving the fictional roles behind, and prepares to reflect upon the fictions just created. De-roling signals the essential paradox of the dramatic experience—that of the continuity of the me and not-me, of the actor in relation to the role. In leaving the dramatic role, the actor resumes a life in a parallel universe that is less obviously masked and stylized. Because drama therapy treatment in role can become quite complex and confusing, the therapist needs to insure that the client de-roles each character and each object. While under the spell of the role, the client loses distance and has difficulty reflecting upon the drama.

There is no such rarified position as a fully de-roled human being. Behind all masks are more masks. The aim of de-roling is not to fully transcend one's personae, but to shift from one reality, that of the imagination, to another, that of the everyday, for the purpose of reflection. Another way of looking at de-roling is as a shift from a more affective, physically active mode to a more cognitive, reflective one.

The steps in the role method do not necessarily proceed in a linear fashion. As a client works with a problematic role, he might discover, as George did, that the problem really lies on the other side. The CR then becomes the role and needs to be clearly named and worked through in itself. At the place marked as step four, the client is encouraged to locate a guide figure. Many, however, begin therapy with a guide figure intact or temporarily lost, one that usually is based upon a nurturing or idealized parent.

Steps five and six of the role method are reflective and point to a cognitive component of the approach. Following some form of enactment clients are asked to reflect upon the roles they have played and then to link the roles to their everyday lives. Many drama therapists believe that enactment is healing in itself and that reflection is at best unnecessary and at worst counterproductive. I believe that reflection and verbal processing are potentially as important as enactment in leading to healing. However, I do recognize that verbal processing would be inappropriate with certain populations with limited insight and verbal capacities such as autistic children and severely mentally ill or mentally retarded adults.

The final step, that of social modeling, implies that once a role or configuration of role-CR-guide has been changed, the client becomes a model for others within his various social environments of home, work, play, etc. When George goes to an upscale cocktail party given by wealthy art dealers, many of whom he has encountered previously, feeling insecure each time, he is fearful that they will see him as a failed artist. But since therapy has helped him to revise his self-conception, he is able to go as a competent artist whose business and self-promotional acumen is a work in progress. The dealers react positively to his altered self-perception and engage him in conversation. At the same time, peers at the party who think of themselves as failed artists see

George in a more relaxed state and wish they could be more like him. George then, in his transformed state, becomes a role model for them.

I begin both a group and an individual session in a variety of ways. Most often, I greet my clients and wait for them to verbalize or non-verbally indicate their present state of being. Sometimes, especially with a new group, I will lead them through a physical warm-up and help them locate a role. One exercise I use often is to ask the group to move through the room and let go of tension through breathing and stretching and extending. I ask them to focus upon one body part and allow a movement to extend from, for example, their belly. I ask them to play with the movement, adding a sound and letting a character emerge. Once the character is established, I help the group develop it further through improvisational interactions in role, brief monologues, and finally, a naming of the role.

Once individuals in the group are warmed up to their roles, we work through these roles by means of storymaking or sculpting or free play in small groups. Or individuals can work toward locating counterroles and guide roles and setting up improvisational scenes among the three.

The form of identifying the three roles is generally effective, especially in higher functioning groups. This approach can become more confusing with low functioning or highly medicated groups. In that case, I generally begin work with a single role. If and when there is an opportunity to move to the other side of the role, I will ask individuals or a full group to locate and take on the counterrole.

With this model in mind, I will utilize a range of techniques, generally staying within the scope of projective techniques (see Landy, 1994). With individuals as well as groups, I will use sandplay and free play, mask and puppets, drawings and sculpts, storytelling and storymaking and playback theatre. Most recently, I have found that work with stories provides a clear structure within which clients can locate and work with their roles and subsequent counterroles and guides. If any of the three are missing, the story structure provides a frame in which to locate the missing pieces.

In treatment, I also make use of psychodramatic techniques including doubling, role reversals, mirroring and sharing during closure. I try to avoid the often direct reality orientation and intense cathartic nature of psychodrama unless I sense that clients have distanced themselves too much from feeling and need to tell a direct story with a maximum of affect. In groups I also make use of sociometry in order to discover certain underlying dynamics and to encourage members to make often risky choices.

With some clients who have difficulty organizing their lives because of borderline tendencies or addictive dependencies, I will use a modification of cognitive-behavioral approaches. My aim will be to help them develop effective coping strategies. In terms of a role approach, I often ask them to identify a role that they need to play and to specify its behavioral qualities. I help them practice playing the role in therapy as a rehearsal for moments in everyday life. I model this kind of work on the approach of George Kelly (1955) who developed a form a treatment called fixed role therapy.

In working cognitively, my goal is to help individuals reconstruct their mental schemas and find appropriate roles and counterroles to structure their lives. Through this work, a conscious effort is made to locate an inner guide figure, a kind of reliable central intelligence that can effectively direct the show.

The Role of the Drama Therapist

The drama therapist working through the role method needs to be flexible and responsive. Generally speaking, the drama therapist serves as guide and model, standing over and above the client, encouraging him, finally, to find his own guide. It is inadvisable for the drama therapist to become too distanced as this may provoke too much transference on the part of the client. When moments of transference do occur, the drama therapist can take on the transferential role and engage with the client, encouraging him to take on an appropriate counterrole. In the example I offered above of Joe, both therapist and client enter the domain of father and son as they visit a metaphorical baseball game and sing the evocative song, *Take Me Out to the Ballgame.*

In general, the drama therapist neither encourages nor discourages transference. When it appears, the drama therapist should be prepared to do one of two things. In the first instance, she takes it on in the form of a role and encourages the client to take on the counterrole. Both in their respective roles then enact a brief drama. Following the enactment, they derole and discuss the experience. In the second instance, often in a group process, the therapist helps the group to shift the transference from the therapist to the group thus empowering the group to work through the drama of transference on its own. For a full discussion of this second approach, see Eliaz (1988).

The model of distancing very much guides the interaction of therapist and client (see Landy, 1983, 1994, 1996a). The therapist will assess each moment and make instantaneous judgments as to how close and how distant to be with the client. The determination will be based upon two primary factors:
1. the client's diagnosis and ability to handle closeness and/or separation;
2. the therapist's ability to contain emotion and to deal effectively with his countertransferential reactions within a session.

Although the therapist must be willing to take on various counterroles to the client's roles and engage in a direct form of play, she will most of the time serve more as director and witness to the play of the client(s). One exception is when working with children through play therapy. In this case, the drama therapist will most often engage directly in the play unless the child clearly indicates her wish to play alone. In playing with the child, the therapist will work toward establishing open communication and trust, setting limits, containing emotion, and helping to clarify the theme of the play. The therapist will work through the structure of role-CR-guide to ultimately help the client find a way in and out of each.

When taking a more distanced stance, the therapist will guide the enactment and encourage the client to take on and play out the necessary roles. As an example, George comes into a session and tells me a dream. It is about a villain who sits in a room at the top of a tall tower. He has killed George's wife and George goes up to confront him. The villain transforms into many shapes. In one, he is driving George's car and George puts his hands over the villain's eyes so he will crash. In the front seat is a tough, sexy woman. In the end, George is with his wife who has come back to life. They are both descending the stairs of the tower. The villain is above and spits down at them. It is hard to avoid the spit. The villain is captured and sent to jail.

In working with the dream, I ask George to assume all the roles. He plays the villain, the wife, the sexy woman in the car, the car, the tower and the spit, giving a first person monologue for each role. He also identifies himself, George, as the protagonist. I watch George work. I am fully engaged in his drama, although I do not participate directly. I guide him from role to role, sometimes asking questions so that he will deepen his connection to a particular role or amplify a theme. After his enactment, I lead him through a discussion of the roles and their connection to one another. Finally, I ask him to link the roles in the dream to his everyday life.

Through our work together, George has learned to make the connections. Over time, George has learned to expand his repertory of roles, to deepen his commitment to several key roles and to find a way to guide himself without the fear of crashing. As therapist, I remain present as guide, reminding him to remove his hands from his eyes while he is driving, encouraging him to explore all the dark rooms at the tops of towers, urging him to look at ways to exist as a man among men and among women.

Populations Best Served through the Role Method

I began experimenting with drama therapy in the mid-1960s when I was a teacher of emotionally disturbed adolescents. My task was to teach English and drama, but many of my students were too disorganized and did not have the inner controls to learn how to scan poetry or to memorize lines in a play. Their pathologies ranged from learning disabilities and neurological impairments to severe mental illness and trauma. It took me several years of trial and error to begin to feel any sense of competence. I was learning the ropes, making up the work as I went along. For my students I was a guide of sorts, although very much a work in progress. I was not much older than some. Many had more life experience than I would ever have. And yet, I knew something about the theatre and had a great faith in its healing power. My years as an actor were more therapeutic than aesthetically gratifying as I found a form through which I could express and work through my pain. I was passionate about sharing my experience with others.

Twenty-five years passed before I developed role theory and the role method, and yet the seeds to my work as a drama therapist were planted at that time. I learned how to reach people who were unable to think and feel in a traditional way, who were unable to trust and to communicate and to empathize.

As I have developed drama therapy approaches over the years, I have kept my early experiences very much alive. The emotionally disturbed people I initially worked with remain my models, and when I speak of role-CR-guide or the taxonomy of roles or the role method, I still reflect upon my early work with them. It made sense that when I started to treat individual clients in drama therapy, the first population I worked with was learning disabled adolescents.

During the past 30 years I have worked with a sizable number of people, including those from the following populations: attention deficit hyperactive disorder (ADHD), alcohol and heroin addiction, eating disorders, post-traumatic stress disorder (PTSD), bipolar disorder, sexual disorders, borderline and schizophrenic disorders, physical and developmental disabilities and normal neurotics, among others. My students trained in role method have applied the principles of role theory to the treatment of these and a range of other populations including conduct disordered and incarcerated adolescents and adults, war veterans, sexually abused children, homeless mentally ill and frail elderly.

It is difficult to say which groups respond best to this treatment. On one level, it appears that the higher functioning normal neurotic population is most responsive in that this group can easily verbalize and reflect upon their enactments in role. And yet, there is growing evidence that the role method is also effective in treating lower functioning mentally ill individuals. One recent study (Sussman, 1998) offered evidence, primarily anecdotal, that a group of schizophrenics could effectively invoke and work through a number of roles, then relate these figures to their everyday lives.

It remains speculative as to which groups are best suited to role method as there is no hard research available. The evidence that abounds is largely anecdotal and based in process recordings and clinical observations. The exception is the development of systematic case studies which provide a view of the therapeutic process in terms of the role theory paradigm. Case studies include those of Michael (Landy, 1993), Hansel and Gretel (Landy, 1993), Sam (Landy, 1996), Kerry, Lena and Walt (Landy, 1997) and Fay (Landy, 1999).

Limitations and Challenges

There are a number of limitations to role theory. Like any other theory, it is limited by its own set of assumptions concerning epistemology and such psychological issues as personality structure, health and wellness, therapeutic goals and processes. It challenges the humanistic, existential, modernist assumptions that undergird much of drama therapy, moving drama therapy discourse into a cognitive, constructivist, post-modernist realm. Many practitioners find this particular orientation too theoretical and intellectual.

Role theory does not sufficiently address issues of human development. It relies on a model of the human personality–the taxonomy of roles–that is derived from an art form and has very little scientific basis. The taxonomy itself, no matter how flexible and fluid, remains a reductive system, not easily applicable to the fluid and spontaneous movement of individuals from role to role in everyday life and in therapy.

Role theory tends to have more of a literary than social scientific focus and thus does not lend itself to the development of a substantial research literature acceptable to social scientists. And even as modeled in dramatic literature, it relies almost entirely upon role and character at the expense of theme and plot, sound and sense.

The other side of that argument is that the part of role theory that is derived from sociology and symbolic interactionism has too much of a scientific focus as noted in the development of a substantial research literature (see Brissett and Edgley, 1975, Serifica, 1982). As such, it remains unacceptable to those who insist on an aesthetic perspective and minimize the importance of systematic research studies.

The role method is also limited in that it is based in a single theory that is limited in at least the ways mentioned above. If it were linked more clearly with other approaches it might allow the practitioner more leeway in treatment and analysis. Although role method practitioners do make use of techniques associated with play therapy, playback theatre, psychodrama, Gestalt therapy and related approaches, their primary means of treatment is through projective techniques. This can be a limitation, especially when clients need to work in a direct manner, unmediated by role.

There are two challenges to this and indeed to any method and/or theory of drama therapy. The first is to verify its efficacy through carefully designed research studies. Through research, the method/theory will assert its uniqueness among others. The second is to demonstrate its common bonds with other approaches to drama therapy which would, in a broad sense, further establish the credibility of the entire field of drama therapy.

Case Example

The experience I will describe took place during an intense two-day workshop in Israel. I think that it well represents both the philosophy of role theory and the practice of role method. The focus of the workshop was to explore the spiritual dimension of life. In the beginning, as the group was warming up, it became clear that many were uncomfortable with the topic. The group was comprised mainly of therapists and artists, who primarily considered themselves to be secular Jews. They harbored open resentment toward the ultra-orthodox whom, they thought, tried to impose strict spiritual and moral guidelines upon their everyday lives.

After some heated debate, I helped the group identify several roles: the spiritual searcher, the doubter, the object of the search and the guide. Although I had intended to limit the role choice to three, I recognized the group's need to distance itself from associating God with the object of their search. The fourth role of guide was acceptable to the group because it felt more neutral than God and stood outside the object of the search.

As I reflected upon the choice of roles, I thought that the literal guide was redundant and that the object of the search would easily stand in for the guide. More than that, I imagined that any of the roles could be guide, although the searcher and doubter felt like a clear representation of the role and counterrole.

Following a complex process of storytelling, drawing and improvisational enactment, I asked the group to choose one story to dramatize. They chose Judah's story. Judah was an anomaly in the group—a businessman among therapists and artists. He had never attended a therapeutic or creative workshop of any kind. He remained quiet and withdrawn throughout the first several hours of the experience. On a number of occasions I wondered if he would be able to complete the tasks and enter fully into the process. And yet his story was extraordinary in some way. This is Judah's story:

A man comes home from work early and lies down on the couch to take a nap. He wakes suddenly, as if from a dream, to find the light from the TV blinding him. He tries to turn it off, but he cannot. He is disoriented and in order to regain his balance, he must determine the time of day. He picks up the phone and calls an old girlfriend named Rona. He identifies himself as Robert. He asks her urgently: "Is it 6 o'clock in the morning or 6 o'clock in the evening? Please tell me. I must know!" There is no answer. The man cannot rest. He is desperate to know the answer to his question. The question remains unanswered.

The story baffled and intrigued me and probably the others in the group, for they chose it among many highly imaginative and poetic stories. I noticed that there did not seem to be a guide in the story. Although the man turns to Rona to answer his question, she is unable to answer. I wonder why Judah identified the man as Robert. Was this some form of transference? Did he think that I could help him answer his question or, better yet, understand what the question means? Was I supposed to be the guide for Judah who takes on my name in order to search for a sense of balance?

In terms of role theory, my speculation made sense. Judah, a man who has never experienced therapy or a creative arts experience, felt off balance in his life and his wife, a creative arts therapist, suggested that he attend this workshop. In search of a guide to help him find his balance, he takes on the role of the leader whom he imagines is powerful and wise. Judah hopes that the guide role will help him find the clarity and balance he so desperately seeks. In this example, the role and the guide are merged although, as we shall see, they soon become separate. The counterrole appears to be the ex-girlfriend, Rona, the one who cannot answer the question, the false hope, as many ex-lovers come to be.

After the group chose Judah's story, Judah read the story aloud. Unsure of how to proceed with the dramatization, I asked Judah: "Who is telling the story?" As the words came out of my mouth, I realized that I had no idea why I asked this question.

"Leonard is telling the story," Judah replied.

Something was happening that felt unexpected and exciting. Other presences were about to be revealed.

"Who is Leonard?" I asked.

"I am Leonard," said Judah.

And then Judah told the story behind the story. He was born Leonard in Poland. He immigrated to Israel when he was five years old. At the border, the immigration officer told him that Leonard, the Lion, was not a proper Jewish name. As he was about to enter his new land, he was given the name Judah, the Jew.

An important part of the role method concerns the naming of roles. I recognized that Judah's drama would be based upon discovering the right names for his roles and working them through. In discovering the twin names of Leonard/Judah, a significant role-CR relationship was present. On a whole other level, however, I recognized that Leonard would be Judah's guide, just like Robert. Judah seemed to need several guides. He was in foreign territory. By engaging in this workshop, he had stepped over another border.

I asked Judah to tell Leonard's story. He stumbled but managed to tell this:

> There is a little boy. He is not alone. He is with a group of human beings. I think they are grown-ups but they could be children. Or I think they are childlike. The human beings help Leonard to grow.

I ask Judah to choose three people as the human beings and one as Leonard. He chooses Avi, a very playful and dramatic member of the workshop, to be Leonard. Taking their cue from Judah, the group becomes light and playful. The human beings engulf Leonard and Leonard loves the attention. They circle the room, arm in arm, singing and dancing. They are connected and happy. Judah stays by my side. He tells me that he is happy watching the drama.

I noticed that the human beings are easy guides for the little boy to follow. There doesn't appear to be a counterrole in the story. There is no tension, no strife. It appears to be a picture of the boy before he crosses the border, before the fall, before he was forced to change his identity and be a man.

I asked Judah if he was ready to enact Judah's story. He became more serious as he said "Yes." He chooses Dahlia to play himself. I ask him to help Dahlia enter into her role. But as he begins to instruct her, she stops: "Who am I supposed to be?" she asks. "Am I Judah or Leonard or Robert?"

Dahlia raises a very important question. In terms of role theory, is she to be the role, the CR or the guide? Judah, the spiritual searcher, seems to be the protagonist of the story, the central role figure. Leonard could be either a CR or guide. And Robert would appear to be a guide figure.

Who is guiding whom, I wonder? And then I remember the four roles the group had specified at the beginning of the workshop. The first, the spiritual searcher, is well exemplified by Judah. The doubter could also be Judah in the guise of the storyteller or when he returns home from work, so weary that he falls asleep. The object of the search is unknown, but appears to be the one who can answer the man's question. It might be Rona. And the guide appears to be Robert, the workshop leader whose name is taken on by Judah.

With all the potential role confusions it is no wonder that Dahlia is confused. And then she questions why Judah picked a woman to play a man.

Dahlia is stuck and I ask Judah to choose someone else from the group to help her find her way. He immediately chooses Avi who again takes on the childish energy of Leonard and starts to wail: "I want my Mommy! I want my Mommy!"

Dahlia is energized and plays with Avi. They encircle each other as she tries to contain his energy, his mock expression of fear. Role and CR are finally present, the child in pain and the mother attempting to contain. They have transcended the story line, but something very important is happening and we all feel it. I bring Judah directly into the drama, having him reverse roles with Dahlia. Judah tries to calm the child. He pets Avi and says: "It's OK. You will be alright. You are such a good boy."

I tell Judah to try to reach Rona and ask her the question. He picks Roni from the group to play Rona. But as moves toward her, Avi holds on to him tightly. Judah struggles to break free. He finally manages to pull away, but loses a shoe to Avi.

Judah asks the question: "What time is it? I have to know."

She replies: "It is six in the morning."

But I feel she is the wrong object of Judah's search, the wrong guide, and so I ask him: "Did you ask the right question?"

He replies: "No."

I invite others in the group to enter the drama as Judah/Robert and attempt to find the right question. No one is successful. Judah is not able to accept any of their questions.

Again, I am stumped. How do I end this enactment? What needs to happen? And then I realize that the role-CR tension needs some resolution. The drama now concerns Judah, the searcher, and Rona, the object of the search. I ask all in the group to touch the person with whom they most identify—the searcher or the object of the search. Most all choose Judah. They, too, are searchers who are not clear as to their spiritual questions. How different they are from the beginning of the workshop when most openly identified with the role of doubter.

Needing to integrate the two roles, I ask Avi and Roni to attempt to touch one another. When they do, the drama will end. I ask the group to ensure that the moment of touch does not happen too quickly. They take hold of Avi and Roni and pull them in different directions. I then ask Judah to stand in for Avi. Judah and Roni struggle to break free from the group.

Finally, exhausted, the group allows them to touch. The drama ends, and I work hard to de-role all the participants. Judah is in a heightened state and has trouble letting go of the extraordinary roles of the man who wakes up, of Robert and Leonard, of searcher, guide and child. This form of experience in role is all new to Judah. The full group helps him to breathe, to shake off the magic, to come back to the present moment in time. It is a hard journey back for all.

As we discuss this experience, many levels of role-CR-guide unfold. On the level of the dramatic reality, Robert and Rona become role and CR, the searcher and the object of the search. The question of time is never properly answered and doesn't even seem to matter since it might have been the wrong question to ask in the first place. What seems to matter most is the touch, the integration of the roles. Judah reports that this moment was the most satisfying of all. It could be because of the integration of role and CR which, according to role theory, should have some relationship to Judah's everyday life.

That relationship is discovered when Judah explains that Roni, whom he chose to play Rona, the ex-girlfriend, is in reality his wife. On another level, then, this was a drama about Judah's connection to his wife. The figure of the ex-girlfriend becomes a kind of counterrole that leads Judah back to the strength of his current relationship. Incidentally, I recall that Roni led Judah to the workshop in the first place, hoping that it would move him out of his lethargy and imbalance.

On another level, Judah makes a conscious association of Robert as guide. He becomes aware that he took on this guide role as a means of searching for an answer to his burning question. I ask him to consider ways to hold on to this role as he re-enters his everyday realms of love and work and play.

And finally we are left with the theme of the workshop, exploring the spiritual realm through drama therapy. At the beginning of the experience, I mentioned to the group that I was in the process of researching ways that children see God. It was at that moment that several group members expressed their uneasiness with the topic of spirituality in general, and the concept of God, in particular. I chose not to deal with God in any direct way, but here we were at the end of the workshop and I had a need to link our work with the central theme.

"Was Judah's story dramatization spiritual in any way?" I asked. Many nodded in the affirmative and tried to articulate the mysterious quality of Judah's story and the search for love as a spiritual theme. Some spoke about the question of time and related this to the timelessness of the divine. But the most striking comment was made, finally, by Avi, the one who was able to so easily take on the role of the child, Leonard, before and after the fall. He informed us that God is referred to in Hebrew as *Hashem*, literally, the name. There is a prohibition in the orthodox Jewish faith about speaking the name of God directly. Thus God is referred to indirectly as *Hashem*. Avi said that he saw the drama therapy experience as focused upon naming. Judah's search for the right name and Dahlia's confusion over the names was like the Jew's search for the right name of God. And then Judah recognized that the prohibition against speaking the holy name of God connects to his own prohibition against speaking the name of Leonard, the child that he was a long time ago.

Upon further reflection I became aware that Judah was a man very much in search of a guide, one who could help him integrate not only the name he lost as a child, but also the lost qualities of the child. In the end, he recognized that the playful qualities of the child could guide him in so many ways: to get him through his work, to allow him a restful night's sleep, to keep him focused in the present moment in time, to keep him connected to his wife. The implications of the name, Leonard, remained with Judah. Leonard is not only the child but also the lion, the king of beasts, the one in control of the jungle and the playground.

As the group was disbanding, we all also recognized a final political level. Judah's story is the story of a nation of immigrants who left behind their names, their original roles, to take on new identities and to build a nation in and among hostile forces. For many who have shut out the old roles, the counterroles they have taken on have seemed somehow incomplete. And although the state of Israel has had many powerful guides, no one has been universally accepted. Israel is a country of splits and it has been difficult for many to find integration and balance. Judah found his balance having rediscovered Leonard through the help of a guide, Robert. I should say, Judah had the help of several guides including Avi and Roni.

The final step of the role method concerns social modeling. As Judah takes his new awareness into the many realms of his everyday life, he has the opportunity to affect the lives of others. He has taken one large step toward assuming the qualities and function of the guide.

Two years after this experience, I returned to Israel and again worked with Judah. When I greeted him, he told me that he had changed his name to Leonard. He appeared transformed, more playful and open.

SUMMARY AND CONCLUSIONS

Role theory and role method in drama therapy are separate but intimately connected. Role theory concerns a way of understanding the origins and goals and processes of drama therapy. It is derived in part from the social sciences but primarily from the art form of theatre. As such it provides the field with its central and unique focus as first an art form and then a science. As a theory, it gives a framework in which to make sense of all other aspects of the clinical and research branches of drama therapy.

Role method is an extension of the theory to clinical practice. Although I have attempted to outline the approach in a sequential fashion, I feel that the actual process of therapy moves along a curve or circle rather than a straight line. In the example of Judah we see evidence of invoking roles, working them through, discovering counterroles and guides, reflecting upon the roles and connecting them with everyday life roles, integrating role-CR-guide and speculating among the possibilities of social modeling. And yet, I hope it was clear that the actual process is in many ways murky. In this case, the most important element, the actual turning point, seemed to be the naming. In other cases, the key moment appears in the invocation or working through or reflection. Each case is unique.

Drama therapy is a very small field, a subset of psychotherapy or the art of drama/theatre or the creative arts therapies. Or perhaps drama therapy is a field in itself, derivative as much as all fields, yet indivisible. I think the field is too young to proclaim its independence. But then again, the same had been said about Israel and for that matter, about the United States of America.

If the field is to survive well into this new millenium and if it remains alive as more than a footnote in a textbook of psychotherapy or theatre or creative arts therapy, then it will need a solid foundation in theory and in clinical practice grounded in theory. Role theory and its concomitant role method is one attempt to do just that—to organize discrepant concepts, techniques and practices into a coherent system, one that has the weight and the lightness to travel through time.

Part Two

PRACTICE

Chapter 4

DRAMA THERAPY AND DISTANCING: REFLECTIONS ON THEORY AND CLINICAL APPLICATION

In a weekly drama therapy group of four years duration, three members remained constant: Kerry, a teacher in her 50s, originally from Europe, living alone in New York City, who suffered at the hands of a verbally abusive mother and distant father; Lena, a married woman in her 30s, a counselor by profession, with a young child, who has experienced severe anorexia since the birth of her daughter; and Walt, an artist in his 40s, with compulsive work habits like his father and difficulties defending himself and expressing his feelings.

In my remarks on distancing in drama therapy, I will refer to these three because they well represent the range of distance in terms of their abilities to express and withhold emotion. Kerry becomes quickly flooded with emotion when recalling her relationship to her abusive family. This state of overwhelming emotion is characterized by the term underdistance (see Landy, 1983, Scheff, 1981). When underdistanced, Kerry is unable to work dramatically and consequently think through her dilemma. Underdistance is characterized by an over-abundance of emotion which, when expressed, brings neither relief nor insight.

Walt has a difficult time expressing feeling in the group, although he easily becomes passionate about certain movies, actors, or successful artists about whom he disapproves. At times, when others in the group offer a story about their abusive situations, Walt becomes quite angry at the abusers. Generally, however, Walt expresses himself in a rational, analytical fashion. He is often willing to engage in dramatic action and take on whatever roles might be called for, but, with few exceptions, his dramatic renderings lack affect. Walt's emotional expression can be characterized as overdistanced (see Landy, 1983, Scheff, 1981), which is a state of rationality at the expense of emotional expression. While overdistanced, one tends to remove oneself

57

from feeling.

The third group member, Lena, is empathetic toward others and capable of discharging emotion, though she tends to pull back when things become too heated. When she expresses pain through crying, the crying has neither the underdistanced quality of Kerry nor the overdistanced quality of Walt. As such, Lena is capable of expressing feeling at aesthetic distance (see Landy, 1983, Scheff, 1981), characterized by emotional expression that is clarifying and relieving, rather than obscuring and overwhelming, and that invites an engagement of the rational, reflective capacities.

All three group members have learned to express themselves at aesthetic distance, having experienced a process of drama therapy which allowed them to play with and recognize the extremes. In many ways the history of their struggles to discover effective means of expression is marked by their abilities to move from under- or overdistance to aesthetic distance, also known as balance of distance (see Landy, 1983, Scheff, 1981).

In the early 1980s I began to experiment with the ideas of sociologist Tom Scheff concerning catharsis as they apply to drama therapy. Scheff (1979) conceptualized catharsis not only as an expression of emotion, but also as an engagement of cognition, a balanced state of functioning. Scheff's ideas are based not only on classical psychoanalytic studies of hysteria, but also in more current work in catharsis. One recent influence was Jackins (1965), who coined the term "re-evaluation counseling" or "co-counseling," a form of peer counseling based upon the power of catharsis to relieve distress and restore healthy functioning. But Scheff's concerns were broader than the social sciences. He also turned to theatre and ritual for sources to explain the complexities of emotional expression and its relationship to cognition (see Scheff, 1979).

Drawing upon the work of the Shakespearian critic Bertrand Evans (1967), Scheff looked at the notion of discrepant awareness, that is, the levels of dramatic irony that define the relationships between actor and actor, actor and audience. According to Evans and Scheff, the fact that some are knowledgeable while others are ignorant of certain information creates a tension that permeates drama and everyday life. In identifying with the dilemma of any character of limited awareness, one's own feelings of ignorance are re-stimulated and need to be released. Through catharsis, one releases those feelings and reestablishes a sense of equilibrium.

My theoretical work with distancing in drama therapy has incorporated not only that of Scheff and Evans, but also others in the social sciences and arts. One important influence is that of J.L. Moreno (1946) who spoke of several forms of catharsis in psychodrama–somatic, the physical discharge of emotion; mental, the expression of dimly recalled past experiences; individual, the psychodramatic discharge of a single protagonist; and group, the cathartic experiences of others in the group who have identified with the dilemma of the protagonist.

A more significant influence is that of Bertolt Brecht (see Willett, 1964) whose epic theatre asserted a major aesthetic function of drama, that is, to use style as a means of separating the world and the stage, the actor and the role. This simple separation carries a complexity of implications for drama and for therapy. For it is within the spaces between these levels of reality and identity that understanding and healing can occur. When the actor makes the mistake of confusing dramatic life and everyday life, he not only confuses and manipulates his audience, but also himself. In the extreme, the actor unmindful of this distinction is either delusional or ecstatic, either state of which denies a relationship to an audience.

There have been other trends in performance theory that have called for the possessed actor or the holy actor to function as a shaman, that is, a transitional figure between the spirit world and the world of appearances (see Cole, 1975, Schechner, 1985). However, many studies of shamanic experience will note that even the shamanic performance is enacted with some level of distance. The Brechtian performance is self-consciously distancing in an extreme way, presenting people as types and exaggerating stage lighting, properties and scenery in ways to break the illusion of verisimilitude.

The reason Brecht's theories of distancing are so significant to drama therapy is that the drama therapist works with illusion, obvious illusion, in order to help clients re-cognize bits of their experience that they have been unable to see up-close. When a conventional verbal therapist asks: "Tell me about your relationship with your mother," the client generally responds in a reality-based fashion, drawing upon memories and fantasies *as if* they were real and true. When a psychodramatist asks the same question yet urges the client to chose an auxiliary figure to play the mother, he, too, by implication, urges the client to engage in a similar process of recollection. The drama therapist, however, in applying distance, does not ask for memories or fantasies based upon recalled experience. He, in fact, asks the client to play in a new reality, a playspace (see Johnson, 1991). The *as if* experience is a given, accepted tacitly by both client and therapist as they move in and out of the playspace. The invitation to enter the playspace implies the knowledge that the dramatic reality is different from everyday reality and that the person is different from the persona he will take on in the playspace.

Generally speaking, drama therapists are distinct from psychodramatists in that they tend to work more with distance. That is, they tend to encourage clients to play roles that are not themselves within imagined settings that are not their own. They do this for several reasons. Like Brecht, they want their clients to be alienated from expected responses to daily life events, and by changing the context, they transform the familiar into the strange. Through this alienation, they hope their clients will begin to make sense of the everyday in new ways and view the dynamics of abuse and dysfunction, of repression and unhappiness with new eyes. In seeing clearly, Brecht and others assume that the stage is set for direct action within the everyday world.

But drama therapists are not simply interested in mental or cognitive cathartic moments. They recognize that clients, like actors and viewers in the theatre, also require some form of emotional experience. Clients like Walt and Lena have learned all too well how to avoid direct expression of their feelings and thus remain trapped within an inner world of fear and criticism. They come to drama therapy to learn how to express emotion appropriately. They are not so different from millions of audience members who come to the theatre as a respite from daily life in the home and office and streets, environments that seem to whisper: " repress feeling, appear to be strong when you feel weak, competent when you feel incompetent, cheerful when you feel out of control."

These viewers might think they are in the theatre for escape and there is some truth to this fantasy. But more than that, they come to the theatre for expression. The satisfaction of a good cry or laugh or titillation or shudder is well worth the price of admission. In order for this to occur, the viewer makes an identification with the dilemma of a character—the despair of Oedipus about to blind himself, the frenzy of Medea about to murder her children, the strange eroticism of Titania about to copulate with the ass, Bottom. Through the identification, the viewer imagines herself in a similar situation and faces a paradox—feeling this could be me and this couldn't be me, at the same time. The paradoxical feeling causes tension which calls for expression. The expression, a catharsis of laughter, tears, shakes, arousal, or some other form of somatic recognition, occurs because viewers have been pulled into an aesthetically distanced relationship with the actor. As such, they are able to express feeling without being overwhelmed by that feeling, and to reflect upon the cathartic moment, without fear of shutting down emotionally.

In drama therapy, clients like Kerry, Walt, and Lena are on a search for aesthetic distance. Their most favored means of avoiding expression is to talk about events in their lives and analyze them for each other. Moving into the dramatic mode and getting them up on their feet, even after four years of work, is still met with some resistance and anxiety. Lena is going through a painful divorce from her husband Phil, a successful lawyer, with whom she has been married for 12 years. In therapy she speaks of ways that he has been mistreating her. He wants custody of their child and will use the history of her anorexia as a weapon to prove that Lena is a mentally unfit mother. She tells the group about the meticulous notes he keeps documenting her inadequacies as a mother and his competence as a caretaker. She remains cool as she talks. Walt becomes angry at Phil and begins to get hot, slashing him with obscenities. Walt's anger seems extreme and misplaced. Who is he really mad at, I wonder?

Kerry is quiet, but very emotionally on the edge. She is identifying with Lena's dilemma, having once experienced a painfully abusive and brief marriage that ended in divorce. She is also afraid of re-stimulating so many memories of being misrepresented and overpowered by intimates.

I ask Lena to express her feelings in some way. She replies: "I am angry." I ask her to physicalize anger. She is puzzled. "Can you sculpt anger? Can you create a still life of anger using Walt and Kerry as your clay?"

My intention is to move this group experience to a more archetypal level, rather than offer a psychodramatic dialogue between Lena and Phil. I want to create some distance so that Lena can find a balanced way to express her feelings and thoughts. I recognize that working with the body is a fearful area for Lena.

Lena appears struck.

"Are my directions clear?" I ask.

I am met with silence. Walt interprets for me.

Lena replies, "I don't want to do this."

I do not want to let Lena off the hook. I gently urge her to take a chance. Walt and Kerry are supportive of the risk-taking and acknowledge that the act of invoking anger in a physical form is risky. Lena seems very small. Her head slumps onto her chest and her body appears on the edge of collapse. I model the role of the sculptor, taking the arm of Kerry and shaping it. Lena moves forward and works.

Remarkably, she sets up three tableaux. In the first, she places Walt's fist into Kerry's stomach; his other hand at her throat. In the second, she forms Walt's hand into a gun and forces it into Kerry's stomach. And in the third, she has Walt hold a life-support system of IV lines over Kerry's head.

After each tableau, I ask Lena to take on the role of Anger and express her feelings and to reverse roles, when appropriate, and speak to Anger. Her level of involvement increases with each tableau. By the third, that of the life-support system, she is crying as she speaks about her dual roles of lifesaver and dependent victim. I sense that she is still withholding feeling, so much fearing an underdistanced state.

I prod, "The woman in the tableaux has been mugged, choked and poked with guns and needles. How does she react?"

"She is angry."

"Can you show us how?"

With difficulty, Lena says, "I wish you dead. I want you to be run over by a train. I want you dead!" This is said to the figure represented by Walt holding up the life-support system—Walt as a stand-in for Phil.

Lena's words are spoken with force. They catch her off guard. She is surprised and shaken by her own expression. She cries openly, acknowledging her feelings. But soon, she catches herself, attempting to hold back the floodgates.

"I can't say that."

"What?"

"About wishing him dead. I can't say that."

"Why?"

"I can make things happen by wishing them. I have that power—magical thinking."

The enactment is over. Walt and Kerry have deroled. Hearing Lena's statement leads us all to breathe a collective sigh of recognition. We have been together for four years. We knew that Lena had believed in magical thinking but we thought that she was beyond that or at least not as controlled by those thoughts that would sabotage feeling. Our collective sigh was a complex moment signaling our awareness of Lena at an earlier stage and an acknowledgment that she was in it again and needed support (life support?) to help her move on and express her will to survive.

Lena at aesthetic distance opened up for me a chain of images I had seen before in group: Lena as so merged with her mother that once when pushed beyond her limits she ripped off Mother's necklace and felt like she was ripping out her mother's heart—and her own; Lena, whose mother was a Holocaust survivor, living by her wits in Europe, scrounging and hustling in order to survive the devastation of her family and faith; Lena, whose father took pictures of Nazi atrocities and hung them on the walls of her home; Lena, who married Phil when she was 19 and gave herself up to his image of the perfect woman; Lena, who put on 50 pounds during pregnancy and after the birth of her son declared, "Now I don't ever have to eat again;" Lena, whose mantra was for so long: I am devouring myself; Lena, who abused her body by systematically starving herself on and off for years until her family and husband kidnapped her and forced her into treatment; Lena, who resisted treatment yet learned to trust and to discover her expressive abilities while working with a creative arts therapist in the hospital; Lena, who pulled the plug on herself time and again by refusing to eat; Lena, who earned a Master's degree and worked with disadvantaged young people desperately in need of life support.

We spoke of the image of Lena as "hooked up," Walt's expression referring to a state of spontaneity and focus, of being fully connected to a task or object as in art-making, prayer, and marathon running. Lena understood hooked up as dependent, quite different in intent from Walt's understanding. Throughout her work in drama therapy she struggled with her dependencies upon mother and husband and feared that if she separated from these "life supports," she would die. At the same time, she feared that if she were in the role of the life support, akin to playing God, she would be overwhelmed by her responsibility for holding another's life in the balance.

In distancing herself from the actual dynamics of Lena and Phil in everyday life and by abstracting that relationship in dramatic form, Lena was able to view her dilemma in a new way. She would risk death by letting go of both sides of the line. She would make the move toward an independent life. She would cut the cords of her dependency more and more. In fact, once she was publicly able to announce her desire to separate from Phil, a remarkable thing happened—she menstruated for the first time in four years, for the first time since her eating disorder became severe. In Walt's words, now she was hooked up, in the flow, connecting her feelings with her body—blood and guts.

Lena's enactment also had a strong effect upon Walt and Kerry. Walt was able to look at the contradiction between being hooked up to his creative work, that is, in the flow, and hooked into a compulsive dependence upon technical perfection and a fear of having to sell the object of his perfection. So desirous of that flow, Walt fell back to earth again and again as he stumbled over his need to control and repeat. Walt was a photographer who was so technically adept that he prepared his own emulsions, inventing ways to stabilize that most unruly of jellies upon the surface of toxic metals. He photographed decaying, crumbling by-products of industrialization and gave them new life by transposing them onto lustrous metallic surfaces, primarily lead, which contained high levels of toxicity. He was in many ways an alchemist who could transform the detritus of reality into objects of art, but who had difficulty doing the same with his life. His self-image was highly negative and try as he may, he could not find a way to view himself as competent and worthy. In reflecting upon Lena's drama, Walt took a further step into understanding his own dilemma as an addict dependent upon transforming chaff into gold.

At the end of one drama therapy session, when the possibility existed that

Walt might be able to see himself as competent and worthy, he exclaimed: "I am running out of good negatives!" Although his remark referred to his photography, the metaphor allowed him the distance to understand how difficult it is to feel a sense of self-worth. As he ran out of good negatives, he was compelled to consider some good positives in his life, to let go of the hooks that supported his dependency upon alchemical perfection and control.

In one of Walt's most poignant sessions, he accepted my invitation to work metaphorically, leaving behind the safe closeness of the minutia of everyday life. He recalled a play he once saw: "It was about a psychopathic killer who captured a young boy and was about to kill him. Instead, he kills himself. The boy is safe. But he does this strange thing—he starts to become the killer. The kid turns into the psycho!"

As Walt told this story, he became full of feeling. I asked him to name the feeling, and as he spoke, he moved further and further away from it. So I asked him to enact the final scene of the play, playing both characters and holding onto the feeling as much as he could. His enactment was subtle and fluid. He was hooked up to his feelings in both roles. The group gave him very positive feedback and again, he began to search for "good negatives," stressing how he could have given a better technical performance. I brought him back to the drama, trying hard to remove distance from his feelings.

"Would you address the boy directly," I asked, setting up an empty chair. He struggled but Lena spontaneously sat in the chair and assumed the role of the boy. She said: "Speak to me. I am lost in the desert."

Walt replied, simply, "You are a good person. You will find your way out. You deserve it. You're not crazy. You are a good person." And he cried, at aesthetic distance, feeling thoughtfully and thinking feelingly. He got the point that he was talking to part of himself, the child who carried a legacy of poisonous blood. And he acknowledged the reality for the first time that he was capable of letting go of the many years of self-criticism and loathing. He was prepared to state publicly: "I am good person. I can find my way out of the desert."

Kerry needed the most distance of the three. Each of her reality-based stories of neglect and abuse brought on an overflow of emotion. But, most significantly, as she began to assert her needs for acknowledgment and care, she began to receive care. And this receiving brought on an even greater sense of pain and loss. "Why didn't I get cared for when I needed it most?" she said, directly. The child part of her was so starved that any little scrap of food was a mixed blessing—both a feast to a hungry child and a slap in the face to a shamed adult full of memories of abusive feeders.

Kerry shared a dream about a woman of color who is severely hemorrhaging. Although she gets weaker and weaker, she tries desperately not to draw attention to herself. Kerry runs for a doctor to help her. The doctor says: "There's nothing wrong with her. Leave her alone. She'll be alright." In commenting on the dream, Kerry noted that the doctor failed to speak the horrifying hidden agenda which was: "It is OK to let the woman bleed to death."

Kerry was full of feeling when she told the dream, almost on the edge of underdistance. She had just been, in fact, rejected by a lover whom she had planned to live with, and the betrayal set off a string of associations referring back to her abusive early family life. I sensed that she needed a greater degree of distance in order to make the connection with her past. I asked her to name the woman of color in the dream and she said: "Anybody and everybody." She called the setting: "No identity; out of time." These responses were further ways of distancing herself from specific evoked memories. In the more abstract realm of distance, where characters are Anybody and settings are out of time, Kerry's thoughts became clearer as she recalled a specific incident some 25 years earlier:

> I was working as a teacher in a small city. I was pretty lonely there. I missed my period for two months but didn't tell anybody. I didn't know anything was wrong. One late afternoon after school, I went into a closet and heard a terrible sound. I had no idea where the sound came from. I looked at the ground and blood was all over the floor. I didn't even feel it. I closed the door and just stood there. When somebody passed, I asked her in to look at the ground. She was a kind colleague who somehow got me over to the local hospital. I was covered in blood. She got the head nurse and then the doctor. The head nurse said: "You won't be staying in this town very long." They did the surgery and I left right away. I stayed with a friend who took me out for walks. We never spoke about the abortion. The man who made me pregnant was a casual lover, someone I used to cover up my depression. I wanted to apologize to him for being pregnant. I never returned to my job at the school.

In telling this story, Kerry was able to clarify her dream and her identification with the woman of color, a pariah, an "anybody" of "no identity." In that she recalled her past experience in a state of aesthetic distance, Kerry could feel her pain even as she understood how her recent rejection re-stimulated a train of memories of neglect and abuse from the past. In the telling and consequent acceptance by the group and the therapist, Kerry became a somebody with a clear past and clear reasons for feeling despondent. The shedding of her blood was not in vain. Her wounds ennobled her in some way now that they cold be exposed and held by a supportive group.

Aesthetic distance for Kerry was often discovered in the identifications she made with the dramas of Lena and Walt. Of all three, Kerry covered the greatest emotional territory, probably because she began group as the most underdistanced. Within the safety of the playspace she was able to address several of her former abusers: mothers who could not nurture, doctors who could not heal, lovers who could not love, and ask for sustenance. As difficult as it was, she even learned how to accept sustaining care when it was offered. In playing the role of the victim in Lena's drama mentioned above, she was able to hold on to the thought that she was and still is a victim to past abuses, but that she has the ability to play the counterpart, the victor, the one who can say: "Enough! Let go of your stranglehold on me. Let me breathe. Give me my due!"

These ideas on distancing had informed my clinical work in drama therapy for 15 years. My ideas began to shift as I incorporated role theory into my work, noticing that clients in drama therapy find their levels of distance within the formal boundaries of role (see Landy, 1993). They play out their feelings through taking on personae—victim and victimizer, supporter and supported, alchemist and everyman. Not only do they play out their issues in role, but they do so in a stylized way. That style of enactment offers information about their ability to express emotion and to reflect upon experience in a way that is similar to an actor's experience in finding an emotional/cognitive relationship to a character in a play.

In the first several years of work in the drama therapy group, Kerry often re-experienced abuses suffered as a child. During those moments she became flooded with emotion, with no way to battle the currents and return home. While in this overdistanced state, she became fully merged with her real-life roles, disallowing her reflective part to make an appearance. On the other hand, in playing an adult victim or victimizer, Kerry managed a more stylized presentation, less based upon a real-life rendering of the experience. In Lena's drama she played the sculpted figure of a victim with a gun poked in her belly well as the style helped distance her from the flood of tears associated with the helpless child of her memories. Even in telling her own story of loss and neglect in the hospital, she became narrator rather than actor in her personal drama. Through this stylized separation, she was able to find meaning in the present reality of her life.

Drama therapy is a powerful method of healing because it provides a way to re-experience pain, sometimes overwhelming pain, through the safety of aesthetic distance. In its most pure sense drama therapy is play, a representational process of holding, as it were, a mirror up to nature, of moving in and out of the looking glass. Children play spontaneously in order to master a bit of reality, in order to test out their feelings and thoughts by projecting them onto imaginary objects. Adults, too, can harness the power of play as a means of making sense of their lives, as play embodies a distanced world, a make-believe world, one of endless possibilities. One way to experience that world and all its medicines is through drama therapy wherein all are invited to summon such figures as Rumplestilskin (or, indeed, to play Rumplestilskin) and test out their own abilities to spin straw into gold.

Chapter 5

A CROSS-CULTURAL APPROACH:
DRAMA THERAPY IN TAIWAN

No-Self'
Is 'True-Self.'
And the greatest man
Is Nobody.
CHUANG TZU

In December, 1995, I set out on a one-month journey to the East. I was invited by the Chinese Theatre Association of Taiwan to present workshops and lectures on drama therapy and to create a piece of theatre to be performed to a Taiwanese audience. This paper is an attempt to describe that journey in the context of my reading of the Chinese philosophy of taoism. Further, I will relate that cultural understanding to my work as a practitioner and theorist of drama therapy and attempt to show how my experience within a Chinese culture has helped to sharpen my understanding of role theory in drama therapy.

PREPARATIONS

There was a small part of me that felt prepared. As a student of *tai chi* on and off for the past 20 years, I was at the time of my journey fully into the practice, having discovered a generous teacher in my town. As a scholar, I filled myself up with classical Chinese literature, history and current Chinese cinema. But the larger part of me, although curious, felt ignorant. Chinese culture seemed as vast and unfamiliar as its enormous land mass. All my images of things Chinese appeared oversized—so many people, so many dynasties, so much land, so many contradictions among religious practices and between spiritual principles and political realities. The strangeness of the language and the arts, of the customs and the rituals, was daunting.

I had two hosts. One, Hsiao-hua, was a retired military officer who taught theatre in a military college. Hsiao-hua had been my student in New York 13 years previously and had found my class in drama therapy to be an important antidote to his sense of alienation within a foreign culture. The other, Margaret, was a university professor of theatre from one of the most prominent Taiwanese families. Her father had been a celebrated political and military figure in mainland China and continued to enjoy his elevated status when he emigrated to Taiwan. These people were more than gracious hosts; they became my guides and interpreters, not only of the language, but also of the history and culture of Taiwan and of China. And not incidentally, in their own contradictions of warrior/artist and socialite/scholar, they well exemplified the yin/yang paradox at the center of Chinese culture.

My journey began months before my arrival in the correspondence with my hosts concerning the content of my lectures and the topic of the play. For me, the lecture part was easy, but the choice of content for the play was challenging. Previous to my visit, Peter Schumann and the Bread and Puppet Theatre were invited to Taiwan and created a pageant-like production based upon the Chinese myth, "Mending the Sky" (see Chung, 1994). In his characteristic mytho-poetic-political style developed over some 40 years, Schumann (see Brecht, 1988) folded his stylized masks and puppets and formal sense of theatre as sacrament within the sparse content of the story of Nu Wa, a god who gathers found objects in nature to repair a hole in the sky and prevent the destructive flooding of the earth. In his own way, secure in his theatrical vision of inclusion, Schumann seemed able to negotiate the cultural divide of East and West with ease. As for me, distanced by time from the act of creating theatre, insecure in my abilities to negotiate cultural boundaries, I read the book on the Bread and Puppet Theatre's visit to Taiwan (Chung, 1994) and prayed for inspiration.

Like Schumann, I decided to work from a traditional Chinese text and dramatize it with a group of actors. As a drama therapy experience, I intended to work on the piece improvisationally, examining the connections between the fictional roles and images in the text and the lives of the actors. Further, I planned to involve the audience directly in some way yet to be determined. Several models I had in mind included: playback theatre (see Salas, 1993) where audience members are invited to come up and tell a story from their own lives, which is then dramatized by a group of actors; forum theatre (see Schutzman and Cohen-Cruz, 1994), where audience members are invited on stage to offer an alternative solution to a dramatized problem; and various psychodramatic and drama therapy workshop approaches, where action is frozen and group members are asked to double for or reverse roles with the protagonist.

My first task was to choose a text. I began by reading several anthologies of Chinese myths, legends and stories, most of which remained too distanced from my experience. I finally discovered one, "The Infection," that was very appealing in its ironic twist of conventional morality. The fable-like story took place in a fictional village where it was the custom that young virgins preparing for marriage were required by their elders to have sex with an outsider in order to purify themselves for the marriage bed. The virgin carried an infection within her body which could only be expunged if she passed it on, through intercourse, to her non-betrothed. He, then, would hold the infection that would kill him. Was this a metaphor for AIDS, I wondered? What an odd rite of passage—a virgin rids herself of her virginity in order to become pure. Was this a reversal of the Western male notion of sowing one's wild oats before marriage?

In the story, the hero/virgin saves the life of a stranger, despondent and down on his luck, whom her father has chosen as the object of the ritual. Because she cannot bear to murder him sexually, she sends him on his way and is herself banished by her father to face a certain humiliating death. Through several twists of fate, the man's life is transformed and he repays the woman by magically saving her from her deadly infection.

When I sent the story to my hosts, they rejected it as preposterous and culturally inappropriate. I was disappointed in my hosts' reactions and felt ashamed that I transgressed a cultural boundary. But time was running out and I had to move beyond my personal affront.

My hosts and I sent several ideas back and forth, but none seemed to connect. As the trip was approaching and I was becoming more and more concerned with the lack of clarity, Margaret recommended that I create a piece based upon the character of Ji-gon, whom she characterized as a trickster god, similar to the Western figure of Robin Hood. The idea intrigued me and as time was running out I asked for guidance regarding literature. She mentioned that there was one book which contained all the stories of Ji-gon and would sent it to me by express mail. I breathed a sigh of relief until the book arrived in the mail. It was a dense volume in Chinese and I was illiterate. I summoned all my Chinese speaking acquaintances who offered to translate small portions of the large book, then threw up my hands and gave myself over to what I later learned was the philosophy of *wu wei* or non-action, an essential tenant of taoism.

Days before I boarded the plane, I had this dream:

I am climbing a steep and high flight of stairs. There are many people in front of me. I hold my 7-year-old daughter's hand and with my other hand I hold a wheel. It is a struggle to get to the top. When I arrive, there is a narrow landing. A bed takes up most of the space. A baby with a pig's face is in the bed. Half a mustache grows out of its nose. It is placid. I have no space. All the others are gone. There seems to be no way out or down. I feel tentative and off balance. I expect the worst–a fall. I hold on to my daughter but drop the wheel to maintain balance. It falls a long distance and I am afraid that it will hit someone below. It does not. I teeter but manage to hold on.

The dream seemed very Western to me. It is about a struggle to get to the top, ahead of my competitors, and a realization that arriving there is a shaky and confusing experience. When I arrive, however, all the others disappear and the dream shifts in tone, becoming more Eastern. For one, I am connected and stay connected to my firstborn child, who becomes my guide. The scene at the top becomes abstract and contradictory. The human baby is an animal. It is also half of a grown-up man with a mustache. In this odd, space-less place of role and counterrole, I feel off-balance and expect disaster. Ironically, I drop the wheel while holding onto my daughter. In taoist terms I surrender my balance in order to regain balance. The dream ends with an image of paradox–a shaky balance.

In an Eastern sense, I think of the images in the dream as parts of me. I am a flight of stairs and a group of people climbing to the front; I am a seven-year-old daughter and a 52-year-old father; I am a wheel and a young girl; I am a narrow landing and a large bed; I am a baby and a pig, a smooth face and a mustachioed one; I am space and no space; I am falling and standing, afraid and secure; I hold on and I let go. In the links between these seemingly opposite roles and images, I exist. In understanding the dream in this way, I was able to continue with my journey accepting of my inaction and ignorance of all the Chinese gods and traditions. I was to be a visitor to a strange place. When I arrived, I could count upon my guides for translation. And, in trusting the wisdom of my dream, I could rest assured that one more guide would be present–the daughter figure, leading me by the hand, empty of cultural expectations and of worldliness, unsophisticated and unformed. The loss of the wheel in the dream baffled me. What did it mean? In the *Tao Te Ching* (Mitchell, 1988), I found this one year later:

We join spokes together in a wheel.
But it is the center hole
that makes the wagon move.

In letting go of the wheel, I relinquished my grounded knowledge of the West, of drama therapy. In opening up to the center hole, the nothingness, I allowed the possibility of movement, of new knowledge. Unwittingly, I was

beginning to understand taoism which I would see as central to my understanding of Chinese culture. To my greatest surprise, I would eventually
understand my own work in drama therapy more clearly through this very
paradoxical lens.

The taoism I came to understand was more in the tradition of philosophical Taoism (see Smith, 1962). The ancient philosophy filtered down from the
fourth century B.C. through the teachings and examples of Huang Ti, Lao-
tsu, and Chuang-tsu, and was very much embedded in the ancient texts, *I
Ching (The Book of Changes)* and *Tao te Ching (The Way and Its Power)*. The *tao*,
popularly translated as path or way, is seen by Huston Smith (1962) as having 3 meanings: the way of ultimate reality, which is transcendent and name-
less; the way of the universe, which is the driving force in all nature; and the
way people should order their lives, a more Confucian emphasis upon social
norms of proper behavior. The *tao* is limitless. It is *tai hsu*, the great void; *tai
chi*, that which is simultaneously infinite and finite; *tai i*, that which changes,
and *t'ien* the source of order (see Blofeld, 1985). It is based upon an acceptance of ambivalence and contradictory forces at play in nature. The human
being is viewed not as center of the universe but as a part of nature, a work
in progress, a seeker of balance. The natural and supernatural worlds, which
are all part of the same *tao*, are comprised of two contradictory energies—yin,
embodying soft, yielding, feminine qualities, and yang, embodying hard,
rigid, masculine qualities. Human life, like the life of nature, is predicated
upon a changing relationship between the yin and yang energies. The taoist
philosophy is not actually a dualistic one where yin and yang remain on
opposite sides of the circle, but one of dynamic movement. In fact in the
ancient symbol of yin/yang, the circle of light, the yin energy, has a point of
darkness or yang; and the circle of darkness, the yang energy, contains a
point of yin. The two poles are separated by a sinuous S curve rather than a
straight line, suggesting the dynamic relationship between yin and yang. As a
philosophical system, taoism admits other schools of thought, including
Confucianism, although, in a strict sense, it differs from Confucianism in its
concerns with matters of the mind and spirit.

One of the central concerns of taoist philosophy is the letting go of pre-
conceived notions of success and failure, of worldly possession and of intellectual property. In the *Tao te Ching* there is frequent reference to *wu wei*, the
power of spontaneous action or non-action, that is, an attention to process.
Huston Smith (1962) refers to *wu wei* as creative quietude. In recent years,
taoism has becoming popularized as an alternative philosophy for Westerners
who feel the need to resist the advance of scientism and technology (see
Heider, 1986). Further, recent theoretical developments in physics have led

to a taoist understanding of the physical universe as dynamic and paradoxical (see Capra, 1975), comprised of hard matter that is full of space, and space that is endlessly shifting.

The ancient wisdom of the *I Ching* has been recapitulated in the contemporary study of archetypal psychology, where forms of being are seen as ubiquitous throughout culture and history. Taoism stands in contradistinction from materialism, yet for all that it is not, it also is everything that does not see itself as the truth and the ultimate. The tao is ultimately indescribable and mysterious. It is being, pure and simple.

A Stranger in a Strange Land

Although I had some sense of Taiwan as a culture in transition, I was not prepared for the extent of contradictions I would find. The country had been under martial law since Chiang Kai-shek arrived with his armies in 1949, having been deposed as ruler of mainland China by Mao Zedong. Martial law reigned until 1987, when Chiang Ching-kuo, the son of Chiang Kai-shek, lifted many of the restrictive laws and allowed exchanges between people of Taiwan and China. Just three months after my visit to Taiwan, in March, 1996, the first free election in the state's history took place. President Lee Teng-hui won by a considerable margin, which reinforced the sense of cultural ambiguity since no one really knew Lee's politics. Was he for an independent Taiwan with its own language and culture or for unification with mainland China, asserting a common Chinese language and heritage? Was he for an even more Westernized system of values, a more traditional culture, or one in-between, in keeping with the Chinese tendency to incorporate changes? Taiwan entered the 1990s as a culture in transition, if not crisis, politically, economically, and spiritually.

According to Andrew Solomon (1996), "[Taiwan's] crisis in identity is reflected in . . . the country's increasingly conflicted art (p. 29)." Solomon was commenting upon the choice of expression in painting, linking forms including traditional brush painting and post-modern conceptual art to particular political ideologies. In my experience with Taiwanese theatre, I found the same ambiguities. Traditional Chinese opera was flourishing on the stage, in special schools for the training of young opera performers, and on television. Alongside that, conventional popular drama was available in the larger venues, like the national theatre where current Broadway and West End fare was showcased. Further, a growing contingent of academics and artists were encouraging the performance of more experimental forms of theatre. In 1995, for example, the American director, Richard Schechner, was invited to Taiwan to direct a post-modern version of Aeschylus' *Orestia*. Taiwanese post-modern companies like Cloud Gate Theatre, a dance-drama troupe, were also creating a vision of a culture in transition, deconstructing classical texts to explore contemporary issues.

But before I even encountered the art, I was dazzled by the contradictions on the streets. I stayed at a Western-style hotel. It was Christmas-time and young Taiwanese hostesses were dressed in Santa Claus costumes. Muzak played in the elevators which I shared with Asian men in business suits and Texans in cowboy hats. Outside, the street was lined with exclusive shops—Gucci and Tiffany, endless banks and department stores. But just around the corner, I found myself pulled into a fantasy of old China. Throughout the narrow, teeming alleys were cooks and butchers, tiny restaurants and shops unfolding onto the streets, a cornucopia of fried fish, plucked chickens, steamed dumplings, live eels and snakes, herbs, roots, and medicines of indescribable sorts.

I was drawn to a concrete playground with one lone, barefoot child sliding down a stone sliding pond. Next to the slide was an old dilapidated building surrounded by red and yellow lanterns. The door was open and I walked in. Before me was a miniature temple. Candles and incense were burning on an altar. Odd Chinese puppets with abundant facial hair sat behind dirty glass. Three large expressionistic masks rested alongside the figures. Plates of rotting fruit lay on the altar. Next to the fruit were mysterious strips of paper and prayer rods. Below was a fireplace-like opening in the floor.

My excursions to the temples were to become more and more frequent as I tried to get closer to my fantasy of traditional Chinese culture. While on the way to these mysterious and seductive back streets, I always moved through the more Westernized broadways so familiar to me. These passageways, I began to realize, were also important parts of my cultural journey. My education was truly one in yin and yang. Like a good meal in Taiwan, the elements were harmoniously balanced. This notion of balance, which had so informed my understanding of drama therapy, was to become ever more prominent in my work in Taiwan.

Rehearsals—Finding the Form

The first rehearsal, which was to be a warm-up to the group, took place at The *Kuo Kuan* School on the outskirts of Taipei City. The school was a concrete structure, cold and stark. As I entered the grounds, I noticed a basketball court, with two boys playing, both with such short-cropped hair that I imagined them as young Buddhist monks in training. I would see these and other young students at the school often peeking in at rehearsals. I would catch glimpses of them in tights and tutus on the school's enormous proscenium stage, tumbling on hard stone floors in classrooms, applying intricate make-up to become monkey kings and other traditional Chinese opera role types.

Rehearsals would take place in an oversized rectangle of a room—cold and damp, with concrete floors barely covered with foam mats. At our first meeting, I was presented a company of 36—actors, students, teachers, social workers and other mental health professionals. The company was chosen by a group of theatre professors from a pool of 100 applicants. Members of the group did not know one another; three members came from Malaysia, having responded to a notice in a Malaysian newspaper.

I began by warming-up the group and introducing the role method of drama therapy, wherein individuals are asked to invoke roles, name them, and begin to explore their qualities through improvisation. I subdivided the group of 36 into six groups of six and had them work with the roles they had invoked. Immediately, a cultural problem arose. Having done hundreds of classes, workshops, and clinical sessions involving the spontaneous evocation of roles, I was used to a certain range of role types, generally related to my taxonomy of roles (see Landy, 1993). In this case, I needed translation on two levels—both verbal and cultural. The latter was critical when roles were chosen that did not conform to my Western-devised taxonomy. At the beginning of the rehearsal process both of my hosts whispered the verbal and cultural translations to me at the same time. The translations were literally going in one ear and out the other, which made me quite dizzy as I attempted to concentrate fully upon the array of images enacted before me—snake and mosquito in one improvisation, a spiritual search for meaning in another, a blind man's discovery of the world of appearances in a third. The final role was especially poignant in that I felt like a blind man in need of a staff of guides in order to see the culture clearly. The role further connected on a personal level in that my son was born with a visual impairment. In many ways, I was like my son. And like him, I found a way to adapt. Both son and daughter, safe at home in a culture they well understood, guided me.

Following these early experiences in warming-up the group to the role method, in warming-up myself to Taiwanese culture, and in attempting to create a positive group dynamic, I inquired as to their understanding of Ji-gon, the trickster god. Before I describe their response, let me provide some background to the character. Ji-gon is a taoist monk who first appeared in Chinese folklore in the Sung Dynasty. He is a reincarnation of a monk of extraordinary power, one who slays dragons. Ji-gon is quite an anomaly among holy men as he disobeys the rules of his religious order and, unlike his colleagues, he leaves the monastery to commune with those of the streets and towns. Like his spiritual forefather, Ji-gon also has supernatural powers of healing. He is not only a healer, but also a trickster, one who is independent and carefree. His favorite targets are the affluent and well-heeled. To many working class and poor people, he becomes a Robin Hood figure, who takes from those who have to give to those who have not.

Ji-gon lives simultaneously in the material world, helping the dispossessed, and the spirit world, from which he draws his magical powers. He is both holy and profane, monk and profligate, child and elder. In fact, Ji-gon often appears in stories, drawings, and even on a popular Tiawanese television program as a childlike figure dressed in colorful robe, fan and hat. In many ways, Ji-gon represents many of the paradoxes inherent in Chinese culture which so very much is about the search for harmony in body and spirit, in hearth and heaven, in female and male. My attraction to this character was in his representation of a multitude of roles and counterroles. This trickster god seemed to embody the essence of taoism as a philosophy of paradox.

In continuing my workshops and rehearsals, I realized my most pressing need was to discover a form for the play of Ji-gon. My yang, Western part was always thinking ahead, forming and shaping, worrying that time was running out. The more I pushed for form, the more my company of actors pushed against imposed structures. They came for the drama therapy work, the process, not the performance. There was still so much I didn't understand. My hosts were at odds with the actors. They were pushing even harder than I for the production and critiquing workshops as if they were rehearsals of a known text. They pushed and I pushed while the group pulled. As I pushed, I began to become aware of myself pushing and that slowed me down. I walked the streets each day and took in the power of the taoist temples. It was all there. I listened to the company, especially the young voices of Ji-gon.

In the streets I saw theatre everywhere. An old crone with silver teeth sold sweet potatoes. She was a fortuneteller and offered me a vision of good luck. Outside a Buddhist temple, an old beggar approached me for a few coins. Thinking I was on the Bowery of New York City, I refused, then wondered: "What if he was Ji-gon?" Up the street was a political demonstration. I turned a corner and police in riot gear lined the pathway, clubs in hand. I recoiled, then realized that they were like props. There was no threat and I walked through the lines unnoticed and safe. A woman stood at a brick stove on the street burning paper money, paper houses, paper boats. I was told that even the dead need their material comforts. At the Lungshan Temple, I bought sticks of incense, lighted them and prayed three times to the sky gods, the earth gods, and the temple gods. I threw the divining blocks, asked secret questions, all of which were answered as I would have wished. Nearby, I visited the Chiang Kai-shek memorial and, getting lost, wandered into a room that was an authentic reproduction of President Chiang's office. Behind the desk sat the President, a perfect wax figure dressed in military tans, a benign smile on his face, pen in hand, signing a document in perpetuity.

Back at the hotel, I watched American television broadcasters forecast the weather in Bangkok, and I delighted in a stunning replay of the 1952 World Series between the New York Yankees and the Brooklyn Dodgers. For an instant, I was transported back to Ebbets Field, a cultural monument long gone. In the moment, I was, indeed, a stranger in a strange land.

Each morning, I would awake too late to join the group of local people doing *tai chi* in the Sun Yat-Sen Memorial Square. So I would practice the form in the small health club attached to the hotel, where young Taiwanese executives labored on tread mills. I was still struggling with the form at this time, still trying to master each intricate movement and integrate the movements with my breathing. I was far away from realizing my goal of *wu wei*, that is, allowing the meditative movements to flow as if by no force at all on my part. As my teacher taught me: "The mind moves the chi; the chi moves the body." Unfortunately, my mind remained cluttered. I was reminded time and again how the form of my play was still missing and it was up to me to find it. In my *tai chi* exercise, at least I knew the form although, in thinking about it further, I realized that I knew the form externally, in my mind, but did not know how to enact it with chi.

One day in a taoist temple, I came across a dozen or so figures, life-size, all costumed and made up (see Figure 1). They represented gods, heroes, mythological and historical figures. I stayed with them for a long time. There was a form in their arrangement that struck me as theatrical in the most natural way. They were lined up like objects on an assembly line, like trees in a forest. There was both a randomness and an order to their arrangement. They seemed both ready to go out somewhere and well settled in for eternity. Looking at them brought me into awareness of myself as onlooker. I was a drama therapist trying to create a play in a language and for a culture that was beyond my grasp. In front of me were giant figures that had no particular meaning to me at all. Yet the meaning of who I was in relation to them was clear—my form was drama therapy. I moved in it and breathed it each day of my life. That was my *tai chi* and I was a master. My *Tao Te Ching* was an understanding of the way that process works as written down in a book containing a method and a taxonomy.

The Taxonomy of Ji-gon

I reached a transitional point. The company was eager to proceed. They did not need me to teach them about Ji-gon or other aspects of their culture. All I had to do was present the taxonomy and ask them to fill it in with their cultural experience and offer to help move the cultural to the personal levels within the given limits of time and intimacy. The group, as mentioned above, was divided into six sub-groups. Each sub-group focused upon one domain of the taxonomy and chose one role and its counterrole therein. Each choice was to relate to one aspect of the multitudinous Ji-gon. From the somatic domain, Group 1 choose the doctor who, like Ji-gon, serves a healing function. As a counterrole, the group chose the patient, one who is in need of healing. From the cognitive domain, Group 2 chose the role type, trickster, a character directly related to Ji-gon in its qualities of mischief, anarchy, and playful wisdom. As their counterrole, they chose the pedant, an ignorant fool who thinks he is knowledgeable.

From the affective domain, Group 3 chose the helper, a loyal friend who serves a function of support and service to a hero, and the helpless one as the counterpart. From the social domain, Group 4 chose father and daughter, and from the spiritual domain Group 5 chose the roles of god and demon. The final Group 6 chose the role types of performer and audience from the aesthetic domain. In trying to specify our theatrical task and its relationship to drama therapy, we came up with the central question: What is the connection between a cultural role type, Ji-gon, a culture, Taiwan, and a personal search for meaning?

As the rehearsal process continued, we worked through various drama therapy techniques to explore the relationships between and among these roles through sandplay, improvisation, storytelling, movement and mask-making. Each group created one characteristic mask to represent its role and counterrole type. Individuals were challenged to look at their personal issues as reflected through the roles of Ji-gon.

During one sequence in sandplay, a young Malaysian man, whom I shall call Chen, set up a scene in the sand among three figures: Ji-gon, a mother and a father. Chen, as narrator, told of an abusive relationship between the mother and father. He also mentioned that in his personal life his mother was abusive toward him and his father often served to rescue him from the mother. In the sandplay story, the mother was a gossip and had an adulterous relationship with another man. Ji-gon took off with another woman and it was not clear to me whether she was actually the mother. I asked him with whom he felt most identified. He responded Ji-gon because he had the freedom to do whatever he liked, without responsibility to others. He also mentioned that he saw Ji-gon as kind. I asked if there was a contradiction between kindness and a sense of total freedom. He could not respond. Was this my question, I wondered, my need to resolve ambivalence? I asked him about the mother figure in the sandtray. Was there any connection with himself? He said no. I asked him to take on the role of the mother. He could not. In a group of 36, in a workshop situation, I let it go.

During group discussion of this work, as others were speaking of their connections to the figures of father and mother and Ji-gon, Chen spoke of feeling homesick and guilty about not communicating with his mother in the weeks he had been away from home. He began to cry and the expression built to an overt sobbing. I gathered the group close and invited those who identified with him to put their hands on his shoulder and share their own feelings. Many did so with ease. One man spoke of moving from the south and experiencing a loss of family and friends. Several offered friendship. The group was bonding. This crisis was essential. I recognized the cultural reticence to express feeling openly, especially among strangers, and the importance of creating a cohesive group which became an acceptable container for feeling. Someone mentioned that the group was beginning to take on a quality of Ji-gon, that of the healer.

The Western notion of psychotherapy as helping individuals to discover ways of solving their own problems is, for the most part, alien to Asian people. Because the Eastern sense of psychological healing was still strange to me, I was surprised that after this particular session people approached me for advice. They offered stories and sought my guidance. One began: "I am a nurse supervisor and some of my nurses can't get along with each other. They do not accept my authority as they should. What should I do?" And another: "I know a Catholic woman with young children. Her husband went to work abroad in the United States, and while away he had an accident and died. She has not been able to tell her children. What should she do?"

Who am I? I wondered. Back home after a workshop or group therapy session, I would never get such questions. In facilitating an open group process in Taiwan, I became endowed with wisdom. I became trustworthy and wise and yet I was still sitting with my own sense of cultural confusion and ignorance. I still was unclear about the story in the sandtray. Who was this Ji-gon? What was I to make of the abusive mother and rescuing father? Why was the protagonist unable to take on the mother role and why did he break down in speaking about his separation from her? In the barrage of unanswered questions, I forgot the form. When asked I wanted to answer. But in being pulled toward answers, I lost the *tao*.

Before we ended, one person asked: "What if during our performance, someone breaks down, loses control? What do we do?" I responded quickly, "You do what you just did. You support each other. The group will know how to take care of itself." Was this a sufficient answer, I wondered? Maybe I should have answered in a more taoist way:

Practice not-doing,
and everything will fall into place. (Mitchell, 1988)

The Form

The form of the play was finally created. I returned to what I knew best—the role method of drama therapy. I let go of trying to be more Chinese, more taoist, more knowledgeable, more in control, more free of my hosts. I discovered what was right there before me—a group of people learning to bond with and to trust one another, a theatre space upon which Chinese opera was performed, and an archetypal role, that of Ji-gon, rich in ambivalence. In that this was to be an interactive experience between actor and audience, I set up the space in such a way that actor and audience sat together around a large rug, upon which traditional opera is performed. The action would take place on the rug and move in and out of the audience space. The group created 12 masks, representing one role type and its counterpart from each of the six domains. Each mask was made twice—once on a human scale and once as an oversized icon, fastened to an eight feet bamboo pole. The giant masks reminded me of Peter Schumann's work with the Bread and Puppet Theatre. Their style brought me to a further appreciation of aesthetic distance as moving one's consciousness from the personal to the archetypal. In drama therapy terms, the giant masks of role and counterrole would exemplify in broad strokes the therapeutic goal—awareness of the possibilities of a paradoxical existence.

The 12 giant masks were positioned upstage in a large box. Keeping with the opera-like feeling of the theatrical event, we borrowed a group of four young women musicians, students at the Kuo Kuan School, all who played traditional Chinese instruments. The musicians created original musical themes which corresponded to the qualities of the individual role types.

During the Prelude, one actor entered and introduced the concept of drama therapy to the audience, describing the process of creating the play. A second actor entered and explained that we chose Ji-gon as the central role and theme of the play, because he embodied the many contradictions within Chinese culture and within many individuals in Taiwan. Further, she established a contractual agreement with the audience, inviting them to contribute to the play and allowing them the right not to contribute. While she was speaking, one actor, Chen, took on the role of Ji-gon by donning a yellow hat and poked fun at the speaker, urging her to accept the fact that this was his play, not hers. The two playfully sparred until Ji-gon relinquished his role and returned to his place in the audience.

The play had four sequences of action and an epilogue. The form loosely followed that of the role method. The first sequence, for example, began as actors set up a banner which read: "The Invocation and the Naming." The action performed corresponded to the first two parts of the role method, invoking the role and naming the role. In the play, one group entered at a time, e.g., that of doctor/patient. Members of the group choose counterparts in the audience and sculpted them in role. They then placed their masks on the audience members and enroled them with the words: "You are the doctor (patient, etc.) and your function in life is to heal the sick." Having enrolled members of the audience, the actors then took back their masks, enroling themselves as doctor, patient, etc. In doing so, they invoked their roles and named them. In connecting with members of the audience, the actors warmed-up the audience to the roles that would later be seen as part of Ji-gon, in the hopes that they would join the actors later in developing the play (see Figure 2).

The second scene corresponded to the section of the role method that concerns a working through of the role and a discovery and working through of the counterrole. During this part of the drama therapy process, clients move their fictional roles into enactment and invent stories while in role. In the play, this scene was called "The Roles and Stories of Ji-gon." The roles, as mentioned above, were already invoked and named. Each group chose one story about Ji-gon and proceded to dramatize it. Throughout the stories, Ji-gon solved all problems and healed all wounds through wisdom or trickery or magic. Of the six stories chosen, the one most surprising to me was that of "The Chalk Circle," which I had known as Bertolt Brecht's *The Caucasian Chalk Circle*, concerning a wise trickster judge who resolves the conflict between two women, one treacherous and priviledged, the other innocent and poor, over the custody of a child. I was not aware that this was an old Chinese story and seeing it enacted by Taiwanese actors brought to memory an essay written by Bertolt Brecht in 1936, "Alienation Effects in Chinese Acting" (see Willett, 1964). This was a pivotal essay in that it was the first time Brecht used the term *verfremdungseffekte*, referring to the distanced form of acting he observed in Chinese theatre. His notion of aesthetic distance as a means of aiding viewers to separate themselves from expected emotional responses to theatrical events would play a key part in my understanding of the drama therapy process. The fact that he based this understanding, in part, upon a Chinese theatre aesthetic further reinforced my need to learn more from this rich culture.

In the enactment of "The Chalk Circle," Ji-gon became the judge. He was played by Chen with great baudy humor, well keeping with the trickster quality of Ji-gon. Throughout "The Roles and Stories of Ji-gon" each group chose a storyteller who set up the story, directed it, and froze the actors upon its conclusion. But more than this, the storyteller presented the story as his own, as if he embodied all the characters. He would begin: "This is my story." Having established a frozen tableaux at the end of the story, he then invited audience members on stage to double for those characters with whom they identified. Following that, he again repeated, "This is my story," and proceeded to make a connection between each character on stage and his own life. He ended by articulating his connection with the Ji-gon character.

The stories dramatized provided me with much insight into Chinese culture and its taoist underpinnings. A key story, which I will call "The Laughing Grandfather," is a good example. The story presents the vision of a happy family. Three generations live together: the husband and wife and daughter, the husband's sister, and the grandmother and grandfather. They are all good-natured. The daughter watches television while the adults go about their business of keeping house and working. The storyteller challenges the domestic tranquility by taking on the role of demon and casting a spell upon the family. He brings bad temper to the grandmother, naughtiness to the daughter, boredom to the father, obsession to the mother, and incessant chatter to the sister. In these alternative roles, the family members plague one another. The taoist harmony is destroyed. But one person is spared—the wise grandfather. He takes on the role of Ji-gon by donning the yellow hat, and teaches the others to laugh. Having learned laughter, the family rediscovers its harmony.

Through this story, I saw the traditional family structures and a dualistic view of family life as either content or miserable. Further, I saw the powerful need for a wise elder to restore balance. The view of the elder as healing through laughter was particularly appealing to me. Ji-gon as trickster offered a refreshing alternative to the self-righteous position of many of the moralistic elders within Western Judeo-Christian traditions.

Following the dramatization, the storyteller invited members of the audience on stage to double for the actors. During this section, I was always a bit anxious that the audience would be too reticent. I was told time and again that because of the cultural reticence, I should not expect audience participation. However, the actors worked hard at encouraging people to come up and their efforts paid off. People made identifications with the father, the mother, the sister and, most often, with Ji-gon as grandfather. A poignant comment in role of the mother was: "I always feel like crying when the parents fight."

The sequence ended as the storyteller articulated his own identifications with each character in "The Laughing Grandfather." He ended by speaking as Ji-gon: "I don't like to be a big mouth and use my words to influence people. Laughter is the best medicine."

The third sequence was called "Who is Ji-gon and what does he want." It related to the role method in its examination of an understanding of the role and its counterpart in terms of quality, who one is in role, and function, what one wants in role. This scene would use a highly stylized approach in conceiving the figure of Ji-gon as a container of the contradictions of role and counterrole. Two from each group would enter, representing the group's chosen role and counterrole, e.g. father and daughter. One would enrole by taking a giant mask from the box and striking a sculpted position onstage. The second, unmasked, would assume the role of questioner and guide, attempting to help her partner explore the many roles contained in the one. She would do this by repeating the question: "Who are you." When satisfied that her partner had responded fully, she would continue: "What do you want?" (see Figure 3).

Theoretically, we were making the assumption that Ji-gon as one role, e.g., father, embodied a multitude of related qualities and that it was possible to access some qualities that lie underneath the surface. The further part of the experience was not only to recognize the myriad of qualities, but also to clarify the various functions of roles, that is, motivations underlying one's role-playing.

Taiwanese culture appeared to me to be very proper and sedate, at least on the surface. Public expressions of affection were generally unacceptable and families exerted much pressure on young unmarried people to remain chaste and safe in the bosom of the family until married and even then, to remain close to the family unit. The expression of sexuality was frowned upon. The only signs on the streets were garishly colored, oversized barber poles, spinning wildly on a diagonal arc, pointing to an upstairs brothel.

Given the generally repressed sexual norms, the drama therapy experience allowed some to release a bit of erotic energy. One woman, enrolled as a demon, when asked, "Who are you?' responded: "I am Ji-gon." Then again: "I am a dancer of god." Then: "I like to swim naked." And after several further responses to the same question, she ended with: "I am woman." Her action, worked through in rehearsal, seemed to have a liberating effect. The mask moved freely with her, like a dancing partner, as her guide moved her though her expression. Her final response to the question: "What do you want?" was a simple: "I want attention, recognition, focus upon me." From my Western point of view, I thought long and hard about this unabashedly open display and call for attention, especially given the cultural taboos. How different from the individualistic, narcissistic norms of the United States

where the cry for attention is blurted out on every radio and television talk
show. Many in the company lived well within their cultural rules, but the
dancer of god proceeded with abandon. This was a rare opportunity to
unmask behind her mask, to participate in the pleasures only given to the
gods and the prostitutes. Many in the company had trouble with this section,
avoiding a descent beneath the surface. They, too, were supported in their
choice, like each member of the audience, to be or not to be.

The most challenging moment for me came on the last night of the performance. Chen enroled as the father. When asked, "Who are you?" he
replied as follows: "I am Ji-gon . . . I am the father . . . I am the son . . . I want
my mother . . . I have no role . . . I am nobody." At this point, he threw down
his mask, fell to his knees and began to sob. There was a tension in the room
as great as I have ever experienced in the theatre. His partner froze and did
not know what to do. A part of me felt responsible for setting up a potentially volatile, unsafe public experience without proper controls. My host,
Margaret, sitting to my right, became agitated and said to me: "You must stop
the performance." My first reaction was guilt. Thinking about the story of
"The Infection" that I had sent her months ago, I felt again that I had transgressed a cultural boundary. I was finally found out as an imposter, or at least
an imposer of things foreign. I had to stop the play or things would truly spin
out of control. But in an instant, I found the *tao*, the *tai chi* of the moment. For
years my instruction in *tai chi* was based upon the principle, "yield and overcome." I could not intervene. It was not my role. It would have contradicted
all I had learned about Chinese culture and taoism up to that point. Yield and
overcome, I thought. I responded to Margaret; "The group will help itself.
They will find a way." Even as I said those words, I mistrusted myself, fearing that I was wrong. But just then, another actor entered and held the young
man in his arms, helping him up. Another picked up the giant mask and
placed it back in its container, alongside the other masks. Several actors
entered and joined the group to restore order and move on. From imbalance,
balance was again restored. From pain a new order emerged. The actor who
had tested the safety of the group process in rehearsal had done it again in
performance. The group was prepared. It knew the form. It indeed took care
of itself. As for me, in the face of my judge, I took no action. Later, I reflected upon the *Tao te Ching* (Mitchell, 1988) which says:

If no action is taken
Harmony remains.

This sequence of the play was clearly the most charged. It released libido, narcissism, pain. Some were playful in their responses; some rather serious. All seemed most drawn to this part of the play, heavily identified with the trickster Ji-gon, the one who could break all the rules, live the life of his choice, honor his culture and transcend his culture, use his wisdom to rescue himself and all others in need. Through this section, the group answered the question: "Who is Ji-gon and what does he want?" For them, Ji-gon was the yin and the yang, the self and the other, the holy god and the sensual human being, the female and the male. And he wanted what the group wanted—acceptance and harmony. In tossing away the mask of father, Chen committed yet another taoist act of Ji-gon. He discovered the son beneath the father and the non-being beneath the being. From my point of view, nothing exists beyond one's roles. When one expels all roles, one is lost, delusional, dead. Yet, in re-thinking this point of view, perhaps beneath all the roles is the void, the other side of being that is also part of the tao. This helped me to understand the meaning of *wu wei* and the sense that my theory of role in drama therapy can only make sense by allowing a notion of nothingness to be present at all times as a therapeutic and performance option.

Following each dyad's performance, audience members were invited onstage to express their connections with the roles. Because the actors were so intense, it became somewhat difficult for audience members to enter into the scene. Those who did tended to give rather basic and/or humorous statements. One young man said of the naked dancer: "I want to swim with her!"

The final sequence was called "Unmasking Ji-gon." My inspiration for this scene was my many afternoons in the Taoist and Buddhist temples. My intention was to create a kind of theatrical altar, with many of the roles of Ji-gon present. I wished for the actors to have the opportunity to let go of the fictional Ji-gon but to hold on to those qualities that might be helpful in forging ahead with their own lives. In terms of the role method, this section applies to the ability of clients to view the connection between the fictional roles they have played and their everyday lives.

The section began as one group entered and placed two actors, representing role and counterrole, on a low platform. Each actor was given the appropriate face mask to wear and the giant mask to hold as a kind of scepter. The dyad graphically represented two paired roles of Ji-gon, variants of trickster and pedant, doctor and patient, helper and helpless, father and daughter, god and demon, performer and audience. Members of the group, one at a time, approached the altar and spoke to the dual effigies, articulating several differences and similarities between the fiction of the roles and the everyday reality of their lives. Then they attempted to close by letting the paradoxical Ji-gon go even as they held on to certain identified qualities. The group finished by removing the face masks and giant masks from the actors and presenting them to members of the audience. As each actor approached an audience member with a mask, he said: "Please hold this for me. It is my ability to (for example) forgive my mother. Please take good care of it."

One actor who played the grandmother in the story of "The Smiling Grandfather," addressed the demonic figure on the altar as follows:

> As the bad-tempered grandmother, you made the family suffer. I have a bad-tempered mother. You made me aware of my mother. I was always afraid of her. But even though you are bad-tempered, you can still take care of the family and help create a bond. Thank you for letting me see this. I can see that I am not trapped by my mother's bad temper. You allowed me to shout, to express myself openly and to reach beyond myself. I hope my shouting is not too overwhelming to face my difficulties.

This speech was quite extraordinary in its confessional quality, quite unlike any expectation I had about working within a Chinese culture. Yet, it reinforced my sense that many in the group needed to express feelings in some safe fashion. Because the culture did not have a tradition of psychotherapy or of introspection in art and religion or, for that matter, of individual self-expression, many held onto strong feelings with scant opportunity for release. The experience of working on the Ji-gon project in drama therapy provided a sense of release for many through a safe and acceptable form. But there was still so much that I could not comprehend concerning the process. What was the experience of those who were not forthcoming with their emotional expression? What did the audience think and feel? Was this experience perceived as a Western attempt to impose a psychology of theatre upon an Eastern audience or an attempt to integrate a Western form with a more Eastern taoist-inspired vision?

At the end of this particular scene, the actors joined hands and said in unison: "This is our story." But the story was not over. As the co-creator, I needed to say something through my mask of Ji-gon. To do so, I wrote an epilogue, the only speech I actually composed for the play.

My version of Ji-gon is, as follows:

> This is my story. I am the healer. I heal by telling my stories and daring to play all my roles. I heal by laughing at all the foolish things we do in our everyday lives. I heal by changing. I can be a god or a demon, a man or a woman, an audience member or a performer. I am the part of you that is most oppressed, most silent, most ashamed. I am your voice. I heal by telling my stories and daring to play all my roles. I embrace my contradictions. I am Taiwan and China, KMT (Kuomintang) and DPP (Democratic Progressive Party). I am Wei Jingshen[1] and Mao Zedong,

---

1. Wei Jingshen is a prominent Chinese political dissident who was sentenced harshly by the Chinese government when I was in Taiwan.

Chiang Kai-shek and Lee Teng-hui. I am Buddhist, Taoist, Christian, Muslim and Jew. I am black and white. This is our story. We are the healer. Our name is Ji-gon.

I presented this speech to the group one week before performance. It was translated on the spot and several of the company read it aloud in Chinese. It was read with a passion that shot through my body. It was Christmas eve in the Kuo Kuan School. Outside our rehearsal room, the students were celebrating by performing the many arts of their school. Scenes of Taiwanese opera and acrobatics, karioke, a mix of traditional and modern dance swirled around and around. Young people in red and black face paint and wild yellow silk costumes wandered about, boys with long hair slicked back practiced their best Elvis routines (Presley or Costello?), canned rock music blasting from the loud speakers followed the live twangs of the traditional Chinese instruments. In our rehearsal room, the company engaged in a ritual of honoring their teachers with gifts and offerings of dried meats and lotus candies. With the sound and sense of that final Ji-gon speech still buzzing in my head, I tried to take it all in.

I had arrived at the top, I thought, referring back to my earlier dream. The wheel had fallen and I was teetering on the edge of two cultures. This was my story of the familiar and the strange, the form of drama therapy that I knew and the forms of an ancient culture, large enough to contain all contradictions, that I did not know. Ji-gon was my guide and had been my guide all along. In preparing for this trip, he appeared in my dream as a sleeping pig with a moustache (the long dark hairs of the Chinese gods and heroic figures in the temples represent long life and wisdom), as my daughter, as the figures in the story, "The Infection." And in Taiwan, he was Hsiao-hua and Margaret, the company of 36, the Buddha-like students at the Kuo Kuan School, the sobbing young man from Malaysia, the young woman who wanted to dance naked and the prostitutes in their garrets. This was his story. And this was my story.

Following the performance on December 31, all involved gathered to derole and discuss the process before going out together for a celebratory Western New Year's meal. The final feedback from the group was quite powerful. I will mention two comments. One woman said:

> At the beginning I rejected this group and thought I could handle my difficulties and problems myself. Why do I need therapy from others? At the end of the first performance I found that I loved and enjoyed the whole process. It was a very comfortable feeling. Thank you for letting me dare to face my own difficulty, my need to reject such a group.

And one man said:

> In this group I learned to open myself. I believe that everyone who knows me would
> be very surprised how much different a person I am after this experience. I seemed
> to find the happy boy in my heart.

Not all in the company were so touched. And even those who felt moved
were about to be abandoned by the power and comfort of the group and its
leader. Collectively we recognized these realities and allowed them into the
mix of feelings. As one gift, I was presented with the yellow hat of Ji-gon,
signed by all in the company. It would remind me of the possibilities of living the paradoxical life of yin and yang, of East and West.

Through this experience, I came to know my own work and my own life
better. Like the woman above, I found that I loved and enjoyed the whole
process. And like the man, I learned to open myself and find the happy boy
in my heart. Since this journey, I have been actively attempting to articulate
a taoist understanding of drama therapy. I discovered that my role theory was
taoist in spirit, aiming toward helping clients live among their several ambivalent tendencies, yet limited in practice to working with two elements–role and
counterrole. From the *I Ching* I discovered with the aid of my teacher, C.T.
Wu, that each hexagram, each sacred form of wisdom is comprised of threes.
It is the third piece that keeps the ying and yang propelled in their dynamic
relationship. Without the third, the two opposite forces might seek balance
too quickly and too easily. The third part leads the yin and the yang to the
center, the borderline, the threshold where creative possibility abounds. This
third piece, which I now call the guide, is, I think, an essential factor in understanding the relationship between role and counterrole as this dyad affects
healing through drama therapy.

I conclude with this thought–in the West, I am often challenged on my
assumption that there is no central Self or core to the human being and that
through drama therapy, one does not essentially concern oneself with alter-
ing or healing the Self and one's conceptions of it. In Taiwan, among those
raised within the cultural reality of a philosophical taoism, the rejection of the
Self was a non-issue. Many Easterners who have not embraced Western forms
of monotheism, clearly view being as holistic with no one center of the person or the universe or the cosmos, no God of judgement waiting to condemn
an inauthentic act, a wayward thought. For me, this philosophy was a great
relief. I could relax and fold into my many personae with an ease that often
escaped me. Ah, but then I was also aware of the other side–the fear not of a
harsh and punitive God, but of transgressing the Confucian laws of proper
decorum. Perhaps it is natural to the human condition to demand certainty

from some central source—whether psychological, political or spiritual. In Taiwan I learned more clearly than before that such a source is inexorably paradoxical. And I even learned that it has one ancient name that I can embrace—*tao*. *Tao* is not the Self or God or the State or the Father or the Mother. And it is.

At the beginning of the role method is the invocation, the calling into being of a role, and the naming of the role. At the beginning of the *Tao te Ching* (Mitchell, 1988) are these two verses:

> *The tao that can be told*
> *is not the eternal Tao.*
> *The name that can be named*
> *is not the eternal name.*

> *The unnamable is the eternally real,*
> *Naming is the origin*
> *of all particular things.*

In Taiwan, we engaged in a process of drama therapy that touched many of us. And we created a product, a play about an Eastern trickster god who had a name, Ji-gon. By the end of the process, the actor portraying Ji-gon offers the thought that one persona is all persons, one name is all names. Implicit in this is the thought that the particular and the eternal are linked in some inexorable way. In the end, most of us involved agreed. I flew home on New Year's day, having celebrated the Western New Year's eve the night before. Somewhere over Japan, a voice on the plane's loud speaker announced that we were passing through a new time zone and, once again, it was the first minute of the new year. I was twice blessed.

Chapter 6

FATHERS AND SONS

I am a father and I am a son. I also happen to be a therapist who works a lot with sons and fathers, though rarely together. I recently became aware that many if not all of the men I treated had come to therapy to find their fathers. For some, however, the goal seemed to be the opposite–to let go of the pervasive and powerful presence of their fathers. I reasoned that the discovery and the letting go are two sides of the same dilemma–the struggle to locate a male identity shaped so profoundly by an imperfect mentor.

As a father and as a son, I fall into the struggle of my clients. As they tell their stories, I find myself drifting in and out of reveries about my father and my son. This paper is a personal one as I try to make sense of those reveries, and it is a professional one, as I work with the stories of my clients. My aim in the work is the kind of reconciliation and re-union that connects the figures of father and son in a way that allows for a wide range of paradoxical feelings–sweetness and bitterness, acceptance and rejection, love and shame. And it becomes increasingly clear that each man I work with becomes at some point a son or father to whom I play a counterrole. When our therapeutic exchange is effective, we learn more about the most complex male dynamic of all.

The Swing

I had a powerful dream following a particularly challenging group in which one woman said tearfully that she felt judged by the group and unsupported by me. She felt that I had exposed her vulnerabilities and offered no help. The dream is set initially in a garage and my father-in-law tells me I have to take in some lawn furniture that has become contaminated by his germs. We are then outside in the yard and my father-in-law is sitting on a large wooden swing with a back support, the kind I used to see in my youth on front porches in the country. The swing begins to move on its own power and I watch its ascent into the sky. But rather than come back down to earth, it continues to rise, further and further away. My father-in-law says to me: "How am I doing?" I can see that he is becoming frightened as the swing spins out of control. As the swing moves higher, I notice that it is attached to a tree trunk. Its rough bark is very visible. I grab unto the tree in an attempt to pull the swing back down to earth, but it moves even higher. I assure my father-in-law that I will save him even though I am quickly losing hope. In one final burst of strength, I manage to successfully halt the ascent of the swing. But suddenly the swing begins to dive, and my father-in-law comes crashing down to earth. I am afraid that he is dead, but I hear his voice and know that he has survived.

In thinking about the dream, I realize that the three roles of father, son and healer are linked. For one, I easily find myself having trouble letting go of a client or group experience in which I feel unable to rescue or at least ground those who have spun out of control. And that difficulty leads me to my father. In the dream the figure actually becomes my father-in-law who is in many ways an inversion of my father. My father-in-law is alive and well, leading a very full life while my father, who died in 1985, always took the safe, middle ground and rarely allowed himself the opportunity to spin out of control.

As son to my father, my function was to listen to his war stories which he told me regularly since my childhood. They were stories set in the foxholes of War World II and the equally threatening mine fields of the family sweatshop. The stories were moral struggles of good guys and bad guys. Despite the fact that the Nazis lost the war, the theme was usually the same—good guys finish last, even though they hold the moral high ground. The ambiguity that I sensed, especially in my youth, had to do with my father's insistence that it is always better to be a good guy, even though that role often leads one to feel like a coward and a failure.

As son, I was never sure what my father wanted me to do with his stories. I sensed that they came out of his pain, but I was just the son, unskilled in the art of doctoring. In my early years, I had the feeling that he wanted me to be his healer and that healing was part of the requirements of a son. Now that I am older I realize that he probably just wanted me to listen and witness uncritically as he knew that I was good at both tasks. He also needed someone to hold his pain as he unburdened himself. The story I best remember is this:

> When I returned home from the war, I was sick as a dog-TB in my chest and crazy thoughts in my head. The family was all gathered around and said: "Thank God you're home safe and sound. That's all that matters. Let's forget about the war now that it's over." And they forgot about it.

I tried to comply with my father's wishes. I was a good son but my good intentions came with a price. The price was my guilt for feeling helpless, not good enough to compensate for the emotional unavailability of my father's family, the same price that I still pay as a professional healer when clients let me know that I have failed them.

In the dream, I am faced with a father figure who is out of control, a condition of great anxiety in my father's life. He has contaminated the furniture, the object that can hold him. I am supposed to put the furniture away in a safely contained space, the garage. But one piece of furniture gets loose and I cannot contain it, just as I cannot contain the father. When he asks me: "Robert, how am I doing?" I don't know how to respond. He is not doing well. He is in danger and is frightened. I could answer: "You are in trouble and I will try to help you," a line I wish I could have spoken to my real father. But I remain silent, watching him spin more and more out of control.

I recall feeling frightened in the dream. I am spinning out of control, fearful that I can do nothing to save the father and that if he disappears, it will be my fault. But I don't lose my power. I am not impotent. I seize a tree trunk, one that is quite vivid and sensual. I can feel its rough texture and I grab hold and pull. In thinking about the image, it feels phallic, masturbatory. The way to rescue the father is through the penis, the mark of masculine connection. As I pull, the father moves higher. I temporarily lose hope of the rescue, the ultimate climax. But finally, it happens, according to the law of nature—whatever goes up must come down. The ejaculation has occurred, the great father has fallen to earth. I am relieved.

In working with dreams, I make the assumption that all images are part of the dreamer. I am the garage and the yard, the contaminated and uncontaminated lawn furniture. I am the tree and swing, and I am the son and the father. Each image stands in relation to its counterpart and in trying to make sense of the dream, I attempt to discover ways to live within the sometimes messy connections. In-between the image and counter image is a transitional space (see Winnicott, 1971). The guide figure lives in this realm. It is the figure that links the two and helps them move toward balance. In my reading of the dream, the tree becomes the guide, standing between the father and the son. If conceived as a phallic image, it is the masculine bond. In the dream, the sexual metaphor refers to the emotional complexity of rescuing, a concurrently fearful and pleasurable moment, one that takes the rescuer to lows and highs of excitation and release.

Does Man Help Man?

There was a time in my life as a theatre director that I worked with a number of lesser known didactic plays by Bertolt Brecht. One was a section from *The Baden Learning Play About Understanding* (1929) called "Does Man Help Man?" It was an expressionistic clown show featuring the systematic dismemberment of one clown by two others. The one who is dismembered, Herr Schmitt, claims that his various body parts cause him pain from which he seeks comfort. In order to rescue Herr Schmitt, the brutal others agree to help, hacking off limbs, torso and finally head. As it turns out, the cure is worse than the disease and poor Herr Schmitt is not only relieved of his pain, but his life. Brecht's intention was to highlight the social and political nature of relationships. His conclusion was that human relationships are often brutal, a quality that lurks just behind the mask of help. My interest in working on the piece was a more psychological one, and I wanted to find a way to answer the question of the piece in the affirmative–Yes, help is possible!

When I initially worked on the piece, I saw it as about the relationship between men and women. The Others became archetypal misogynists, objectifying and abusing the innocent sexual object, Ms. Schmitt. At some point, however, I moved away from a feminist interpretation and saw this play in terms of the relationship of father and son. And I wondered whether it was possible for one to help the other without cutting up the body, without cutting off the feelings, without stifling the spirit. As I drifted from theatre to therapy, the question remained. The following case examples concern my attempts to say: Yes, help is not only possible but necessary to heal the other and to heal the self and to heal the primal bond of man and man, father and son.

Blue Horizons

Phil, a 28-year-old man, came to see me because he experienced a pervasive feeling of detachment. He recently married and within a month had an affair with an old girlfriend. It was painful to carry around his secret so he confessed to his wife and began the difficult journey toward reconciliation. Phil needed guidance in many facets of his life–in family and in business. He wanted to clarify several conflicting roles and feel more attached to his wife, friends, colleagues, mother and especially to his father.

His parents divorced when he was very young, and Phil feels that an affair on the part of his father led to the break-up. Phil was raised primarily by his mother, although he has regularly visited his father. He finds his relationship with his father painful and somewhat hopeless.

At several key points in his adolescence, Phil confronted his father and ultimately defended his own point of view regarding money, education and future direction. Phil feels that because he was able to assert his needs, his father felt defeated and has since refused to offer any opinions at all. Leaving behind the role of guide, the father has lost a meaningful way to father his son. The father lives an independent and isolated life and has successfully managed to keep his world and work simple and contained.

During our first session, Phil told a story he called "The Buddha and the Opportunist." The following is a synopsis:

> The Buddha lives on an island in the middle of the ocean. It is isolated but he has everything he needs—food, nature and beauty. He hasn't discovered anything new in 12 years. He is completely content. That's what it means to be the Buddha. The Opportunist is a high-powered businessman on vacation aboard a cruise ship. The ship sinks in a storm, and he survives by swimming to an island. He is used to having all his needs taken care of by others, and he becomes very worried. But he recalls camping as a child and knows that he will survive. In the distance, he sees smoke and follows it. He finds the Buddha sitting by a fire and tells the story of his shipwreck. The Buddha is unmoved and offers no solution. The Opportunist is furious, but he is also resourceful. He builds a boat and sets sail.

I ask Phil whether there is another character in the story and he says: "Yes. While the Opportunist is at sea, a little bird flies by, a swallow. The Opportunist then knows he is close to land. He follows the swallow."

"What happens to the swallow?" I ask.

"The swallow may be lost at sea," he replies. "If the swallow is lost, then the Opportunist is lost and will never return home."

From this first session, I have the sense that Phil is struggling with two parts of himself—the spiritual, passive part and the secular, commercial, active part, both of which feel incomplete in themselves. Both seem to require an integration. The swallow serves the purpose of a guide figure that can hold the two together, but it has a tendency to lose its way. I conclude that the guide is unclear in Phil's inner life and that perhaps an external guide is also elusive. In the absence of a father whom he frightened away, I will need to stand-in, and I must have the strength to withstand his confrontations. I hope that I am not expected to have the wisdom of the Buddha and the aggressiveness of the Opportunist, for my father did not leave me these skills. I feel more comfortable as the swallow who can stay attached to the land, even though he sometimes gets lost at sea.

Phil remains in therapy for six months, meeting with me once a week. Whenever he mentions his relationship with his father, I try to get him to deepen his exploration, but he veers away. We speak about writing dialogue for a talk between himself and his father, and he even outlines a four-act play with alternative conclusions. But he is unable to move beyond the outline. There are always other things to deal with—problems at work, marriage, travel plans.

One summer weekend, I go to the beach with my family. My children bring their bikes and my son, Mackey, wants me to ride with him. I am very tired and find an excuse. He wants me to swim with him, to read to him, to have a catch with him, to do any of 100 other things that a father can do with a son. He talks to me about his latest Nintendo® video game and about the book he is reading. The more he wants engagement, the more I want to detach.

Late in the day, I think about my son and wonder why I am have having trouble connecting to him. And then an image of my father comes before me. It is somehow confused with the face of Mackey. It is as if they are both far away, flying off into the sky, expecting me to rescue them. I will not. I cannot. I feel like a child although I am a grown man and my son is 9 years old.

When I put Mackey to bed, I tell him that tomorrow we will take a long ride along the sea. And I sing him the song I sing each night, naming all the important figures in his young life, and ending with his name, the most important of all.

When I return, I have a session with Phil. He comes to see me once every two weeks now. He rarely mentions his father. He is blocked and has nothing to say. I ask him to tell me a story, and I listen as I have listened with mixed emotions to all the repeated tellings of my father's stories over so many years. He calls his story *Blue Horizons*:

> Once upon a time, there was a bike-rider. He lived on his bike—eating, drinking, having sex, traveling. One day he got a flat tire. Someone had left a beer bottle in his path. He didn't have the right tools. He was out in the middle of the desert. He was angry that he didn't have his repair kit. He kicked his bike but then regretted it. He didn't know how to fix the tire and how to get out of his bad mood. He parked his bike and began to walk. It was 30 miles to the nearest town. Since there were no cars coming, he walked off in a random direction, into the desert. He soon got lost and things got worse and worse. He was hungry and thirsty. Above a dune, he saw some smoke and followed it. He came upon an old man sitting next to a cactus, cooking lizards on a stick over a fire. Although the old man didn't see or hear too well, he was sharp. He spoke very little. He handed the biker a bottle of water. He didn't have a tire repair kit and the biker got mad at the old man for not seeing the gravity of the situation. Soon, the biker relaxed and the old man spoke: "I have lived in the desert my whole life and don't see why it is important to ever leave the desert." The biker eats some lizard and drinks some water and spends some quality time with the old man. At nightfall he walks back to his bike. A pickup truck appears on the road, and he hitches a ride into town. He fixes his tire and goes to bed.

I asked him to name the roles and images in the story and he mentioned the long, straight road, the old man, the biker, the cactus, the lizard and the flat tire. I noticed that *Blue Horizons* was a recapitulation of *The Buddha and the Opportunist* and that the characters had many of the same qualities. The one difference is that the bird has been replaced by a pickup truck that brings the biker back to town. There is now a clear sense of a helper and of a moving on. It intrigues me that after the biker returns to town and fixes his bike, he goes to sleep. I wonder what he will dream about—the old man? the town he will return to? And I wonder about the blue horizons, noting that there are more than one horizon. Phil sees the different horizons as conflicts, especially that of youth and age.

As we were about to end, Phil mentioned that the story was based on a real incident. He and his brother had gone to an obscure beach town over the weekend, and he had actually gotten a flat tire while far away from the town. As he described certain features of the landscape, I recognized it as the same small beach town I had been with my family. I asked him the name of the town and he confirmed that it was the same. I told him that I was in the same town at the same time and that if I had known he was in trouble, I would have brought my repair kit along to help fix the tire. He was pleased.

Before he left I told him that he had forgotten one important piece of the story when he named the roles—the repair kit. "Sometimes," I said, "the repair kit doesn't appear all by itself. It can be brought along by a helper."

As he was leaving, Phil told me that it was time to tackle the issue of his father. I agreed. On my way home, I made a pact with myself to never refuse the offer of a bike ride with my son.

Trouble in Paradise

One day, I got a call from Emma. She told me she had just discovered drug paraphernalia hidden in the room of her 28-year-old son, Leo. When she confronted him, he confessed that he was shooting heroin. She asked me to help and I agreed to see Leo. I expected a frightened, defensive young man, but Leo shined like the sun. He was tall and strong with long straight hair. He greeted me warmly and genuinely. He was bright and reflective. I couldn't imagine him hustling for heroin on the streets.

In our early work, Leo seemed so clear and focused. He articulated goals and strategies to remain clean and sober. He spoke openly of his spirituality, his love of nature and love and respect for his mother and his two fathers. He played the good son splendidly. He was also the good client, arriving early and paying in cash, embracing me warmly upon coming and going, praising the therapy for keeping him on track.

And yet Leo stayed on the surface. His stories of wise men and elders were too facile and romanticized. Where was the pain, I wondered, and what in the world led this lovable and loving young man into the streets to risk death for a moment of euphoria?

In our four months of work together, I tried to patch together a few clues. Leo came from a hippie background, from parents who lived communally with others on a country farm. The adults on the farm regularly smoked marijuana and experimented with psychedelics. Theirs was a lifestyle of art and nature, of peace and love. But there was trouble in paradise. When his father took on a lover, his mother began a relationship with the landlord. When the dust cleared, the family shifted. Leo at five had a new father who would live on the farm with his mother. His biological father also remained on the farm, living with his new wife. Because of prior arrangements and philosophy, the couple was granted permission to remain on the land virtually rent free. In the minds of the adults, all would be well.

During important moments when the surface cracked, I learned about disappointing relationships with friends and lovers. Living a long distance from home, far from the protection of his mother, Leo played the innocent to young women and men who ultimately betrayed him. And when betrayed or abandoned, he became self-destructive. He chose fringe people as friends, some of whom engaged in high-risk behavior, one of whom introduced him to hard drugs. Reflecting on the cycle of loving and losing he once remarked: "Good guys finish last." I immediately thought of my father.

Leo rented a modest room in a friend's apartment and kept mostly to himself. He was in debt and worked hard to free himself from his financial burdens. He took on various physically demanding jobs and would arrive in soiled clothes, often fatigued from a long day of physical labor. On some days, I would find him in the waiting room half-asleep. Toward the end of our work together, he would be so tired that he could barely engage with me. He was slipping away. All the while, he claimed to be clean and sober, his only temptations the long nights of loneliness and boredom.

As his creativity waned, I tried to engage him more directly than usual. He spoke of having a guardian angel who rescued him from many close calls. I wanted to be a stand in for that figure and guide him back to the exuberance I experienced when I first met him. When I asked him more about the guardian angel, he said: "It protects the part of me that has a purpose—to fulfill my destiny."

As he spoke of destiny and of his belief in past lives, I felt a sense of hopelessness. What possible good is therapy for a person who believes that his consciousness is predetermined? I again heard the voice of my father who smoked two packs of cigarettes a day and always told me, "When your time is up, your time is up." There was nothing to be done, no rational sense to be made of this life. "It's funny," he'd tell me, "you'd never know who would break down in battle. You'd think it would be the weak, skinny kid, scared of his own shadow. But it was often the tough one, the big brute of a guy with all the bravado of a bully."

Leo was big and strong, confident and hopeful when I met him. Was it his destiny to die in the streets of an overdose like a weakling? If this was his destiny, I wanted to intervene, empower Leo to take action. After the war, my father went on to the battlefield of the family business. The enemy was two-fold—his bullying, brutish partners and the cowardly part of himself that was afraid to fight back. Unable to act effectively and clinging to the hope that the good guys would prevail, he went through the motions, like a good soldier, following orders but afraid to take command. "One day," he told me, "somewhere in France, my commanding officer wanted to promote me to platoon leader. I refused. I couldn't take on the responsibility of leading men into battle and watching them die."

For all his war stories, my father told me very little specific information about battle. I always wondered if he killed German soldiers and what it was like. I wondered if he ever came face to face with the enemy and how it felt. I realized that Leo had avoided speaking about the experience of getting high on heroin. I had conjured up images of squalor and disease, of homeless people nodding out on street corners, of emaciated prostitutes dying of AIDS. But eventually Leo told me of warmth and light, of a transcendence of boredom and pain, of a feeling of ecstasy beyond anything he had ever known, of a spiritual connection to all things. "Why would I deny myself that?" he asked rhetorically. "Why would anyone?"

I had no answers nor did he expect any. I was there to listen to his stories and was glad that he offered something to me. I suspected that he was glad to speak to me. But then one week he didn't show up. And another week passed. I called and he told me he was sick. He sounded very far away.

A day later I got a call from Emma, his mother. She had discovered that he was using heroin again and had been for some weeks. She was distraught and defeated. So was I. I wondered where was his father.

I remained in touch with Emma and Leo for several months by telephone. Leo checked himself into a drug rehabilitation program and worked daily with a tough, no-nonsense counselor, a demanding drill sergeant. The program was based upon a 12-step model and Leo did well. His mother began to calm down and soon Leo left town to seek his fortune. He called and said good-bye, and he thanked me for the work we did together. He also assured me that the failure and deception was his alone. I thanked him and wished him well. Despite his assurances, I was left with a sense of failure. I could not be the guardian angel he needed just as I could not steer my father clear of his pain.

During this time in my work as a therapist, I was almost exclusively seeing men who felt abandoned by their fathers, and I struggled mightily to take on the role of the good father for them and help them slowly repair the damaged connection. I was conscious of doing all I could to stay connected to my son, Mackey, but I was, in fact, very far removed from thoughts of my father. I had not thought of Leo in many months until one day I received a call from his father. It was, actually, his stepfather, the landlord of the farm who had taken up with Emma when Leo was very young. His name was Bill and he had, in fact, raised Leo as a son since he was five. When Bill told Leo that he was searching for a therapist, Leo insisted that he see me.

I soon learned that Leo had a serious drug relapse that led to an arrest and incarceration. Since then, he had joined an excellent, spiritually-oriented 12-step program and was fully committed to the task of becoming clean and sober. Interestingly, the first step in the program is an acceptance of one's helplessness in the face of the disease of addiction. But Leo would move beyond his helplessness as he climbed the steps. He would take action and change his destiny.

On the Farm

Bill came to see me because he needed to make a decision. On the surface, the decision concerned whether he and his wife, Emma, should move back to the farm. Within a short time, it became clear that the pressing decision was not about moving but about finding the strength to remove Charles, Leo's biological father, from the farm. It seems that when the families shuffled, Bill, Emma and Leo became one unit and Charles and his new wife became another. Bill agreed to allow Charles to remain on the farm, rent-free. Emma convinced him that it would be better for Leo to be connected to his father. And Leo, being the good guy, embraced the counter-cultural philosophy of peace and love. All the while, Bill harbored a great resentment toward his rival and toward himself for denying his impulse to expel Charles.

Charles was a writer who made a minimal income from his work. As an artist, he expected to be supported by others throughout his life. He viewed Bill as one who would do so unquestionably. Bill, however, also saw himself as an artist and had experienced success as an actor, although the bulk of his income came from producing plays. Within a short time of our first meeting, Bill identified several major role conflicts in his life. On one level he saw the conflict between the artist and the landlord. At a deeper level he began to see the conflict between the roles of the vanquished—the weak male, the failed artist, the substitute father who is forced to support the real father; and the victor—the strong male entitled to set the rules on his own land, the artist and bread-winner, the responsible, authentic father. At the deepest level, Bill's conflict seemed to me to be about the part of Bill that felt good and moral and responsible, and the part of him that felt bad and immoral and guilty for feeling that way. Not incidentally, I linked Bill's dilemma to that of my father. I recalled he was an excellent card player and had so much at stake in being good that even when he won money from his friends he would purposefully lose so that they would not feel bad.

Bill and I played with classical images of male warriors—Greek kings fighting the Trojan war, cowboys shooting it out in a gunfight, baseball players locked in a fierce pennant race. Once he was clear that he had to get Charles off his land, he proceeded to take the long road toward victory, confronting not only the wounded and wrathful Charles and the criticism of the former occupants of the farm, but also his own self-doubts and guilt. Underlying all was the fear that he wasn't good enough to be a father, that after all, it wasn't his sperm that created Leo, that after all, it was his immaturity that led his adopted son to heroin.

I asked Bill to tell me stories about his father and I learned about a respected and admired physician who devoted his time unselfishly to help the needy and infirm. In a wistful moment, Bill said: "I wish he was more loving to me." To help Bill become aware of how he was seen by his father, I asked him to take on the father role. In role he said: "I've been concerned about Billy's ability to be a man in the world. He should find a way to exercise his maturity."

In our work together, Bill confronted the imagined criticism of his father and began to think and act more like a mature man in the world. He successfully confronted Charles and negotiated a move from the farm. He embraced a clear image of his father as loving but limited in leading him toward maturity. He told me a story that occurred shortly before his father's death. He had invited his father to spend a weekend out of town. Late at night, Bill awoke to find his father sitting in a chair by the fire, gasping for air. He asked to be taken to a hospital immediately. Bill quickly surveyed the situation and realized that the fire had diminished the oxygen supply in the room. After opening the window, Bill put out the fire. His father could breath again. He was saved by his son.

When she discovered Leo's drug paraphernalia, Emma was devastated. Bill recognized that his son needed help and supported Emma's calls to therapists. Throughout his ordeal, Leo stayed in close contact with Bill, who eventually joined an Al Anon group for parents of addicted children. Charles, however, remained on the sidelines, as always, calling Leo when he, Charles, needed help. After about a year of our working together, Bill informed me that Leo was coming home for a vacation and asked whether I would like to see him. I casually mentioned that perhaps all of us could meet for a session and Bill liked the idea very much. As did Leo.

The three of us met for one session. I was a bit anxious because I still felt that I failed Leo. At some level I hoped that by helping Bill, the father, I would also be helping Leo, the son.

After the small talk about the weather, Leo mentioned that he enjoys becoming silly with Emma when he is home and that her sense of humor is so much more satisfying than Bill's. Bill was surprised. Leo continued by saying that when Bill gets together with his friends, he, too, becomes silly, but the silliness is based upon intellectual subjects, like Beowulf.

Bill said that he tends to withdraw when Emma and Leo become silly, feeling like the false father, an outsider to the biological family. At that point, Leo turned directly to Bill and said: "But you are my real Dad. Charles was never there for me. I grew up with you and you took care of me."

Leo spoke with great clarity and emotion and even authority, as if he were the father. All the while, however, Leo played the role of the good son trying to connect to the father.

At some point, Bill and Leo spoke of their common need to play the bad boy in order to get their needs met. Again I thought of a Brecht play, this time *The Good Person of Szechwan*, about Shen Teh, a prostitute with a sweet nature who receives a gift of money from the gods because, despite her profession, she is a truly compassionate and moral person. Because of her goodly nature and her inability to refuse anyone, she is exploited by a number of greedy people and is about to lose her inheritance. The only way she can survive is to take on the disguise of an aggressive, hard-nosed businessman. By playing the bad person, she is able to allow the good person to live.

Both Bill and Leo dared to be bad in order to maintain their integrity. In finding the strong, aggressive part of himself, Bill is able to resolve a conflict that plagued him for more than 25 years. He will force Charles off the farm and will feel more fully entitled to the roles of father and husband. In choosing Bill as his real father, Leo will face the pain of his rejection by and separation from Charles. He will continue to struggle with the connection to a caring and supportive community of parents and peers who will challenge him to maintain his sobriety and maturity. In taking these assertive paths, both Bill and Leo undo their co-dependency with Charles. Bill would no longer feel the need to support Charles' elevated status as artist. Leo would no longer feel the need to support Charles' elevated status as father.

Toward the end of the session, I ask father and son to make up a story together. After some hesitation I give Leo the first line: "Once upon a time there was a father and son." Leo begins but quickly passes off to Bill. In his story, Bill brings father and son to a cabin in the woods. At nightfall, they decide to build a fire. The son goes out to get firewood but it is too damp. Leo picks up the story and says: "So without dry wood, they decide to burn Beowulf."

"There just happens to be a stack of Beowulfs in the house and they burn well," says Bill.

Bill moves the story forward and brings the father and son into dialogue around the blazing fire. They talk man to man, on an equal basis. They profess their love for each other. Bill is moved to tears as he tells the story.

I ask Leo to tell the end. Leo affirms the love in the story between father and son but needs to veer away from a closure that Bill very much wants. At the end Leo says: "And suddenly Goldilocks and the three bears appear at the door." In shifting the tone, Leo returns to the silly jokes that alienate Bill. Why can't he just embrace this moment, I wonder? Perhaps he is not as clear as he let on that Bill is the real Dad. Maybe this is why Bill feels insecure in his father role. Why does Leo choose *Goldilocks and the Three Bears*?

I could only speculate that Goldilocks is an intruder on the happy family of bears and that maybe Leo is not truly comfortable with his sense of Bill as the true Dad. Maybe Bill will always be an intruder on Leo's happy idyll of a family living on a hippie commune in the 1960s in love and peace, getting stoned on the marijuana they grow on their land. It may be that this idyll keeps Leo from growing up and assuming adult responsibilities. It may also be that the idyll has just as firmly affected Bill who has felt entrenched in a cloud of immaturity, a self-fulfilling prophesy inherited from his father.

It could be that Charles was the intruder, the pariah artist who lived for himself and his work and expected the world to take care of him. Or maybe Leo, himself, is the intruder, the junkie, the one who shakes things up in order that they will all deal.

Although the story ends in a jokey way with Goldilocks, it begins with another joke on Beowulf. Interestingly, Beowulf is the classical hero, an outsider who arrives at a kingdom plagued by monsters, slays the dragons and establishes a new order for all. If he is an intruder at all, he is one who is desired. In the story told by Leo and Bill, Beowulf, the book, is a vehicle for fire. Beowulf is also the substance of Bill's house of books which perhaps need to be burned in order to equalize the men.

I recall an earlier story where Bill puts out the fire to rescue his father. In the present story, the father and son build the fire together, a fire that is fueled from an old story of heroes. The old heroes are gone. The old romance of the good life on the farm is gone. What remains are two men, father and son, building a fire together and keeping it burning as they share their stories and ritually secure their bond.

In the end, I am left with this meeting of men and I am part of it. I am not son and I am not father. I am in-between, the one who again holds the stories. But this time I do it differently from the way I held my father's stories. I know what needs to be done and I can do it. I am the one who assumes that connections between father and son can be made. I am the one who presumes to facilitate that connection. I am the spirit of the campfire, warming the imagination, lulling fathers and sons out of their defensive, narcotic sleep into the heat of communion.

Leo returned to his new home alone and continued traveling the path of the 12-step, self-help program, remaining clean and sober, remaining connected to his father, Bill, and mother, Emma. His status as intruder upon the family has transformed, his goals accomplished.

Bill and Emma still puzzle over their next home site, but the farm is empty, ready to be sold. The power of Charles as intruder has diminished. He, too, has moved on and continues his search for the pure artistic form.

A Reflection

Reflecting on my work with Phil, Leo and Bill, I think of the fictional characters in their stories—*The Buddha and the Opportunist, The Biker* and *The Old Man in the Desert, Beowulf, Goldilocks and the Three Bears*. And I think of the themes of the stories—the shipwreck and the bike ride and the search for a male mentor, the dueling over land and paternity, the building and putting out of fires, the walk in the woods and the sharing of stories and jokes around a ritual campfire, the slaying of dragons and the feelings of respect and love.

As a drama therapist, I assume that the archetypal and mythic roles and themes offer a path to the inner life of the client. Phil, the biker, is searching for a wise father as represented by the Old Man in the Desert and the Buddha. Leo, the real life addict, is searching for a way to let go of his dependence upon a fantasy father, whether artist or warrior. Bill, in putting out fires and building fires, is searching for a way to be both father and son.

In working with their old stories and creating new ones, these men will let go of their fathers and find their fathers. And in doing so, they will find ways to better father themselves and their sons, and assume the male identity that is so profoundly shaped in the meeting of father and son.

On the Line

As I write this essay my son has been away at summer camp for two weeks. It is the first time that he has been away from home. I am happy to have the time alone, to do my work uninterrupted by the demands of the children. I don't think much about Mackey, and when I call him on the phone to assure myself that all is going well, he answers my questions in terse grunts. He is completely uncommunicative, but he is content in his temporary home in the woods.

Soon it is visiting day. I am apprehensive, not so much about his comfort level at camp, but about my ability to connect with him. When we meet, he leaps into my arms and I hold him. We bruise each other's scalp with our knuckles, a rough male greeting. He shows me around camp, we play tether ball, and we take a playful swim in the lake. All is well.

Before I leave, he wants to show me the climbing wall, a wooden structure as high as the highest tree, straight up into the sky, with diagonal slabs of plywood haphazardly placed for grasping and climbing. Fear shoots through my body. I would never had tried to scale the wall at his age or at any age. But Mackey at nine carefully secures the twisted straps of his harness and checks in with his two counselors on the top and bottom of the wall, guides who will insure his safety and success. As Mackey climbs higher and higher without a sound, I am left behind. As I let go of my fear and realize that this is Mackey's moment, I remember my dream of the swing. If Mackey were to call out: "Dad, how am I doing?" I would have answered: "Great, just great." This reality is so much better than the dream. Mackey is free and so am I. I do not have to rescue my son, because he is not in trouble. He is harnessed and he is safe. He climbs higher to reach a summit. I am his father and I love what he can do separate from me. He is out there climbing toward the blue horizon and I am below, marveling at his courage. He is my hero.

Although lost in my reverie, I notice that the guide at the top of the wall harnesses Mackey to a wire, the zip line, and Mackey leaps off the top of the wall, flying through the air, along the entire length of the zip line, with the greatest of ease. When he returns to earth, I want to lift him off the ground into my arms again, but there are others watching and so I hug him, just for an instant. Soon it will be time to say goodbye for the final two weeks of camp.

Before I leave I ask him: "Mackey, have you built any campfires?"

"No," he tells me, "the weather has been too damp."

I think of all the books I have on my shelves and imagine that they would burn with great ease. But my son doesn't need my books and my heroes. He will wait for the weather to clear and with the help of his counselors and friends, he will burn the dead branches from the trees.

When I wave goodbye to my son, I feel at peace, connected to him and to the world. He knows how to climb up and swing down. He trusts the laws of nature and the support of his helpers. Maybe my father was wrong when he told me that good guys finish last. Mackey is a good guy and he is doing well. Although he was born with a physical disability, it is not his destiny to be disabled. But then my father wasn't telling me about my son or even about my experience as his son. He was telling me about himself and his sense of dis-ease.

When I was very young, my father would sing to me. I loved his songs which were often light Yiddish ditties that made me feel full of life. The one song I remember best, however, is *The Ballad of Samuel Hall*, an old folk song about a murderer about to be hanged at the gallows. Samuel Hall looks down at the crowd and in a rage curses all those who have betrayed him. Having seen my son climb the wall and fly back down to earth, it was time to let go of Samuel Hall, the part of my father that felt so unprotected in the war and so denied in the home. And it was time to let go of the legacy passed on from Sam Hall to my father to me.

There is a lifeline that connects fathers and sons, enabling them to rise and fall, to go out in the world to seek maturity and to return safely home, repeating the cycle again and again. Sometimes it gets all tangled up and sometimes it is down altogether. So afraid to climb, I lost the connection to my father so many times throughout my life. His lines to me were his stories and his songs. Many years after his death, I still hold on to them and try to use them in new ways to scale new walls and find new ways back down to earth.

My father was a sweet and bitter guide who taught me how to listen to stories and read between the lines. Unwittingly, he taught me how to hold on and how to let go. He is with me in my office, by my side, on my shoulder, in my heart each time I ask a man who is a son or a father to tell me a story.

Part Three

ASSESSMENT

Chapter 7

HOW CHILDREN SEE GOD

When I was 22, I studied literature at a prestigious American graduate school. I was surrounded by high-powered intellectuals, many of whom were prominent in their fields. They were like Talmudic scholars who devoted their lives to *midrash*, the art of interpreting texts and offering commentary. And like the old wise men wrestling with their holy books, the measured pronouncements of my professors, I believed, would have profound implications on how we lived our lives.

Toward the end of my first year of study, I became distracted, unable to mine the gold of the venerable old texts. It was the 1960s and the world was changing fast all around me. I was losing my sense of balance and needing to break out of the academy. One night I had a vivid dream. A group of holy men dressed in black are in a room, discussing the true nature of Christ. They are highly skilled in the art of interpretation. I am a young boy hiding behind a chair in a doorway. I feel ignorant as I try to make sense of their words. What do I, a Jew, know about Christ? What do I, a young man about to lose his sense of balance, know about God? As their debate becomes more and more intellectual, they seem to become removed, distant. As I strain to listen, I become agitated. They believe nothing that they say; they are empty. The intensity builds: the words less intelligible, the figures less visible, my heart racing, my head pounding. And then, suddenly, I am knocked over by a brilliant flash of light. I awake instantly and sit up in my bed. I am shaking. My first thought was that I had just seen Christ. My second, much more frightening, was that the vision was a trick. It was the devil that had planted this dream, intending to lead me astray and renounce my religion.

On one level, the dream seems clear to me. I was young and experiencing an identity crisis. I needed a break from the intellectual life which at the time felt false and empty. My spiritual identity was shaky and I was unsure of which god to follow. Even when confronted with a revelation, I quickly became confused. This was, I reasoned, only a dream, and at the time, I had no clue how to read a dream.

Over the years, I have become a better reader of dreams and have found ways to understand their connection to everyday life. In my work as a drama therapist, I have come to understand that the substance of dreams is the stuff of the imagination–images, feelings, rhythms, motifs, stories and roles. When Shakespeare writes: "We are such stuff as dreams are made on," he implies that the essential matter of human life is the imagination.

My work as a drama therapist has been to help clients freely access their imaginations, learn to read their extraordinary tales and build firm bridges between the two realms of the image and the empirical world, the representation and the thing that is represented.

People generally seek therapy because they are in some kind of crisis. One way of understanding crisis is as an inability to bridge the gap between image and reality. This may be because one lives too much or too little in the imagination. At 22, when I had my vision of a real or false god, I indulged fully in my imagination. The world outside was for the most part unintelligible. I had no means of building the bridge between the two and without a proper guide, I floundered.

Over the years, I have learned more about bridge building, and I have learned more about living on borders. I remain, however, baffled about true and false gods. My early dream stays with me because it remains unresolved and mysterious. It serves as a prelude for the following research.

Several years ago, my daughter, Georgie, eight years old, returned from school and told a story about a conversation with her schoolmates. The girls were discussing religion and one turned to Georgie and said: "You know, you Jews killed Jesus Christ." Georgie brought the story home. We all discussed it at the dinner table–Georgie and her six-year-old brother, Mackey, my wife and I. My wife and I spoke of the importance of religious tolerance and made it clear that such remarks are hurtful and unacceptable. Both children listened a bit to our lecture but remained silent. Perhaps they were too young to understand anti-Semitism and religious intolerance. Perhaps my wife and I were too insistent and intense.

The next day, my son drew a picture. It was of a figure in a cage with a sad expression, surrounded by several images of the crucified Christ. He labeled his picture "Jew," and told this simple story: "The Jew is in jail" (see Figure 4). When Georgie saw Mackey's drawing, she did one, too–Christ on the cross, being tormented by a figure with a sword (see Figure 5). Although she claimed that the tormentor was a foreigner, I noticed that he bore a strong resemblance to Georgie. Both children seemed to be struggling with their understanding of the episode in school. Although they could not verbalize

Figure 1. Taoist Gods.

Figure 2. Actors Warm-Up Audience to the Roles of Ji-gon.

Figure 3. Who Are You and What Do You Want?

Figure 4. Jew in Jail

Figure 5. Who Killed Christ?

Figure 6. That Shadow Behind Us.

Figure 7. The War in Heaven and in Bosnia.

Figure 8. God and His Enemies.

Figure 9. The Satanic Verses.

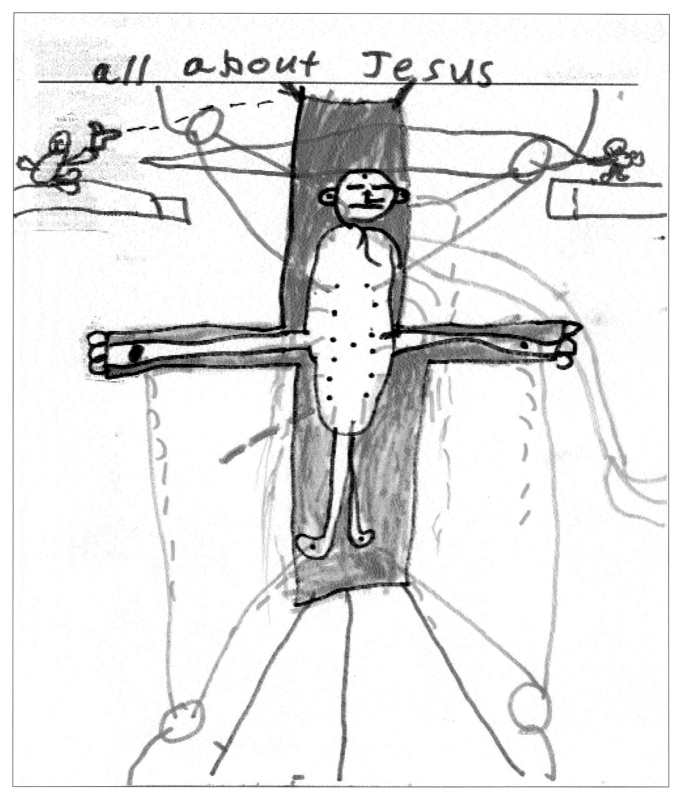

Figure 10. All about Jesus.

Figure 11. God Lives in the Soul.

Figure 12. The Two Nests or Unfinished Business.

Figure 13. The Two Trees.

Figure 14. Fairy and Frog.

Figure 15. The Girl Who Shined as Bright as the Sun.

their feelings, they could well express their fears. Georgie feared that she might be seen as the killer of Christ. Mackey feared the same except he took it further. Not only has he committed the murder, but he is punished for it. He becomes the Jew in Jail surrounded by reminders of his sin—images of the crucified Christ.

All of this was very powerful for me and with the encouragement of my friend and colleague, Sue Jennings, I decided to resume a project that had remained dormant for many years—a search for God. I suppose there were two motivations for my research. The first had to do with that early dream and my confusion over real and false gods. The second motivation had more to do with the question of intolerance and hatred. Why were my children learning in school that their god was lesser than another's? This question had personal implications for me, born during the end of World War II to an extended family of East European Jews traumatized by the holocaust. And it also raised broader political and moral concerns about wars fought in the name of land and religion.

My children's drawings and stories provided a model for a workable method of research. I would interview children and ask them to draw God and to tell stories about their drawing. My general research question became: "How do children see God?" Aware that my work with children would be a way to sharpen my own perception, I also asked: "How can we, as adults, invoke our own images of God and learn how to read them." And finally, as I neared the end of my research, I raised the question: "Why does it matter?"

My methodology expanded one day when Mackey came into my room with a drawing of an abstract red face attached by tape to his shirt. "Do you know who I am Dad?" he asked. "Who?" I replied. "God," said Mackey. "And what is God saying?" I asked. In his best imitation of Moses confronting Pharaoh, Mackey responded: "Let my people go." And then I had the final piece of my interview—I would also ask the children to take on the role of God and speak from God's point of view to a particular other.

Before I started out, I decided to limit myself to children between the ages of four and 12, old enough to articulate their ideas and young enough to retain a direct connection to the life of the imagination. I wanted to interview as wide a range of children as possible from many cultures and spiritual traditions, from different economic and social backgrounds, from peaceful countries and countries at war.

I started close to home and to my delight discovered the whole world in microcosm. Within 50 miles of my small town north of New York City, I met with children whose backgrounds were Christian, Jewish, Muslim, Baha'i, Hindu, Buddhist, pagan and atheist. As I ventured out into the world, I interviewed more children from a variety of countries or asked for help from others living far away—teachers, artists, therapists, social workers—who would implement my questionnaire to children. In all, I collected more than 600 interviews.

Although it is difficult to summarize what I discovered, I will offer several of my general findings. First, God lives. There is an old Hasidic saying that God is present wherever people let him in. The children I have interviewed let God in. They see the living God not only in the framework of conventional religious traditions but also in terms of a spiritual consciousness independent of institutionalized religion.

Second, God has many definitions and forms and transforms readily. God can be feminine and masculine, one and many, hidden and revealed, anthropomorphic and abstract.

Third, God is as much a creation of children and indeed, all of us, as God is a creator. Throughout the research, I discovered ironically that it is God who is created in the image of man. In interviewing the children I learned that for many creating God is a powerful and healing act. This observation has therapeutic implications in that many of the children appeared to be working through concerns and fears about mortality and immortality, war and peace, bigotry and kindness, poverty and plenty as they drew their pictures and told their stories.

And finally, I learned that God is vulnerable and very human. God has enemies. God gets lost and lonely. God works hard and becomes tired. Sometimes God gets weak and loses heart and requires the special power of the child to make him whole again. Not only is man the creator of God, but also the restorer.

To provide a brief overview of the children's responses, I have selected a number of statements from the interviews and a number of drawings. Many of the statements are in response to specific questions, as follow:

What Is God?

God lives in glass and is shaped by the wind.
—a seven-year-old Christian girl from South Africa

God is a ray of light that shows us the good way.
—a ten-year-old Jewish girl from Israel

Allah has no form but power.
—a nine-year-old Muslim boy from India

God has huge ears so he can hear when the children cry and everything that people say.
—a seven-year-old Lutheran girl from Germany

God's tummy is red and that means he is very holy.
—a five-year-old Catholic boy from Northern Ireland

God has black eyes so at night nobody will see him.
—a seven-year-old Catholic boy from Northern Ireland

To me, God is everything, and God is a girl and a boy, and God loves everything God makes.
—*a seven-year-old Jewish girl from the USA*

You can look in the nun's notebook. Everything about God is in there.
—*a five-year-old Catholic girl from Italy*

Where Does God Live?

God lives on a flying cloud.
—*a nine-year-old Catholic boy from Mexico*

God lives seven skies high.
—*an 11-year-old Muslim boy from Bangladesh*

Even I know where God lives. I took an airplane. He lives with the shepherds.
—*a five-year-old Protestant boy from the USA*

God is in the world but we don't see him. We feel him in the stomach when he knocks.
—*a seven-year-old Jewish girl from Israel*

What Happens When You Die?

God sees to it that everyone who dies and goes to heaven has his own little cloud. Every cloud can be opened like a jewel case, and inside there are a lot of things that can be taken out, just like from Mary Poppins' bag.
—*a ten-year-old Catholic girl from Italy*

Not everyone goes straight to heaven. You can go to hell or puberty or something.
—*an 11-year-old Catholic girl from Northern Ireland*

How Does God Talk to People?

I can't understand God because he speaks in ancient Greek.
—*an eight-year-old Greek Orthodox boy from Greece*

God speaks in Latin. If he spoke in English, I would ask him if I am on a list for heaven.
—*a ten-year-old Protestant boy from Northern Ireland*

God speaks to humans in the feelings. He says that love and friendship are the most important things in the world.
—*a nine-year-old Catholic girl from Croatia*

How Does God Create Life?

God caused the big bang that formed the earth and the first humans.
—*a ten-year-old secular boy from South Africa*

I wonder if God ever gets pregnant? He probably beams babies out of his head and puts them in the mothers on earth.
—*a nine-year-old Catholic boy from the USA*

God made dinosaurs. Nobody knows how they got killed. He makes new things if they run out.
—*a six-year-old Baha'i girl from Canada*

Heavenly Father and Jesus split the earth and put all the people who believe in them in it and closed it up. After the earthquake, they open it up and make a whole new generation.
—*a nine-year-old Mormon girl from Canada*

What Happens If You Disobey God?

If I disobey God, God will turn me into a soldier.
—*a ten-year-old Taoist boy from Taiwan*

What Happens When God Gets Angry?

When God's angry, he throws thunder and lightning. Last night he got angry at someone, probably a priest who did something wrong in church.
—*a nine-year-old Christian Orthodox boy from Bulgaria*

What Is God's Work?

God shines love on the whole of earth.
—*a ten-year-old Catholic boy from Nigeria*

God uses his magic to give his child a teddy bear.
—*an eight-year-old Eskimo girl from Canada*

The Goddess of Mercy protects the earth.
—*an eight-year-old Buddhist girl from Taiwan*

God protects us under a shell, like the turtle. He rejects broken hearts, war and injustice.
—*an 11-year-old Catholic girl from Spain*

Do You Believe in God?

I believe in God but don't pray as the temple is usually shut.
—*a six-year -ld Hindu boy from India*

I believe in God because there's no one else to believe in England, and I don't want to upset my Mum.
—*an eight-year-old Pentecostal boy from England*

When less than 100 people stop believing in God, he dies.
—*an eight-year-old Jewish boy from the USA*

What Is It Like in the Presence of God?

All is peaceful around the young Buddha. There are no enemies, no bad things. Just calm.
—*an eight-year-old Taoist boy from Taiwan*

The sun walks behind God. The lamb runs after him.
—*a ten-year-old Hindu girl from India*

Where Is God?

God is up there, and he spends his time going around in circles.
—*a nine-year-old Gypsy boy from Greece*

God is in my heart, peeping out and saying hello.
—*a six-year-old secular girl from South Africa*

Is God Whole?

God has a very big heart, but he is missing a little part. My heart is full. I give that missing part to him.
—*an eight-year-old Catholic girl from Mexico*

During the past several years, as the crises in the Balkans escalated, I became fascinated and confused. In collecting my interviews, I found a number of compassionate responses to the material and spiritual devastation.

Wanda, a 10-year-old Italian girl questions the suffering and offers a vision of love. She draws a picture of a poor boy sitting in a city street, begging for money (see Figure 6). Behind him is the outline of God, a large man with a beard, supporting the young beggar.

Wanda describes the boy as a six-year-old named Sinsha who lives in the suburbs of Sarajevo, destroyed by the war. She tells this story:

> Sinsha was sitting for hours on the sidewalk. The chill was making him shake. He gazed at the hat, left on the ground for money. It was empty and that increased his hunger. Just a few months before, the war wasn't there. Sinsha thought about the smiling faces of his parents and the shout of his little sister, but the horrible memory of that bomb that destroyed his house and killed his family made him feel bad. A voice said: "Remember that you are not alone. I will always be there to help you." Sinsha knew that reassuring and familiar voice and said: "Lord, I am cold and I haven't eaten in the past 2 days. Make it that someone notices me." The voice remained silent but after a few minutes a United Nations patrol passed and seeing the boy cold and numb had compassion and after they gave him food, they took him to a camp for poor children. Sinsha understood then that the love of God is also found through the acts of humans.

Wanda names her story *That Shadow Behind Us* and says that God's only enemies are those who are unable to love but who hate and make war. Wanda sees God as an invisible force of love that transforms evil into good.

Sinsha, Wanda's alter-ego, is rescued by God, the holy shadow. But Wanda and many Italian children know that others across the sea have not been so lucky. Their God has not kept them safe from the realities of war and displacement. And yet these Italian children keep the faith. They know that there is a holy shadow behind us that will find a way to mobilize the compassionate acts of human beings.

I want to mention one more response to the Balkan wars, this one by eight-year-old Anita who left Bosnia for Austria in search of a better and more secure life. She comes from a working class Muslim family.

Anita draws a picture of God in pencil. He sits on a chair surrounded by angels (see Figure 7). Two most prominent are called Roserrot and Evalischen. She tells this story about the drawing:

> Everywhere there was war. God wished it so. The angels didn't like it. But then one day God said: 'War finish! I don't want this war anymore.' There was a little fight between the angels, because one wants war, the other doesn't. Evalischen is the peaceful one. Roserrot wants war. The angels go to God and he says the war was over. Then the sun shined nicely and everybody made their own houses nicely again.

Poignantly, Anita relates this story to her experience in Bosnia:

> There also was war in Bosnia. And I was there, with my aunt. There was a woods up there and the trees were a bit further away from our house and they shooted on a tree. You can still see it. And they shooted and the tree had no leaves. It still has no leaves, no more leaves, no more leaves on the tree.

Anita sees the contradiction between war and peace in the figures of the angels. She also sees it in terms of a debate between two figures she adds to her picture, the devil and the guardian angel, perched on either side of God's head. The guardian angel helps God defeat the devil. But he is not banished forever from the heavenly kingdom. Anita says: "When he is away, there are little pieces of him, like dust. He will come again when he has something bad to say or to do."

After the celestial war, God decides on a plan:

> Everywhere should be peace. The children should be happy, and they should get many presents for Christmas, all that they desire. In the end, when all the enemies are away, the sun will shine and winter will come. God sends the angels to Santa Claus, because he needs help. The angels will throw the presents to all the children through the chimney.

Curious, the interviewer asks Anita whether there is Christmas in the Muslim religion. Anita refers to her religion as Ali Allah. She mentions that Christmas is celebrated in her new home but that in Bosnia, she celebrated Ramadan.

Anita's spiritual world is a rich one. Although Muslim, she also depicts a Christian world with a visible God in the center. Anita sees God as a peacemaker yet one who allows dialogue, debate and dissension. There is evil in the world which needs to be combated, yet it is part of the natural order.

I am very taken with Anita's spiritual landscape. It holds together contradictions in a seamless way. The unseen Santa Claus and Ali Allah feel like brothers. Anita's world feels like a vision of Sarajevo before the war, when Muslims and Christians lived in peace.

In leaving Anita's world, I hold onto one very poetic image of war–a tree is shot and gives up its leaves. And I hold onto a vision of transformation–the season of war passes, the sun shines and it is Christmas. And in this season of peace, the children get presents, all that they desire.

Toward the end of my research, I spent time in the Middle East interviewing Israeli and Arab children (see Figures 8 and 9). During part of the trip I was joined by my son, Mackey, then seven years old. In Israel we visited the holy sites most sacred to Jews, Muslims and Christians. At the Western

Wall in Jerusalem, Mackey and I wrote prayers on small pieces of paper and carefully placed them in a crevice between two ancient stones. Without prompting, Mackey turned to the wall, his hands on the smooth stones, to say a prayer. I stood behind him, my arms circling his small body and did the same. And then, very simply, I became aware of the presence of the spirit. It was a brief and gentle moment—a feeling of heat that emanated from the base of the spine and spread upward. It was very different from the dream vision I had at 22 which knocked me off my feet.

You may remember that Mackey was the one who drew a picture of a Jew in jail surrounded by several images of the crucified Christ. After a day of visiting sacred Christian sites around Tiberias where Jesus walked on the water and preached the sermon on the mount, Mackey drew a picture he called *All About Jesus* (see Figure 10). In his drawing, a large Jesus is nailed to a red cross. He displays all the stigmata of the crucifixion. Many lines are drawn to and from the body of Christ. Above him are two small figures, one with a gun and one with a sword. Mackey informs me that the figure with the gun is a Jew and the one with a sword is a Roman. And then he tells this story:

> Jesus was walking one day. He went into his tent and opened up his secret book. He saw a Roman coming and the Roman took him away. He put Jesus on a cross with nails. He stuck a big sword in the wall and used it to cut off Jesus' head. The Jew came along. The Roman saw him. He got the big sword and tried to chop off the Jewish guy's neck so he could be put on a cross. The Jewish guy took his gun out. He shot at the Roman to let Jesus free, and he took the nails off with his gun. Jesus' head came off because the gun shot the nails. The Jewish guy caught Jesus' head. Then he got the body. The cross fell and a fire was made from it and the whole place blew up. The Jewish guy escaped with Jesus. He went to bury Jesus so Jesus could rest in peace.

Mackey had come a long way from seeing the Jew as shamed for killing Christ. Not only is the Jew liberated from his jail, but he is the rescuer of Christ. I wonder if it took a trip to Israel to bring Mackey to this shift in consciousness. I imagined that he was impressed by seeing so many soldiers walking the streets of Israel, armed with rifles. I imagined that he was impressed by the apparent power of ordinary Israelis who hardly match the image of the Jew in jail.

Mackey's God is consistent with the vision of many children who imagine God to be wounded and in need of help. In Mackey's mind, as in other children's, the human being restores the celestial being. The Son of God needs the son of man to free him from pain and save his eternal soul.

But this is not all there is to know about Jesus. Mackey and I require more. We return to Jerusalem and visit the Church of the Holy Sepulcher, the site of Christ's crucifixion and burial.

Just inside the door of the church is a stone chalice which is said to mark the center of the earth. Nearby is the holy sepulcher, the tomb of Jesus. Behind the holy sepulcher is a small dark chamber. It is said that within this chamber is the tomb of Joseph of Arimathea. It was Joseph, so the story goes, who took Jesus from the cross and laid him to rest. But in my mind, it will always be Mackey, the liberated Jew, who rescued and restored the Son of God. Mackey, the Jew, is not in jail. He is in the world, at the center of the world, to learn more about the Son of God and to learn more about the Father whose presence transcends churches and faiths.

As I near the end of my spiritual journey, still considering an answer to the question, "How Do We See God?" it occurs to me that God is seen through a medium that, like a bridge, links the spiritual and the empirical worlds. Two mediums that come to mind are the mirror and the window. Looking in the mirror, we see a reflection of ourselves. Of the 600 drawings of God I surveyed, so many appeared to be self-portraits. Some were very literal, others more metaphorical– portraits of the soul. So many children's stories made reference to a god that lives within the human being. One good example is this picture drawn by Joanna, a young Christian Orthodox girl from Bulgaria who says: "God doesn't live in the clouds. He lives in the human soul" (see Figure 11).

Looking out the window, one sees God in a different way. Through the glass, God resides in nature, in the world, in the sky and the heavens. God is different and separate from the human being. Through some windows, for some children, God is so far away as to be invisible. For many steeped in orthodox traditions, it is even forbidden to look.

It could be true that God's presence can be seen both in mirrors and through windows and that one does not need to choose a medium, only the will to look inside and out. My dream at age 22 was a mirror reflecting my inner state of turmoil at the time. In reading the dream now, I recognize all the pieces–the open child and the closed intellectual, the seeker and the doubter, the saint and the trickster. In subsequent years I have discovered other mirrors of the soul and other windows on the world, and as a drama therapist, I have helped others discover the same.

I have learned that it matters very much how we see God. It matters because without the will to see the profound worlds inside and out, we become myopic. It matters because without the will to create new life, our old life ossifies. It matters how we see God because we are godlike in so many ways, even as we struggle with our limitations and our shame, yearning to be more. It matters because when we turn a blind eye, we torment others for worshiping false gods and blame them for our loss of vision. It matters because in too many dark moments in history, too many children have been murdered by those who saw their God as superior. It matters because so many children from so many diverse cultural and spiritual traditions demonstrate that it matters.

I end with a simple story I heard on my travels. A four-year-old boy asks his mother if he can speak to his baby sister alone. The sister is just two weeks old. The mother says yes and stands in the doorway, listening. "Can you tell me what God looks like?" asks the boy. "I have forgotten."

It can become very difficult to accept one inevitable consequence of aging—the separation from the wonder and mystery of the world as seen by the child. In doing this research, I have learned to remember. I have remembered that little boy in a dream long ago hiding behind a chair, waiting for the light. And I have remembered the recent feeling of father and son at the holy wall, connecting with one another in silent prayer, discovering openings in the stone and in the heart and letting in the divine presence. The children have led me back and will lead me forward. I will try not to forget.

It matters how we see God if we see God as the thing most important to remember—the electric presence that exists at walls and in doorways, in dreams and stories, through windows and mirrors, the shadow behind us that can restore peace and harmony.

Chapter 8

DRAMA THERAPY ASSESSMENT: TELL-A-STORY

In a recent article, Alice Forrester (2000) reviews the literature on psychological assessment through role-playing and improvisation. She notes that dramatic approaches to psychological assessment have been applied since World War II when Henry Murray and his colleagues introduced an instrument to measure the readiness of individuals to assume officer rank in the military (see McReynolds and DeVoge, 1977). Forrester covers a number of approaches from the mid-century to the present, summarizing the psychodramatic experiments of Moreno (1946), the more cognitive-behavioral approaches of Kendall (1984) and Bandura (1977), and the drama therapy-based work of Johnson (1988).

One other significant approach in drama therapy not reviewed is that of the puppetry interview developed by Eleanor Irwin and her colleagues (1985), applying a psychoanalytical framework to an analysis of the form and content of children's stories created through puppet play. Most of the instruments reviewed by Forrester, with the exception of those of Moreno and Johnson, are based in theoretical models outside the field of drama therapy.

Since 1997, I have been developing two dramatic assessment instruments. Both are based in a particular drama therapy framework, that of role theory. Of the two assessment approaches, Role Profiles (see Chapter 9, this book) was developed first as a means of extending the Taxonomy of Roles (see Landy, 1993) into clinical practice. In its initial form, Tell-A-Story was part of Role Profiles. As I refined my attempt to assess a client's role system, Tell-A-Story (TAS) became an independent test. Its aim is to assess an individual's ability to invoke roles within a story structure and to view connections among the roles in the story and between those in the story and those in the individual's everyday life.

At this writing, Tell-A-Story has not been sufficiently subjected to tests of reliability and validity. Yet through ongoing experimentation and clinical trials, some promising data has emerged (see Seitz, 2000).

Below I provide the actual test instructions. Following that, I will offer several clinical examples. I have modified certain factual aspects of the clinical work in order to protect the confidentiality of the subjects.

TELL-A-STORY

1. Tester asks subject to tell a story:

   I would like you to tell me a story. The story can be based upon something that happened to you or to somebody else in real life or it can be completely made-up. The story must have at least one character.

Tester can provide appropriate prompts to help subject tell the story. An example is for the tester to set the frame, e.g., "Once upon a time there was a. . . ."

If the subject is not warmed-up, the tester asks:

   Can you tell me one character that seems interesting to you right now? Please tell a story about her/him.

If the subject is still unable to begin, the tester says:

   Move around the room. Focus upon one part of your body. Find a movement that leads out of that body part. Find a character that moves that way. Start your story with that character.

If the subject is unable to tell the story verbally, then she should be encouraged to tell it non-verbally, either through sound and movement or with a projective object, such as a puppet.

2. Following the story, the tester asks the subject to identify and name the characters and/or significant objects in the story.

3. For each character, the tester asks the subject to specify **qualities**. If there are more than 4 characters, the tester helps the subject to select the most important ones. Questions to be asked can include:

   Describe the characters. How do they look (physical/somatic qualities)? How smart are they (cognitive qualities)? How do they feel? What are their beliefs and values (affective qualities)? How social, spiritual and creative are they (social, spiritual, aesthetic qualities)?

4. Tester asks subject to specify **function** of each. Question to be asked:
   In the story, what does each character want most of all? The tester can prompt the subject and can refer to the list of 28 needs formulated as part of assessment research protocol by R. Landy:[1]

Table 1

Beauty	Celibacy	Revenge	Powerlessness
Ugliness	Wisdom	Acceptance	Adventure
Health	Ignorance	Connection	Safety
Sickness	Goodness	Autonomy	Transcendence
Youth	Immorality	Protection	Domesticity
Maturity	Isolation	Exposure	Prophesy
Sex	Intimacy	Power	Creativity

5. Tester asks subject to specify **style** of each, that is, whether the role is presented in a fantasy-based, stylized fashion or a more reality-based one. In theory, a move away from reality implies a distance from feeling. Reality-based storytelling implies a need for more feeling. The optimal state of balance is one where feeling and thinking/reflection are both available. Question to be asked:
   Are the characters real or make-believe? Are they primarily thinking or feeling types or are they somewhere in the middle? Please explain.

6. Tester asks subject:
   *What is the **theme** of the story? What is a title for the story?*

Prompts can include a referral to the list of 28 needs above so that a theme could be, for example, the conflict of beauty and ugliness.

7. **Integration**. Tester asks subject:
   Can the characters find a way to resolve their conflicts and live together in peace? How?

8. Tester asks subject:
   What is the connection between the characters in your story and your everyday life? What parts of you are like the characters in your story? How can these parts live or exist together?

---

1. This list of needs is partly based upon the research of Henry Murray (1938) and partly adapted from the qualities of the roles listed in Landy's Taxonomy of Roles (1993).

9. Tester notes any other subject reflections upon the story and reactions to the process.

10. Tester notes her own feelings and impressions of the subject's process.

CLINICAL EXAMPLES

The Refrigerator and the Bomb

Mark is a bright and creative 15-year-old living alone with his mother in the city. He attends a private prep school with a fine academic reputation. Although he is recognized as talented and even gifted in some areas, he is on the verge of being expelled from the school. His behavior has been defiant and oppositional to the extreme in relation to teachers, administrators and peers. He has pushed too many boundaries and regulations too far and too often. He has been verbally abusive to his mother and at times has threatened her physically. Mark has been treated by a number of therapists and by a psychiatrist. Neither therapy nor medication has significantly influenced a modification of his oppositional and defiant behavior. His mother asks me to see Mark and to determine if drama therapy might help him.

I introduced TAS during our second session. Below is a recreation and modification of the assessment process.

    —Mark, I would like you to tell me a story. The story can be based upon something that happened to you or to somebody else in real life or it can be completely made-up. The story must have at least one character.

    —I don't know . . . .

    —You can begin any way you'd like. Such as, "Once upon a time there was a. . . ."

    —I don't know . . . .

    —Tell me the name of one character that seems interesting to you right now.

    —I don't know. I'm hungry.

    —Could this be a character?

    —What?

    —The one who's hungry.

    —Whatever.

    —Can you tell me a story about a hungry guy.

    —I don't know.

I began: "Once upon a time there was a hungry person. . . ."

Mark continued: "And he couldn't get the food because there was a lock on the refrigerator. The end."

"What happened next?" I asked.

Mark was becoming more and more annoyed. "I told you it was the end!"

I prodded him: "Give it a try."

He responded defiantly: "He tried to break the lock but he couldn't. So he took a bomb and blew up the refrigerator."

"Then what happened?" I asked.

—He blew up the food. Splat!"

Mark refused to identify and describe the characters in his story. I asked him: "What does each character want most of all?" He responded: "Food."

He was unwilling to address the question of style—real vs. make-believe, feeling vs. thinking. In fact, he would not respond to any of my other questions. When I asked him to connect the story to his everyday life he shrugged and turned his back to me. He remained silent until the session ended.

Interpretation

Mark's story is quite minimal and in fact dependent upon my prompts. Mark is consistently resistant to the process of storytelling, and on the surface it would appear that Mark's ability to invoke roles and view connections among the roles in the story is poor. And yet despite his resistance and opposition, Mark tells a very poignant story about his present state of being. Although he refuses to name the roles in the story, they are all present and namable: the hungry person, the food, the lock, the refrigerator and the bomb.

Mark refuses to reflect upon the story at all. My sense is that he is quite intellectually capable of doing so but is unwilling to move beyond his oppositional, defiant state of being. He and I had not had time to establish a trust, having met for just one hour previously. He had no reason to offer up a story for my benefit.

I will attempt to respond to the questions in TAS, offering my interpretations based upon my previous and subsequent work with Mark. Although I often limit the number of roles to three, in this case I will reflect upon all five as they are intimately linked and clearly defined. I note that there is only one human character, the hungry person. All the others are related to the object of his desire, the food.

In my opinion, the hungry person is someone who looks like Mark. I think of Shakespeare's characterization of the conspirator Cassius in *Julius Caesar*. "Yon Cassius has a lean and hungry look. He thinks too much. Such men are dangerous." I see the hungry man as dangerous because he uses extreme measures to get what he needs. He seems to have poor reality testing skills and poor inner controls.

The food is inert, lifeless. It's only value is as an object of desire. The refrigerator is a container. It could just as well be a safe in a bank as a storage place for food. It holds the thing most valued by the hungry person. The lock is an object of frustration that insures that the food will be withheld from the hungry person. The bomb is the most affectively charged role in the story. It has power beyond that of the hungry person. Although it is powerful, however, its power is destructive and frustrating to the hungry person.

In thinking about the function of the roles, I note that the hungry person wants to satisfy his appetite. Although the food is presumably there for the taking, it is locked up and inaccessible to the hungry person. It feels like a charged role to me. On the one hand it wants to satisfy its archetypal function, to be eaten. And yet, it displays the counter quality, not to be eaten or not to be available for consumption. In some ways, it appears to be a forbidden fruit, enticing yet potentially damaging.

The refrigerator's function is to contain the food. The lock serves to frustrate the ability of the hungry man to get the food, but the bomb helps the hungry person get the food. In essence, the bomb's function is to destroy the lock and the refrigerator.

When I look at the list of the 28 needs, I see this as a story about the struggle between power and powerlessness. The hungry person feels powerful as he takes up a bomb to get his precious food. In the end, however, he destroys the thing he most wants and is left feeling frustrated, powerless.

In terms of style, Mark's story is effectively distanced, that is, removed from reality. The style he chooses is quite appropriate for it enables him to present an emotional reality of himself without appearing to divulge anything personal. Being very well defended, Mark had no intention whatsoever of revealing his feelings to me. From my point of view, however, Mark's story is quite emotional. The figure of the bomb offers an indication of the intensity of his feelings. The figure of the hungry person, eschewing all reasonable solutions to the problem of how to satisfy his appetite, resolves his solution irrationally—he will force his way in and in doing so, destroy the hand that would feed him.

I named the story *The Refrigerator and the Bomb*. Mark was unwilling to venture a title or commit to a theme. It appeared to me that the theme of the story was the futility of using force to satisfy one's appetites.

Mark was not at all prepared to answer the question: *Can the characters find a way to resolve their conflicts and live together in peace?* Until he can reconceive of the bomb as a deterrent and think of ways that the hungry person can satisfy his appetite, it is unlikely that he will be able to find an integration among the roles.

It also appeared obvious to me that Mark was unable to view the story as a parable reflecting some aspects of his everyday life. From my point of view, Mark was hungry for an emotional sustenance that he thought was so unobtainable that the only way to get it was through an act of violence, one that would ultimately destroy the thing he most desired.

As I reviewed my notes taken right after the process, I discovered that I, like Mark, experienced a degree of frustration around this task, especially with Mark's growing refusal to answer any of my questions. I realized that if I were to take Mark on as a client he would be quite a challenge and I questioned whether I was up to the task.

As I was reflecting upon the form and content of Mark's story, I thought about his work from the point of view of role theory (see Landy, 1993, 2000). There was a role and counterrole present in his story–the hungry person and the food. I wondered whether there was a guide figure, then came to the conclusion that perhaps the bomb is a guide as it leads the hungry person to the food. However, this guide is a very negative one that doesn't serve the hungry person very well at all. I reasoned that one central aim in therapeutic treatment would be to help Mark locate a more positive guide, one who could help him discover a constructive way to fulfill his needs.

When I first met Mark, I was aware of two assessments from his psychiatrist and his mother. The psychiatrist had diagnosed his condition as oppositional defiant disorder. Previous to my first meeting with Mark, I learned of his provocative behavior at home and school from his mother. My job was to assess his ability to engage in a creative act, storytelling, and to link the fictional characters and themes in the story to his own life. Further, I tried to assess whether he would be a good candidate for drama therapy.

After reflecting upon the experience of TAS, I concluded that Mark was capable of imaginative storytelling and character identification, but that he was incapable of doing so independently. I noted that he was too symptomatic to link the life of the story to his everyday life. And I noted that although he was able to conceive of a guide figure, that figure was ultimately self-destructive. I felt that he was not ready for drama therapy treatment at the time of assessment yet at the urging of his mother I attempted to work with him for a limited number of sessions. I sensed that if he could accept me as a nurturing guide, the treatment had some chance to be successful.

After a few sessions it became clear that my initial assessment was correct. Mark was not ready to engage. In drama therapy treatment, at home and at school he could not find a way to contain the bomb that was his explosive feelings. He required a more intensive therapeutic milieu away from home.

The Man Who Sought Answers for Everything

Coram is a 30-year-old man who lives alone in the city. He is an artist who has not painted for several years. He supports himself by waiting on tables in restaurants. His girlfriend has recently rejected him, and he carries around a deep sense of betrayal and sadness. Unable to let go, he thinks about his lost love obsessively. He seeks therapy to rekindle his creativity and to let go of obsessive thoughts and compulsive behaviors.

It is easy for Coram to tell stories and each time I introduce TAS, he tells a detailed story with many subplots and characters. His stories are fantasies drawing heavily upon mythology and science fiction. It is not so easy, however, for Coram to see the connection between these stories and his everyday life. In my initial assessment during our first session, Coram told the following story:

> Once there was a little boy with red hair as bright as the sun. He was noted by others for his red hair. Some thought he was odd. His parents found that he had powers of perception and a connection to nature. He loved to play in the backyard. He played in a tree stump with magic pebbles and found a blue jay egg. The egg was whole and inside there was a special blue jay that would grow without any nurturing. It would become a dragon, and the dragon would be his companion and he would fly on it away from his parents. He went on a journey and the egg remained in the tree. He forgot about the egg but not the wonderment in the backyard. He met a girl. She also had an egg, a blue jay egg. They shared many stories and found new ones together. A deep feeling came that he had never known before. Maybe she is like the dragon and the egg, he thought. Maybe she is part of the mystical being held inside the egg.

Coram called his story *The Beautiful Boy and the Blue Jay Egg*. He recognized that the story was very much about his connection to his girlfriend, Bree, with whom he felt a deep, spiritual bond. He was disinterested in reflecting upon other aspects of the story. Coram seemed to enjoy the fantasy aspects most of all. The girl appeared to be his guide, and the magical elements of dragon and eggs appeared to be as real as all other roles in the story.

After discussing the story with Coram, I concluded that he would be a good candidate for drama therapy in that he was able to invoke roles through stories and easily access the world of the imagination. And yet I recognized that Coram would have difficulty connecting that world with the reality of the everyday.

After working in drama therapy with Coram for a year, I assessed him again by means of the TAS. This time I decided to ask him to tell the story non-verbally, through miniature objects that he would choose and arrange on a tabletop. Because he used language so readily, at times as a defense against feeling, I wanted him to reveal his inner world more directly through a projective medium.

I had available a range of miniature objects, both human and non-human, reality-based and fantasy-based. Coram choose seven objects: a young woman with a wheelbarrow, an older woman with a basket, a goat, a nun in black habit with a book, a young man in a red cape with a walking stick, a clown and a large dragon.

In the story, which Coram enacted with dialogue, the two women are proceeding down a road when they are stopped by a jester who demands that they pay a toll. When they refuse, he harasses them, insisting that they pay or leave. The young man who is on a quest of some kind, intercedes and helps the women proceed on their journey. He manages to dismiss the bothersome clown to the far border of the scene. The young men tells the women that he is searching for the Dragon Lord whom he hopes can answer the most significant questions about his destiny. He is encouraged to search for the answers by the nun whom he calls the Guiding Angel. She tells him to have faith in the search.

When the Dragon Lord appears, the young man asks his questions: "What is my destiny? How should I proceed in my life?"

The Dragon Lord replies: "I will answer your questions if you turn over the young woman who will live with me and serve me the rest of her life."

The man refuses and the Dragon Lord gives him one more chance: "Then I will answer your questions only if you give me your heart and swear that you will love only me for the rest of your life."

The man refuses a second time and the Dragon Lord in anger rejects his questions. The two fight and the Dragon Lord flies up in the air with the young man holding on for dear life. As the Dragon Lord flies higher and faster, the young man falls. Luckily, he lands on the clown's back and is saved from a certain death. He returns to the women and decides to join them on the path. He is again reminded to keep the faith by the Guiding Angel. The old woman welcomes him back and the young woman opens the possibility they she and the young man might make a life together.

This time, Coram is able to reflect upon his characters and story. He names most all of the characters. He calls the young woman Giselle and refers to her as the daughter. The old woman is the mother. The young man is the traveler. The nun is the Guiding Angel or simply, Faith. The clown and Dragon Lord are given no further names. He omits the goat and omits a reference to the wheelbarrow, basket, book and staff.

He is able to describe all the characters and attribute functions to them. The women are traditional, maintaining the domestic and spiritual business of life. Giselle, although loyal to her family and fearful of the outside world, longs for some unknown adventure. The traveler comes from a faraway land. He is searching for direction, answers to his existential questions. He falls in love with Giselle at first sight, but is a chivalrous gentleman and delays his proposal of marriage.

The Guiding Angel exemplifies the virtue of her name, Faith, urging the traveler to stay on the path and keep searching for the answers to his questions. The clown is a fool and a naysayer. He serves himself above all. And yet, he serves a positive function for the traveler, cushioning his fall and preserving his life.

The Dragon Lord is a magical figure who demands a very high price for his favors. He can grant wishes and answer questions to searchers, but if they do not pay his price, he becomes furious and aggressive.

Coram saw the characters as make-believe with a balance of thinking and feeling characters. Some, like the Dragon Lord, exemplified qualities of both thought and feeling as he was quick to anger but also intellectually driven, skilled at playing verbal games. Coram told the story in a generally distanced fashion with little apparent emotion, and yet he was completely engrossed in the action as if were happening to him in the moment.

When asked about the theme, Coram replied: "He who seeks to find something, finds some things as opposed to everything."

Coram imagined the possibility of integration between the traveler and Giselle, suggesting that they might get married and start a life together. If so, the mother and goat would live with them. The Dragon Lord and clown remain apart from the other four figures.

Upon completion of the story, Coram did not see an immediate connection to his life. But upon reflection, he offered this: "I am the man with so many questions. I think that contentment lies along the road on the journey. The treasures are not always worth what we think when we get them."

Coram called the story *The Man Who Sought Answers for Everything.*

Interpretation

In assessing Coram through his story, I noted that he had come a long way on his therapeutic journey. For one, the central character in his story is a young man ready for a grown-up relationship, as opposed to the little boy of the previous story. Giselle is also a grown-up woman, capable of making her own decisions, as opposed to the girl in the first story who is part of the mystical being held inside the egg. Even the dragon figure is different. This time it is a source of wisdom as well as frustration and struggle. In the first story, the dragon is sketchy, a figure that supports the boy's need to escape from the real world.

Coram's earlier story appears to be that of a pre-adolescent boy fantasizing about an ideal connection to a girl. It is an escapist fantasy far removed from the complexities of everyday reality. The second story shares some of the same fantasy elements and yet it is more mature and complex. The boy has grown and may be ready for a mature relationship with a woman. He recognizes that he has significant questions that require answers, but he also knows that he has some distance to travel before the answers will emerge. The dragon becomes an important guide figure as it is no longer a means to escape from reality as it was in the first story, but a reminder that one must struggle with reality and that profound knowledge comes with a price or, in Coram's words: "The treasures are not always worth what we think when we get them."

I conclude from Coram's response to TAS that he has a growing awareness of some important issues. He knows that he still has a way to travel on the road toward maturity. He knows that he still must struggle with his need to answer all questions. He knows that easy answers are worthless and that it is more satisfying to limit the questions to a few in the hope of finding some answers.

I offer Coram the thought that as his obsessions diminish, he will be more open to the possibilities of mature relationships with others. I think about the images that he did not reflect upon—the wheelbarrow, the basket and the book, all held by female figures. Recognizing their common function as containers, I note that a continuing treatment goal will be to guide Coram toward containing his feelings of abandonment.

I offer Coram the time to keep traveling and the support of a helping hand along the way. I remind him that the characters in his story are also inner figures and that he will need to continue to explore his relationship with the parts of himself that are angry and foolish, immediate and archaic, that make unreasonable demands and that demand simple answers to complex questions.

The Woman in the Tower

Eve, a 50-year-old academic, was recently divorced from her second husband. Her daughter from her first marriage had a promising academic career of her own until she succumbed to drug addiction. After spending a year in rehabilitation, she returned home to live with Eve.

Eve fills her life with many activities, participating in various support groups, political and church organizations. And yet she feels a great sense of failure as wife and mother and regularly experiences bouts of depression.

On our initial visit Eve told the following story:

A long time ago, a woman lived in a tall tower high above the tallest building in the city, above all the things that she used to love. Now the thing that she loved the most was her solitude. When it was still dark, she would descend from her tower each morning and go to work in one of the underground passages that services the needs of the people in the city. After work, when it was dark, the woman was transported back to her tower in a flash, welcoming the peace of her inner sanctum. One of her great pleasures after a hard day of work was to consume food and in those days the preparation of a meal was simple. All she had to do was to program the food control unit and punch in the precise menu and time she desired to eat and that was that. What a life! She loved the new technologies. They were so much better than the ones in the past when she had to think about menus, cook for her husband and children, clean up after the meals, do homework with the kids and put them to bed and hope that she had enough strength to watch on hour of bad TV, walk the dog, brush her teeth, have sex with her husband one night a week if he was willing and she wasn't menstruating, set the thermostat and alarm, find a satisfactory position among the covers and with luck, fall asleep. But that was all over now. She saw to it. All these people went the way of the old technologies. They were like toasters, diaphragms, telephones, all things of the past that consumed masses of time and energy. Things were good now. Under control. No responsibilities. No wasted moments. No ringing telephones. The woman was tired. Her eyes met the soft blue oval of the control panel on the central control unit, and she smiled for the first time all day. She felt so safe.

Eve names the characters in the story: the woman, the tall tower, the underground passage, food, husband and children and the control panel on the central control unit. She characterizes the roles simply. The woman is alone and she wants serenity and simplicity. The tall tower is elegant and proud. It stands above all demands and problems. The underground passage is dark and depressing. It is a necessary evil, a means to an end. It is the workplace and it pays the bills.

Food is a burden to prepare and a pleasure to consume. It serves a utilitarian purpose. Husband and children are like food, a burden and a pleasure, although they are more associated with pain. The control panel is perfect and fully pleasing. It provides safety and comfort.

Eve sees her story as a fantasy. Although there is very little feeling involved, Eve comments on the surprising level of feeling at the end of the story. "Maybe this is really a story about love," she says. "The woman loves the machine that can control her happiness and take away all the pain."

Eve continues: "Maybe this is the theme of my story–the attempt to control the pain in a woman's life, the pain of memory, the pain of relationships.

It reminds me of the 1939 World's Fair when women were told that life would be so much simpler if they used the new technologies—vacuum cleaners and washing machines and dishwashers. In my story, it's kind of like back to the future, a time when machines can even control your feelings. It's scary."

Eve calls her story *The Woman in the Tower*. She mentions that some of the characters are integrated, especially the woman, the tower and the control panel. But, she adds, the husband and the children will always remain separate from the woman; she does not want it ever to change. When I ask her about the underground passage and the food, she replies: "I guess there's a connection between the tower and the underground passage. The woman needs to go underground for work so she can afford to pay the rent on the tower. The food is connected to the woman. She needs it to live and it also gives her pleasure. It's like sex. But she doesn't want to work at it. She wants things easy."

Finally, I ask Eve to speak about the connection between the roles in the story and her everyday life. She replies: "You could say I'm the woman in the tower. Or I want to be that woman when I feel most depressed. I want to rise above it all and not feel the burden of having to take care of everything and everyone. I want more control of my family and my body. That's what the central control unit is all about—control, comfort, even a strange form of intimacy with the thing that can give you the most comfort. The tower and the underground passage are interesting. I like my work, my little apartment, my books, my ivory tower. I get weary of visiting the dark places. I don't think this is about my work, or at least not my academic work. I think it's about my inability to work out my love life and save my daughter. These are my underground passages."

Interpretation

Eve has successfully invoked significant roles within a story structure and demonstrated their interrelationships. She has also been able to link the fictional roles to the reality of her present life circumstances. I believe she will make an excellent candidate for drama therapy as she is able to move fluidly between the realms of imagination and everyday life, using the former as a means to reflect upon the latter.

I note that she limits the presence of human beings in her story and that the only love object appears to be a machine, a thermostat that controls her environment. There appears to be no guide figure available to help her move from isolation to intimacy, from a need to control and defend herself to a hope for letting go and making human connections. Given her feelings of failure as wife and mother, she will need to work with these roles and their fearful negative qualities. The treatment goals will be to help Eve find appropriate guide figures to counterbalance the negative qualities and learn not only to accept the pain of loss but also to let go of the past and seek the pleasures of connection with warm and nurturing human beings.

Conclusion and Research Possibilities

Tell-A-Story is most useful in assessing a person's ability to create characters in stories and to link the fiction of the story to the life of the storyteller. It is also potentially useful in determining whether or not an individual is a suitable candidate for drama therapy. In the above examples, both Coram and Eve seemed well-suited to work through drama therapy. Mark, on the other hand, was less prepared and less ready to engage in individual treatment.

TAS has many research possibilities. The researcher could explore the implications of stories according to the absence or presence of guide figures, counterrole figures or, more generally, human figures. Researchers might look at ways to match specific mental and developmental disorders with the kinds of stories told and characters invoked. Further, researchers might look at the connection between stories and specific treatment strategies, whether through drama therapy or other forms of psychotherapy, rehabilitation or psycho-education.

The next steps in research might be to determine the reliability and validity of TAS and to apply the assessment to a variety of individuals of varying age, gender, ethnicity and culture, physical and mental health status. With a broad range of demographic data, the optimal conditions for applying TAS as an assessment instrument should become clearer.

Chapter 9

ROLE PROFILES: AN ASSESSMENT INSTRUMENT

In the early 1990s, when I developed The Taxonomy of Roles (Landy, 1993), I was asked repeatedly about its application to clinical practice. At the time I really had no idea. My intention in creating the Taxonomy was conceptual—to attempt to reveal the contents of the role system, an internalized configuration of roles that represented the human personality. Although I felt challenged by the thought of applying it to treatment, I initially resisted the idea, hoping that others would do the research to make the transition from theory to practice.

In subsequent years I became interested in clinical assessment and reasoned that if the Taxonomy were to have some practical value, then one meaningful approach would be to develop an instrument based upon the role types in the Taxonomy. As I assembled early versions of the test, a number of my graduate students at New York University researched its possibilities (Fistos, 1996, Tangorra, 1997, Portine, 1998). My interest expanded with the doctoral research of Sherrie Raz (1997), a clinical psychologist, who applied the role types in the Taxonomy to an assessment of undergraduate theatre majors. Her approach was generally to provide a list of all 123 roles and sub-roles to her subjects and ask whether or not they identified with the roles. Raz' aim was to discern the role profile of a group of emerging performing artists.

After completing her doctoral dissertation, Raz refined her assessment instrument so that each subject was asked to match each role in the Taxonomy with one of 11 archetypal categories: father, son, mother, daughter, trickster, fool, visionary, hero, antihero, grandparent-male, grandparent-female. In viewing the personality in such a way, Raz reasoned, the assessor gets a picture of the subject in archetypal terms.

My early attempt to construct an assessment instrument based upon the Taxonomy was similar to Raz' method in that I developed a paper and pencil test in the hopes of creating a piece useful both in clinical treatment and research. Although I did not have the quantitative skills necessary for developing the research component, I hoped to collaborate with others to build a viable instrument to measure the personality in terms of roles.

I called the first version of the test Role Profiles (1997) and limited the number of roles from 123 to 90. Subjects, all of whom were students at New York University, were given the following instructions:

This questionnaire is based upon the idea that there are many similarities between everyday life and the imaginary world of characters in plays, movies, and stories. The questionnaire is intended to explore your personality as if it were made up of such characters. Following is a list of **roles** *which are types of characters commonly found in plays, movies, and stories. Circle the number that best describes how much you act like that role type in your everyday life. Then circle the number that best describes how much you would like to play that role in your fantasy life.*

Then subjects were given a list of 90 roles, in the order presented in the Taxonomy. An example follows:

1. CHILD   Not at all   Just a little   Moderately   Pretty much   Very much

	Not at all	Just a little	Moderately	Pretty much	Very much
In everyday life	0	1	2	3	4
In fantasy life	0	1	2	3	4

Following this first part of the test, testers asked the subjects to reflect upon their responses. Part II of the test involved a more subjective view of the roles chosen and moved the subject into a creative act, telling a story based upon several of the most prominent roles. Part II reflected the framework of role theory and role method of treatment which I had developed earlier (see Landy, 1993). The directions for Part II follow:

1. Tester divides roles in Part I into domains and classifications. Tester then reviews Part I with client and begins to point out patterns of responses. Tester locates all roles responses of 0 and 4 (*not at all* and *very much*), indicating a discrepancy between the client's view of herself in everyday life and in fantasy life. Tester asks client to choose one role with a 0 and 4 pattern.

2. If there are no 0 and 4 responses, tester locates and marks all 0 responses and all 4 responses, with special attention to clusters of 0 and/or 4 within a single domain. Tester also notes other unusual responses, such as no response or a mistaken response, e.g., client says: "Oh, I meant to choose 'not at all'

but instead I put 'very much.'" Tester then asks client to choose one role from the 0 **or** 4 grouping or one that was unique in some way, and work with that role. If client has trouble making a choice, tester suggests one that appears outstanding in some way.

3. Tester asks client to briefly describe the characteristics of the role and then to identify a counterrole, a character type that she sees as opposite to or in conflict with the primary role. Client is also asked to briefly describe the characteristics of the counterrole. If the client has trouble verbally describing the role and CR (counterrole), then she should be encouraged to sculpt the role non-verbally with her own body or with a projective object such as a puppet. Finally, client is asked to identify a third role—a guide or helper figure that can lead the role and CR safely through a dramatic experience.

4. Tester asks client to create a story, play or movie that demonstrates some interaction and conflict between the two roles, mediated by the guide role. This can be done in three ways, depending upon the abilities of the client:
    a. A story is written.
    b. A story is told by client to tester. Tester can provide appropriate prompts to help client tell the story.
    c. A story is enacted with play objects, e.g. toys, puppets, sandtray objects. Tester can provide appropriate prompts to help client tell the story.

De-briefing (all of these responses should be transcribed by tester)

5. Tester asks client to specify **qualities** of role, CR, and Guide. Questions to be asked can include: Describe the role, CR, and Guide. How do they look (physical/somatic qualities)? How smart are they (cognitive qualities)? How do they feel (affective qualities)? What are their beliefs and values (affective qualities)? How social, spiritual and creative are they (social, spiritual, aesthetic qualities)?

6. Tester asks client to specify **function** of role, CR, and Guide. Question to be asked: In the story, what does each character want most of all? The tester can prompt the client and can refer to the list of 28 needs formulated as part of assessment research protocol by R. Landy:

1. Beauty	11. Goodness	21. Power
2. Ugliness	12. Immorality	22. Powerlessness
3. Health	13. Isolation	23. Adventure
4. Sickness	14. Intimacy	24. Safety
5. Youth	15. Revenge	25. Transendence
6. Maturity	16. Acceptance	26. Domesticity
7. Sex	17. Connection	27. Prophesy
8. Celibacy	18. Autonomy	28. Creativity
9. Wisdom	19. Protection	29. Other_____
10. Ignorance	20. Exposure	

7. Tester asks client to specify **style** of role, CR and Guide, that is, level of distance inherent in the roles as seen in the story. Question to be asked: Are the role, CR, and Guide primarily thinking or feeling types or are they somewhere in the middle? Please explain.

8. Tester asks client: What is the **theme** of the story? What is a title for the story? Prompts can include a referral to the list of 28 needs above so that a theme could be, for example, the conflict of beauty and ugliness.

9. **Integration**. Tester asks client: Can the role and CR find a way to resolve their conflicts? How? How does the Guide help or hinder this process? How can the role, CR, and Guide live together or exist together?

10. Tester asks client: What is the connection between the fictional roles and your everyday reality? What parts of you are like the role, CR, and Guide in your story?

Role Profiles was given to several groups of graduate drama therapy students at NYU who critiqued the test and helped further refine and modify its shape over a period of three years. With their help, I became aware that the test was cumbersome and unfocused. There were too many roles with too much redundancy, too many tasks to accomplish in one sitting.

Late in 1998, I separated out the storytelling process so that, in effect, Part II became a separate test, called Tell-A-Story (see Chapter 8).

My graduate students remained critical of Part I and led me to try alternative approaches. One was to move the text from paper and pencil to card sort, asking subjects to sort the roles, written on index cards, into groupings representing the domains in the Taxonomy.

Joe Tangorra (1998) was the first to use a card sort of the roles, all those listed in the Taxonomy, applying the instrument to an understanding of the role profile of pedophiles. James Tranchida (2000) also used a card sort although he limited the number of roles to 70, consistent with my latest formulation. Tranchida's approach involved interviewing a group of undergraduate drama students to discover if the domains in the Taxonomy were, in fact, valid. Of the six domains–somatic, cognitive, affective, social, spiritual and aesthetic–Tranchida discovered that the somatic and social domains corresponded best to my framework, especially roles that dealt with sexual orientation, age, family and social class. However, when left to their own devices, most subjects invented their own domains, many of which had only a loose connection to the six in the Taxonomy.

In the summer 2000, I brought the instrument to Israel to work with a group of students and professional creative arts therapists. By this time Role Profiles had evolved into a card sort test with the following directions:

*This experience is intended to explore your personality as if it were made up characters commonly found in plays, movies, and stories. You will be given a stack of cards. On each card is the name of a **role** which is a type of character you have probably seen in movies and plays or read about in stories. On each card circle the number that best describes how much you act like that role type in your everyday life. Then circle the number that best describes how much you play that role in your imagination.*

Note: The tester shuffles the cards before each test to insure a random order of roles.

CARD SORT

1. Tester gives the subject seven large cards with the following labels:

    1. Body
    2. Feelings
    3. Mind
    4. Social Life
    5. Spirituality
    6. Creativity
    7. Other

2. Tester tells subject: *Arrange the cards into six groups according to the given names. If a card does not fit into any group, place it in the group named* Other.

DISCUSSION

1. Tester reviews each grouping with subject, naming the roles in each group, and asks subject to discuss the choices made. If subject needs guidance, tester can ask subject to clarify each role according to its qualities, function and style. Tester asks subject to discuss the connections among roles, if any. If there are cards placed in the *Other* group, tester asks subject to explain why.

2. Tester asks subject to discuss patterns of response within each group according to the chosen degree of role-taking in everyday life and imagination. If subject has difficulty being specific, tester points out responses of 0 and 4 (*not at all* and *very much*) within a single role, indicating a discrepancy between the subject's view of herself in everyday life and in imagination. On the other hand, tester looks for other patterns of response, e.g., a consistent pattern of 0's and/or 4's (or any other numbers) within both everyday life and imagination. Tester discusses the implications of a continuity between everyday life and imagination with the subject.

3. Tester also looks for clusters of 0 and/or 4 (or other repeated patterns) within a single grouping. Tester notes other unusual responses, such as no response or a mistaken response, e.g., subject says: "Oh, I meant to choose 'not at all' but instead I put 'very much.'"

4. Tester notes any other subject reflections upon the process.

5. Tester notes her own feelings and impressions of the subject's process.

When I began to work with this version of the test, it became clear that it was again too cumbersome. My students and subjects in Israel wanted something more direct. I was able to respond by first eliminating the domains altogether and then translating all 70 roles into Hebrew in collaboration with my students and peers. But I still needed some organizing framework in which to sort the cards. The framework needed to be consistent with the parameters of role theory. In taking the next step, I came up with four categories: I Am This, I Am Not This, I Am Not Sure If I Am This, and I Want To Be This.

With this new format, I gave the test to a group of Israeli drama therapy students and professionals. As we critiqued the test, it seemed that it was finally clear, direct and time limited. I modified this version slightly and added sections describing ways to analyze the results. Role Profiles 2000 was intact. I will present the test in its entirety and discuss selected responses from a number of subjects. First, the test:

PART I

Instructions to subject: *This experience is intended to explore your personality as if it were made up characters commonly found in plays, movies, and stories. You will be given a stack of cards. On each card is the name of a role, which is a type of character you have probably seen in movies and plays or read about in stories. Please shuffle the cards thoroughly. Place each card in one of four groups that best describes how you feel about yourself right now. Each group is labeled by a large card which says:* **I Am This, I Am Not This, I Am Not Sure If I Am This,** *and* **I Want To Be This.** *Try to group the cards as quickly as possible. Any questions? When you are ready, begin. Be sure to place each card in one group only.*

ROLE TYPES *(each one will appear on a separate index card)*

1. CHILD
2. ADOLESCENT
3. ADULT
4. ELDER
5. ASEXUAL
6. HOMOSEXUAL
7. HETEROSEXUAL
8. BISEXUAL
9. BEAUTY
10. BEAST
11. AVERAGE PERSON
12. SICK PERSON
13. HEALER
14. SIMPLETON
15. CLOWN
16. CRITIC
17. WISE PERSON
18. INNOCENT
19. VILLAIN
20. VICTIM
21. BIGOT
22. AVENGER
23. HELPER
24. MISER
25. COWARD
26. SURVIVOR
27. ZOMBIE
28. LOST ONE
29. PESSIMIST
30. WORRIER
31. OPTIMIST
32. ANGRY PERSON
33. REBEL
34. LOVER
35. EGOTIST
36. MOTHER
37. FATHER
38. WIFE
39. HUSBAND
40. DAUGHTER
41. SON
42. SISTER
43. BROTHER
44. ORPHAN
45. CONSERVATIVE
46. RADICAL
47. OUTCAST
48. JUDGE
49. WITNESS
50. HOMELESS PERSON
51. POOR PERSON
52. RICH PERSON
53. WARRIOR
54. BULLY
55. SLAVE
56. POLICE
57. KILLER
58. SUICIDE
59. HERO
60. VISIONARY
61. SINNER
62. PERSON OF FAITH
63. ATHEIST
64. SPIRITUAL LEADER
65. GOD
66. SAINT
67. DEMON
68. MAGICIAN
69. ARTIST
70. DREAMER

PART II: DISCUSSION

1. Tester asks subject to name the roles in each group and to discuss the choices made. The following questions can serve as guidelines:
   a. *As you look at the groupings, what do you see?*
   b. *Are there any surprises?*
   c. *Which roles seem most or least important? Explain.*
2. If the subject misses some charged roles, the tester can make reference to those that the subject has rejected or isolated or puzzled over or moved from one group to another.
3. Tester asks subject to discuss the connections among roles, if any.
4. Tester asks subject to discuss patterns of response within each group, between two groups or among the four.
5. Tester asks subject if there are any other aspects of the role profile that seem significant.
6. When discussion is completed, tester asks subject to remove cards from groupings and reshuffle the deck. In closing, tester ascertains mood of client. If client is feeling anxious, tester suggests ways to help resolve or further explore issues.

PART III: RESULTS

There is no right or wrong way to organize the cards into groupings. However, consistent with Landy's role theory, the tester is looking to see whether the subject is able to view himself in a balanced way. Balance would imply a relatively equal distribution of roles between "I Am This" and "I Am Not This," and a lesser quantity of cards in the grouping "I Want To Be This." If there are few entries in "I'm Not Sure If I Am This," the subject would be relatively clear as to his identity. If the grouping becomes large, this may be an indication of immaturity or uncertainty or role confusion.

It is important for the tester not to impose his own judgement upon the subject, but to ask pointed questions in an attempt to help the subject make sense of his role profile. There are, however, certain guidelines the tester can follow in documenting the results of the role profile. The guidelines will be written in the form of questions. In writing up the results, the tester will attempt to answer these questions and add any additional material in terms of the subject's form and content that is deemed relevant. In answering the questions, the tester should note the reflections of the subject as well as his own reflections.

1. How does the subject respond to the directions? Does he ask for more clarity? Does he jump right into the process? Does he manifest any anxiety or resistance to the process?
2. How does the subject sort the cards? How does he decide upon the grouping? Does he sort quickly or slowly, deliberately or impulsively? Does he engage with the tester during the card sort? How does he use time and organize space?
3. Which roles has the subject placed in each group? How many are in each group? Are the groups balanced or unbalanced?
4. Are there any charged roles, that is, roles that seem to be troubling or confusing or evocative of some emotional response? What are they? Where does the subject eventually place these roles? How does the subject react to these roles?
5. Which roles seem most and least important? Why?
6. What is the connection among roles within a single group? Are there contradictory roles within a single group, i.e., mother and father within the group, "I Am This"?
7. What is the connection among roles within different groups, i.e., in the child in "I Am This" and the adult in "I'm Not Sure If I Am This"?
8. Is the subject able to discern patterns, i.e., a view of the connected roles he plays in his family, or does he see the roles as disconnected and fragmentary?
9. Is the subject able to recognize his own identity within the roles and groupings or does he see the results as arbitrary and meaningless?
10. Is the subject able to discern certain contradictions among the roles, i.e., hero and average person, and accept that two or many contradictory roles can be part of his role profile? Or does the subject tend to dismiss contradiction and attempt to view himself in a singular way, i.e., the visionary hero-artist on a spiritual quest?
11. How does the subject dismantle the groupings and reshuffle the deck? Is there a willingness to close the process or to delay the closure? What kinds of feelings are expressed? Is the subject in a balanced or unbalanced state? Does he express what he will do with the results of the test?

PART IV: ANALYSIS

Any analytical judgements should be tentative at this point. However, some interpretations of the content of the role profile can be made based upon the patterns of response:

1. If there are a relatively equal number of roles in groups "I Am This" and "I Am Not This," then the subject is presenting in a balanced way.
2. If there are a relatively unequal number of roles in groups "I Am This" and "I Am Not This," then the subject is presenting in an unbalanced way.
3. If there are more roles in the group "I'm Not Sure If I Am This" than in any other group, then the subject is presenting in an unbalanced way. The imbalance may be due to immaturity or role confusion.
4. If there are a large number of roles (more than 5) in "I Want To Be This," then the subject may be clear about life goals or may be unable to realize present states of being.
5. If the tester notes a charged role, that is, one that troubles or confuses the subject, and the subject denies its importance, then the role might be too threatening for the subject. The tester can note that the subject needs more work on this role. If the role is particularly charged, then the tester might recommend therapy for the subject.
6. A good indication of balance is when the subject is able to articulate which roles are most and least important and why. If the subject is not able to do so, this might be an indication that the subject needs help in prioritizing and focusing on aspects of his life.
7. If there are many contradictory roles within a single group, this might mean that the subject is comfortable with role ambivalence or that the subject is very confused and needs help in sorting out contradictory tendencies.
8. If the subject is able to make meaningful connections among roles in different groups, then he is presenting in a balanced way.
9. If the subject is unable to discern patterns among roles, this might indicate a disorganized thought pattern or depressed mood.
10. If the subject views his role profile as arbitrary or meaningless, it might indicate a sense of identity crisis and need for treatment, or simply a poor match between a particular subject and this particular test.
11. If the subject feels stimulated after the test and is able to see ways to use the experience of role profiles, he is generally in a balanced state. If he is unable to reflect upon the test and feels numb or depressed, then he is in a state of imbalance and might need therapy to help move toward balance.

In giving Role Profiles 2000 to a new group of graduate students at NYU and several other non-students, there was still some confusion as to the meaning of some of the roles, especially avenger, visionary and spiritual leader. On the one hand I felt compelled to simplify the language–for example, to change avenger to one who wants revenge. However, I decided to retain a single word description for each role as much as possible. If the subject is unclear about the meaning of a role, I offered, she should use her judgement and place it in the grouping that appears to be most appropriate.

Some students also raised issues of semantics and cultural interpretations and biases. Some seemed very literal in their responses and others abstract, thinking about the role metaphorically. Acknowledging differences based in interpretation of language, cultural conventions and cognitive styles, I asked all subjects to shuffle and deal, confident that a profile of each subject's role system would emerge to some degree.

The number of subjects in the early research samples was relatively small, approximately 30 each year for three years. Rather than attempting to generalize from the responses, I have chosen three subjects who took Role Profiles 2000, two graduate students and one non-student, to illustrate the dimensions of the test and point toward some interpretation of the results.

Faith

Faith is a 27-year-old Caribbean-American female, who works as a therapist in a large city hospital as she completes her graduate studies. She grew up in Trinidad with her mother and two brothers. Her father left her family when she was very young. She is highly intelligent, soft-spoken and committed to her strong Christian beliefs.

When taking Role Profiles, she carefully and thoughtfully looked at the cards and placed them in their respective categories. Faith worked in a very orderly fashion, leaving one inch of space between each card. Commenting upon the symmetry, Faith noted: "I'm very neat and organized, as you can probably see." Due to the symmetry, a few cards were especially notable because they were placed either off center or facing away from the others.

Faith worked very quickly. When finished, she was asked whether she wanted to make any changes. In a rather swift and orderly fashion, she picked up *Mother* and *Pessimist* and moved them to different categories. *Mother* was the first role card she sorted. She had placed it in the group "I Am This," but now moved it to the bottom of "I Want To Be This." Likewise, Faith had placed Pessimist in the category "I Am Not This," but then moved it to "I'm Not Sure If I Am This." She contemplated all other choices and decided she was pleased.

The following table represents Faith's Role Profile:

Table 2

	A I AM THIS	B I AM NOT THIS	C I AM NOT SURE IF I AM THIS	D I WANT TO BE THIS
1	+Mother	Father	Saint	Warrior
2	Optimist	Son	Child	Radical
3	Wise Person	Magician	Healer	Spiritual Leader
4	Witness	Sister	Elder	Rich Person
5	Helper	Demon	Critic	Hero
6	Heterosexual	Rebel	Egotist	Clown
7	Artist	Lost One	Sinner	Wife
8	Visionary	Orphan	Coward	Lover
9	Survivor	Atheist	Judge (tilted to right)	*Mother
10	Adult	Average Person	*Magician	
11	Worrier	Husband	*Pessimist	
12	Dreamer (tilted to left)	God		
13	Beauty	Homeless Person		
14	Person of Faith	Sick Person		
15	Police	Avenger		
16	Conservative	Killer		
17	Daughter	Beast		
18	Outcast (tilted 90 degrees to left)	Brother		
19	*Innocent (overlapping with Simpleton)	Zombie		
20	*Simpleton (overlapping with innocent)	Adolescent		
21		Villain		
22		Bigot		
23		Miser		
24		Slave		
25		Angry Person		
26		Asexual		

27		Poor Person		
---		---		
28		+Pessimist		
29		Bully		
30		Homosexual		
31		Bisexual		
32		Victim		
33		Suicide		
34				

key: +Removed from this placement
           *Moved to this placement

In the discussion, the tester pointed out that the role of Outcast which Faith had placed in "I Am This," was tilted ninety degrees to the left. She responded by giggling and then explained that she often felt like an outcast because of her attachment to the roles Person of Faith and Conservative. Faith said that she was not able to accept many of the choices made by less devoutly Christian people. Thus, she often felt isolated and alone in her feelings about such subjects as homosexuality, spirituality and love.

Noticing that Outcast had been placed directly next to Brother in the next category, "I Am Not This," the tester asked her if there was some connection between the roles. Faith explained that she was the middle child, between two brothers. She had always felt left out, being female, but she then further explained that her brothers "were the loved ones" in her family. "They got all of the attention from my father, before he left."

Faith also commented upon the role of Judge whose card was also askew. Faith pointed out that Judge, grouped in "I'm Not Sure If I Am This," faced in the direction of "I Am This." She saw an implicit message in this placement, as if she should move the card. When asked if she wanted to move it, she replied that she did not because she did not like to think of herself as judgmental, even though she admitted to owning a bit of that quality.

When asked if she noticed any relationships among the roles, either within one category or between categories, she responded by saying that the "I Am This" group held all of her safe roles. She felt very comfortable knowing that they were part of her. However, she expressed some concern that the roles in the group, "I'm Not Sure If I Am This," were those imposed upon her by other people. She stated emphatically that she did not desire any more insight into these roles, at least not at the present time.

Faith then went on to explain in more detail her placement of roles in "I

Want To Be This." She said that this group consisted of all the roles that would make her a balanced person. When asked if she thought of herself as unbalanced, she responded: "I feel very unbalanced a lot of the time, and I know that if I were to take on some of these roles, I would be a much more balanced person. I need more of the Radical and the Clown and the Lover." When asked if she felt comfortable with all of the roles in this category, she responded: "No. I'm definitely not comfortable with the Warrior, the Spiritual Leader, or the Lover. I don't have any experience with them, so they are very uncomfortable to me right now. The others I've had some experience with, so I'm not as afraid of them as I am these three."

Faith said little about the roles in "I Am Not This." She felt inexperienced with these roles and did not feel the need to integrate them into her life at this point. She felt strongly that she did not share anything in common with the following roles: Father, Sick Person, Bully, Homosexual, Bisexual and Suicide. The latter four clashed strongly with her moral beliefs and led to her self-perception as an outcast.

When asked about the Father role, she explained: "My father left my mother and my brothers when I was very young, and I have not heard from him since then. I don't want to be that kind of person to my children. I can be a nurturing parent, but I will never be what my father was to us."

As to the role of Sick Person, Faith stated that she needs to feel healthy, especially in that she works with sick patients and needs to maintain clear boundaries with them.

Faith continued to comment on the relationships between the roles noticing that Innocent and Simpleton overlapped. "I think, sometimes," she said, "I can be really dumb, but I almost always cover that dumbness up by playing up my innocence or naivete." She offered as an example that when she was growing up, she had no awareness of homosexuality. It was never mentioned in her family, although she knew from her religion that it was morally wrong. As an adult she still struggles with the part of her that needs to remain naive and unaware, even as she recognizes a responsibility to experience life more fully and to accept others.

As she was about to close, she was directed to a grouping of several related roles: Wise Person, Magician, Healer, and Spiritual Leader (Placements A3, B3, C3 and D3) all in the same row, but placed in different categories. After much thought, she was unable to make a clear connection. But then she said that she once thought of herself as a magician: "I used to try to make things disappear, but they don't, do they?"

Finally, when Faith was asked if there were any surprises on her Role Profile, she responded: "Yes, Lover. I'm surprised I put it under "I Want To

Be This." I guess I'm afraid of this role, Lover.""

On the face of it, Faith's Role Profile appears moderately balanced among the four categories. The main discrepancy is that she placed 33 roles in "I Am Not This," as compared to 19 in "I Am This." The difference might imply that there are many parts of herself that remain unexplored or unacceptable. It could be that her experience in the world with the roles not chosen has been limited. Or it could be that she has the need to work out her feelings toward these roles on an intrapsychic level before she is ready to assume their qualities in her everyday life.

There is evidence from her reflections that she has struggled with certain family and moral issues and has yet to discover her full power in the areas of playfulness, family life, sexuality and professional identity. In order for her to fully embrace the power of the wise person, with whom she identifies, she may need to incorporate some of the more affective, irrational qualities of the magician, healer and spiritual leader. And in order for her to embrace the power of the lover, she may need to confront her fears of loving and being loved. Perhaps the magician can help. She may have understood the magician's function only in part. It is not only the magician's function to make things disappear, but also to appear. Magicians restore what they have lost. If Faith has lost some of the lover along the way, perhaps with the magician's help, she can find it again. If Faith has lost her father, she might need some strong magic to at least recover the loving daughter. At the conclusion of her Role Profile assessment, Faith was encouraged to keep looking and, if desirable, to find a guide to help her on her way.

Edna

Edna is a 76-year-old German-American woman who lives with her husband. She has two married children and several grandchildren. Edna works as a secretary in a small town in Delaware and is the breadwinner of the family.

When asked if to take Role Profiles, she seemed very open. Within minutes of shuffling the cards, Edna completed the test. Edna placed 16 cards in "I Am This" and 54 cards in "I Am Not This." There were no cards in the final two categories.

The following is Edna's Role Profile:

Table 3

	A I AM THIS	B I AM NOT THIS	C I AM NOT SURE IF I AM THIS	D I WANT TO BE THIS
1	Worrier	Saint		
2	Helper	Police		
3	Elder	Atheist		
4	Daughter	Brother		
5	Lover	Victim		
6	Person of Faith	Beast		
7	Sister	Radical		
8	Optimist	Witness		
9	Mother	Bigot		
10	Wife	Avenger		
11	Average Person	Outcast		
12	Heterosexual	Critic		
13	Adult	Conservative		
14	Survivor	Warrior		
15	Wise Person	Pessimist		
16	Visionary	Slave		
17		Demon		
18		Coward		
19		Villain		
20		God		
21		Homeless Person		
22		Angry Person		
23		Zombie		
24		Innocent		
25		Egotist		
26		Father		
27		Hero		
28		Husband		
29		Homosexual		
30		Clown		
31		Healer		
32		Magician		

33		Beauty		
34		Miser		
35		Sick Person		
36		Bully		
37		·Judge		
38		Orphan		
39		Rich Person		
40		Asexual		
41		Suicide		
42		Sinner		
43		Dreamer		
44		Artist		
45		Child		
46		Adolescent		
47		Son		
48		Simpleton		
49		Lost One		
50		Killer		
51		Poor Person		
52		Bisexual		
53		Rebel		
54		Spiritual Leader		

When asked to discuss relationships among the cards, Edna replied: "They're pretty cut and dry. I just know who I am and who I'm not. When you get to be my age, you've hopefully done what you wanted. There's no one else I'd like to be right now. I've been all I wanted to be. I know myself and I'm happy."

When asked it there were any surprises, Edna shook her head and said, "No. Like I said, I know who I am and who I'm not. There's no surprises about that." When pressed to comment a bit more about the roles that she is not, she said that the test would have felt exactly the same if the roles of Police, Atheist, Warrior and Zombie had been eliminated.

Edna expanded a bit on her philosophy: "When people are younger, they have more goals and hats they want to try on. They have more time. Once you hit a certain age, you have tried most of the hats, and you know which ones fit."

Edna appeared to be a very balanced person, clear on who she is and who she is not. She also seemed to have no regrets as to her life choices and at 76 years old, did not seem to want much more than she had. She appeared content.

And yet, Edna's Role Profile is even more unbalanced than Faith's with 17 roles as "I Am This" and 53 roles as "I Am Not This." This might mean that her life experiences and circumstances have been limited and given her options, she lived as full a life as possible. In this case, an imbalance of roles between the first two categories does not necessarily represent a corresponding psychological imbalance. On the other hand, the imbalance might suggest that Edna has avoided a number of possibilities in her life, choosing safe, conventional roles through which to present herself. As such she has neither tried on many hats nor examined the parts of herself that are unsure and insecure, whimsical and wishful. If this is the case, she might not know herself well at all, if knowing oneself implies an awareness of one's ambivalences, insecurities and fantasies.

Although I respect Edna's certainty and acknowledge that her self-perception is positive, I tentatively conclude that her Role Profile is unbalanced. And yet, it seems clear from the interview that although she is not very introspective, she is content with her life and most likely has no need to engage in such an introspective process as therapy.

For some, the unexamined life, the life of few questions and ambivalences, is desirable. There may be no need to incorporate the fearful qualities of the Police, Atheist, Warrior and Zombie, among others. Therefore, perhaps it is not completely accurate to say that Edna is unbalanced as to her role choices. I can only, finally, offer a point of view, one that underlies my work in role theory. The roles we take on in everyday life do not exist in isolation but in relation to other, often contradictory ones. To be fully creative and awake to the wonders of the world, it is necessary to wrestle with the tendency to shut down, to play the Zombie. Roles represent not only our behaviors and preferences, but also our ambivalences, uncertainties and aspirations. As Edna chooses to see herself in terms of the former and not the latter, she appears to be psychologically balanced. Moving away form her uncertainties and hopes may be a reflection of her maturity and self-acceptance, a balanced position, or it may be a reflection of her need to banish ambivalence and challenge, an unbalanced position. In choosing not to be a Warrior and then banishing Warrior from the Role Profile, Edna appears to exemplify the latter.

Finally, it seemed sad to me that Edna had expressed no wishes for the future. Perhaps balance is just one measurable aspect of Role Profiles. Another might be an awareness of life goals, expressed in the roles one would like to be. What are the possibilities? How do I get there? Where do I start? It seems to me that there is no correct time or age. It may be at 27 as in the case of Faith, or at 76, as in the case of Edna. It might all be a matter of readiness. And it might all be a matter of willingness to enter the metaphorical hat shop and try on the ones most familiar and most strange and to look into the mirror as if for the first time.

Maureen

Maureen is a 24-year-old recent graduate, now working as a therapist in a large city hospital. Maureen had previously taken the 1998 version of Role Profiles. She reflected upon her role profile after taking Role Profiles 2000 for the second time.

Maureen began her second experience with Role Profiles 2000 by acknowledging a feeling of panic as I worked with her. Following her work she referred to me as her mentor and said: "This wave of panic makes sense to me, when I think about it. After all, I am about to do a thesis on how another former male mentor in my life abused the potential power that can come with mentoring. I have a hard time trusting male mentors or higher-ups. Especially when I know I am about to make myself vulnerable to them. However, I was able to let that panic pass within a minute or so in this case, as I have a certain sense of trust in Robert that has been building for two-plus years."

The following is Maureen's Role Profile:

Table 4

	A I AM THIS	B I AM THIS (continued)	C I AM NOT THIS	D I AM NOT THIS (continued)	E I AM NOT SURE IF I AM THIS	F I WANT TO BE THIS
1	Victim		Egotist		Avenger	Wife
2	Adult		Innocent		Beast	Hero
3	Rich Person	Helper	Asexual		Radical	
4	Rebel	Artist	Miser		Homeless Person	
5	Dreamer	Wise Person	Husband		Poor Person	
6	Elder	Magician	Bigot		God	
7	Healer	Average Person	Suicide		Spiritual Leader	
8	Lover	Witness	Brother		Sick Person	

9	Mother	Daughter* (tilted 90 degrees to right)	Villain		Outcast	
10	Son	*(+Daughter)*	Pessimist		Bisexual	
11	Child	*(+Daughter)*	Father			
12	Optimist	Visionary	Conservative			
13	Simpleton	Lost One	Demon			
14	Beauty	Warrior	Orphan			
15	Angry Person	Survivor	Homosexual			
16	Worrier	Sinner	Judge			
17	Sister	Critic* (tilted to right)	Bully			
18	Clown	Heterosexual	Coward			
19	Person of Faith	Adolescent	Slave	Atheist		
20			Zombie	Saint		
21			Killer			
22			Police			

+Continuation of area covered by width of card (laying on its side)
*Titled to the right

Maureen's reflections upon her work will be given in her own words.

"I shuffled the seventy role cards in my hands and looked down to see what the top card was. It was 'Victim' and for some reason, I did not want to start with that card. I shuffled again. 'Victim' was still on top. I shuffled a third time. Let's just say I am not the world's best shuffler. For the third time in a row, 'Victim' was the first card. It is an extremely charged role for me. It was meant to be, I guessed, so I began by laying it in the category marked 'I Am This.' I continued through the remainder of the cards, most of which were easy to categorize. The one exception was 'Critic.' I set it aside for a moment, as I knew there was another role among the cards that was similar, and I wanted to see it before I decided on where 'Critic' was to go. The other role card I was waiting for was 'Judge.' I looked at them both, thought for a moment, and then decided to put 'Critic' down as something that I was (see Column B, Row 17) and 'Judge' as something I was not (Column C, Row 16). Later, when asked why I did this, I would explain that I often critiqued people's thoughts, but I did not feel I judged them (held anything against them for what I was critiquing). The more I think on this subject, I can see where judging a person's actions could be used as a survival technique. Were a person to creep up behind me on the street, or knock on my front door and not show his face in the peephole, I use my judgement and make safe decisions. Had I thought of this while I had the cards lying in front of me, I would have changed it. Hindsight is always 20/20, I suppose.

"Upon first glance at the cards, I did not see, and so Robert had to point out to me, that the 'Daughter' card was turned completely on its side. Due to lack of space, I had formed two columns of 'I Am This.' 'Daughter' was in the second column and was overlapping three other cards in the first column of 'I Am This' (Column B, Rows 9, 10 and 11). The three cards it was touching were 'Mother,' 'Son' and 'Child.' (Column A, Rows 9, 10 and 11). After having this overlap pointed out, I explained that the 'Daughter' role contains some of the other three in my life story. There are times when I feel like I am less the daughter of my parents and more like the mother to them. There are times when my father and I do things together, that I feel as if I am more the son he never had than I am his daughter. And there are times when I know I am the child or daughter for both my mother and father. Therefore, all three of the overlapping 'Daughter' roles are really quite related to my being the daughter of my parents.

"We went on to discuss poignant relationships between other roles. I talked about the category labeled 'I Am Not Sure If I Am This.' I noticed that many of the roles I had classified under this column were ones I felt were somewhat a part of me, but that I did not feel completely committed to (i.e., Avenger, Homeless Person, Sick Person, Outcast) or were conditional. There was also some element of not being sure whether I actually *was* some of these roles, or if I just *wanted* to be, in my fantasy life (i.e., Radical, God, Spiritual Leader).

"Homeless Person, especially, was a charged role (Column E, Row 4). I was aware of how it had changed placements since the last time I had taken the test. It was formerly in the 'I Am This' category. However, circumstances in my life had changed, even in just the couple months between my Role Profile 2000 tests, which made me begin to question how 'at home' I was feeling. I no longer felt like my home was the city, enormous, loud and fast-paced. On the other hand, I was not feeling completely drawn to the excessively small, quiet and slow-paced life of my hometown in Virginia either. I was not sure where my home was, and I still am not. At this point in my life, I cannot look three months ahead and honestly say that I know where I will be calling home. Facing eviction from the 'home' I have right now, I am not exactly making these decisions by choice. The 'Homeless Person' role is definitely one that I am being forced to take, but that I do not necessarily want. This is one of the reasons why writing about it is so intense right now.

"In contrast to the change of positions of 'Homeless Person,' is the consistency of the 'Sick Person' role, in 'I Am Not Sure' (Column E, Row 8). It has remained in this column since I began taking the Role Profile test in its written form, some two years ago. Though I know I have my kidney ailments, they are *not* constant. I do not live every single day of my life being forced to have to think about them. They recur two to three times a year, and are usually unexpected. Part of why I do not consider them as completely a part of me is for this reason, and also because I do not think I am able to accept the sickness as a part of me yet. Perhaps one day I will be able to accept it more completely. And yet, to a certain extent, I must always be reminding myself, in the back of my head: 'drink your water' and 'eat your oxalates when you eat your calciums.' The modifications I make in my diet are not connected to the kidney problems, somehow. Someday, 'Sick Person' may be moved, though. Hopefully, it will be moved to the 'I Am Not' category, because it will no longer be any part of who I am. But there will always be the chance that it will have moved to 'I Am,' as I may have to learn to accept it as a part of me, in order to become a more integrated person.

"One role that has made a move, I noticed, from the 'I Am Not' category is that of God. For a long time, I had classified it as something that I was not. I always thought it was big-headed for someone to say they were God, although now my opinion of this role has changed. Perhaps, as I explained to Robert in our discussion, I am not THE God. Maybe I am just my own God. I can create and control my own destiny, I believe—or the path that I lead toward my destiny, at least. This is a point of growth for me, a maturation. Part of growing up has been about putting my faith in others to lead me through life. Starting from the time we are infants, we have faith in the fact that our caregivers will take care of us and lead us down the correct path. As I have begun to know more about who and what I am, I have been feeling more like my own God. I am not as reliant on others. I am able to stand up for my own beliefs.

"The appearance of the God role probably relates closely to the Outcast in appearance. My course of study, my career choice, and all of the beliefs that go with it have in many ways made me an outcast. This is so in my social life, and especially in my family. I speak a new language—the language of a therapist. I think in very different ways from them, on levels they are not always aware exist. Though most of my friends and family try to be very supportive and understanding of that, I still feel very removed from them. I find ways of bridging whatever gap there is between us when we are together, but there will always be that difference in thinking and speaking. This is another aspect of me I am slowly beginning to accept.

"One role I was aware of having moved from 'I Am This' to 'I Am Not This' since the last time I took the Role Profiles 2000, was the role of 'Innocent' (Column C, Row 2). When asked to speak more about this, I connected this right away to the role of 'Victim,' the first role I had to categorize (Column A, Row 1). In talking about this, I tried to explain that I no longer feel I am the naive and innocent person—that my eyes were open to many things they were not open to before. This has come up in my own therapy since taking this test, and I have gained even more insight on why I moved 'Innocent' to it's new place. I think there is still some blame toward myself for things that have happened to me, namely the incident between the male superior and I in the past. Why did I stay so still and not fight? I know on an intellectual level, but I am still trying to work through accepting it on a feeling level. One thing I do know is that by moving 'Innocent' to its new place, it was not a way of rejecting something that I thought I was. It is a way of accepting something I am not, for the time being. Hopefully, after more work on myself, I will be able to move it back to its original placement. This is a recognition of a feeling that has been unconscious for a long time. By moving it for a while, it has initiated exploration and eventual resolution, I hope. Though it may not look great where it is sitting right now, it is there to promote my own growth and awareness.

"I noticed many relationships between the two columns of 'I Am This' roles. For example, the rebelliousness in me is definitely a part of the artist in me. This is also so with the Dreamer and Wise Person and the Elder and Magician. In a less positive way, the Simpleton and the Lost One are both related aspects of me. But then so are the seemingly positively-charged role of Survivor and the more negatively charged (for me, personally) Angry Person parts of me. And how can I not point out the relationship between Beauty and Warrior?

"While looking over all of the roles in the 'I Am This' category, I made a remark that, if I could, I would have them all categorized under 'This is Who I Want to Be.' When asked if I wanted to be an Angry Person or a Worrier or a Lost One, I was forced to think more carefully for a moment. I came to the conclusion that the anger and the worry and other roles like this I associate with the emotional side of who I am. They are what make me human. They keep me from being a Zombie, walking through life not aware of or feeling anything. They may not always be the most wonderful colors on my canvas, but they are colorful, nonetheless.

"As far as being the Lost One is concerned, this is what keeps me humble and keeps me searching. I do not envision moving Lost One from the 'I Am This' until I am much older and I know exactly where everything in my life goes. Lost is a strong word, insinuating I may not even know where to turn sometimes. The truth is, I usually do *not* know which way is the right way. But I always know there is *some* way to turn. I may not always choose correctly the first time, but that is part of my philosophy. There is reason behind my search for my oneness. I have reached the lows in the valleys and I have reached the summits of the mountains in my life because I was on a search for my integrated self."

Maureen, like Faith, is young and searching, still trying on hats. Of the three interviewed, she appears to be the most introspective and clear as to her past, present and future. She speaks articulately about individual and inter-connected roles that she sees as clearly part of her "integrated self." I was very impressed with her responses and yet was left with the question of why she did not reflect upon the two roles she placed in "This is Who I Want to Be"–the Wife and the Hero. But there will be many more valleys and mountains to traverse on Maureen's journey. As she finds new ways to make peace with male mentor figures in low and high places, she will learn to better guide her own journey. And as she does so, she will move closer toward the objects of her desire, the roles of Wife and Hero.

CONCLUSION

Role Profiles 2000 is based upon the notion that human existence is essentially dramatic and that people are motivated by a search for balance among their often discrepant roles. As human beings, we have the capacity to take on and enact many roles in our lifetime and discover ways to live effectively among them. But as we inevitably encounter our limitations, that capacity diminishes. Role Profiles 2000 is one way to measure the capacity to be fully human through the language of drama. In positioning role as the central dramatic concept, I hope to reveal a bit more of the personality structure through the elegant notion of self as other. By shuffling the deck and putting one's cards on the table, the card player reveals much about who she is and what she wants to be. In playing with the other sides–the uncertain and rejected parts–she unfolds even more.

The tasks that remain include further clinical trials and research to compare and contrast the role profiles among people of different ages, genders, cultures, mental health and socioeconomic statuses. Establishing a full and comprehensive database should help to validate the efficacy of this new assessment instrument.

Part Four

SUPERVISION

Chapter 10

ROLE MODEL OF DRAMA
THERAPY SUPERVISION

ON SUPERVISION

The process of supervision in any form of psychotherapy implies a relationship among three roles—those of client, therapist and supervisor. On the simplest level, the client reports to the therapist who, in turn, reports to the supervisor. The client and supervisor remain unknown to one another, except as the supervisor hears stories about the client and as the client is (or is not) aware of the fact that the therapist meets with a supervisor to review the client's case. Generally speaking, the three roles are fairly well delineated. The client's function is to seek help from the therapist and to work toward getting better through an extended interaction with the therapist. The therapist's function is to facilitate some form of healing on the part of the client. And the supervisor's function is to help the therapist better serve the client by facilitating a self-reflective, critical process on the part of the therapist.

But this is just part of the story. The clear qualities of each role often shift as the therapist, for example, experiences the role of client as he interacts with the supervisor and as he struggles with his countertransferential reactions, and as the supervisor, identifying with the client, does the same. The client, too, will slip into the role of therapist or supervisor as he discovers his own inner guides. In fact, each role of client, therapist and supervisor can serve as an introject for the others. In many ways, an effective psychotherapeutic process implies that the qualities of therapist, client and supervisor can be held together in a balanced way by each person. Underlying this perspective is the assumption that an optimal psychotherapeutic experience requires a balance of the three roles of client, therapist and supervisor not only on an interpersonal level, but also on an intrapsychic one. On an intrapsychic level, the client would have available an internal therapist and supervisor to guide and critique his progress. The therapist would have available an internal client and supervisor to measure his own effectiveness as a partner in the healing process and as a self-reflective critic. And the supervisor would have available an internal client and therapist to measure and temper the effectiveness of his guidance. Like the therapist, he also needs an internal supervisor to provide a further self-critique.

THE ROLE MODEL IN DRAMA THERAPY

To better explain the convolutions of this role triangle, I turn to a model I have developed to elucidate the process of drama therapy. I have previously written (see Landy, 1993, 1994, 1996) that the goal of drama therapy is to help clients discover ways to live with role ambivalence. I conceptualize role ambivalence as the relationship between a role and its counterpart, which I call the counterrole. An example is the relationship between the part of oneself that feels powerless, the victim, and the part of oneself that feels powerful and competent, the victor. When working with this configuration, the drama therapist helps the client invoke both victim and victor, work them through and discover ways to integrate the two so that it becomes possible to feel powerful and powerless simultaneously without the overwhelming fear of ultimately succumbing to the most extreme qualities of either one.

In working with role and counterrole in drama therapy, I began to notice that when seeking integration, many clients required a third piece, standing outside the role and counterrole. I thought of this third piece as a bridge. I reasoned that people sought therapy because they became struck in a single role, too much the victim, for example, unsure what qualities lay on the other side of their sense of powerlessness. Before they could even consider integration, I reasoned, they needed to know the qualities on the other side of the overpowering role. And, being stuck, they needed a third role as an outside helper to move them along the way. Many children understand this third role as a figure in fairy tales whose magic enables the hero to reach her goals. This magical figure goes by many names–fairy godmother, genie, wizard, good fairy and various gods and goddesses. In my clinical work, I came to understand this figure as the guide.

The figure of the guide became most clear to me in my extensive work with a middle-aged alcoholic woman who had been severely abused by her mother. I will call her Fay. Feeling very much the victim in her adult life, wandering from job to job, finding victimizers at every desk, in every attempted intimate relationship, Fay was unable to locate the qualities existing on the other side of the victim. Intellectually, she knew of the existence of love and care, and she knew that she wanted to feel these qualities. But because of a history of sustained abuse, Fay didn't know how to get to them. She needed a guide.

For several years, in our transferential dance, Fay struggled with me. Rather than a guide, I became her tormentor each time I went on vacation or misrepresented a story told. Each time I could not properly hold her pain or anger, I was her victimizer. I knew, at least unconsciously, that I had to be the guide in order to steer her though the powerful storm of re-victimization. But at times I wavered and discussed her case with my supervisor, revisiting old territory in my psyche concerning, especially, my difficulties holding excessive pain and anger.

Then one day, Fay brought in a photograph of herself as a young girl. She was in the town of her childhood, outside her mother's house, poorly dressed, without shoes, faking a smile for the camera. I asked her to describe the town as she saw it in the picture. The background was a blur except for a distant house. When I questioned her about it, she told me it was Mrs. Smith's house. Fay became very emotional and upon further questioning, she identified Mrs. Smith's house as one of love and care, of comfort and protection. Mrs. Smith was the only example of a good mother that Fay had ever known.

From that session onward, Fay had discovered a guide, one very different from me, the wounded healer who could still re-traumatize, who needed further supervision to still my own countertransferential fears. Mrs. Smith was a fiction based in part on a real character who once lived in a town very long ago and faraway. As fiction, she was safe and magical. As such, she could help Fay safely reach the other side of the victim, the side that was powerful because she was worthy of love and care and attention. Mrs. Smith, the guide, would ultimately help Fay discover a way to live in the ambivalence of feeling despised and unworthy, on the one hand, and feeling worthy of love and care, on the other. Fay's discovery was, for me, a relief, taking away some of the burden of holding her anger. But it was more than that for me—it was a revelation. I saw clearly what I had been intuiting—that in the model of role and counterrole, a piece was missing. This was it—the guide.

During the past several years, I have applied the model of role, counterrole, guide to clinical treatment. In doing so, I attempt first to help clients identify a single problematic role and work with it until it becomes clear. To clarify the role, I ask the client to identify its qualities, function and style. By qualities I mean its distinguishing features in terms of six domains: somatic, cognitive, affective, social, spiritual and aesthetic. Over several years time, Fay came to see the victim part of herself as physically weak and exhausted, as ignorant and learning impaired, as lifeless and unlovable, as socially isolated, as spiritually separated from God and as uncreative and unplayful.

I also ask the clients to speak about the function of the role in their lives, that is, what does the playing of a particular role give them. This victim part of Fay was very large and functioned to keep her asleep and safe from further trauma and abuse. At the same time, it caused her great distress outside the home as she met the world with the expectation that she would fail and that they would be the cause of her failure.

By style, I mean the form of role-playing, whether reality-based and emotional, more abstract and distant or a mix of affect and cognition. Over several years, Fay would play the victim in a realistic, overtly emotional way, with little style and distance. When able to abstract the role qualities and depict the victim as a character in a story, a picture on a piece of paper, a figure in a sandbox, Fay would move away from the profound pain of the victim and slowly discover its other side, eventually locating the house of Mrs. Smith which led to a further disidentification with the role of victim.

Once ready to locate the counterrole or counter qualities of the primary role, and once able to identify a guide, the process of treatment is well underway. In working with counterrole and guide, the client also is asked to specify qualities, function and style. As the client is able to integrate role and counterrole with the help of the guide, the therapy moves toward its final stages.

I have applied the model of role, counterrole, guide not only to treatment, but also to assessment and evaluation. In testing one's ability to invoke these three figures and to attribute qualities, functions and levels of distance to them, I am able to assess one's suitability for drama therapy treatment and/or one's present level of functioning. Further, in analyzing the ability of the client to integrate role, counterrole and guide I am able to evaluate the effectiveness of the treatment.

Application of the Role Model to Supervision: Four Focal Points

In applying the role model to supervision, the supervisor helps the therapist focus upon several role relationships: (1) that of role-counterrole-guide within the therapist, (2) that of role-counterrole-guide within the client, (3) that of the client in relationship to the therapist, and (4) that of role-counterrole-guide in the relationship among client, therapist and supervisor. To better see how this model works, I have constructed dialogues based upon actual supervisory sessions between supervisor and drama therapist discussing the case of Fay. Each dialogue corresponds to one of the four focal points of the role model. To reflect upon the dialogues and attempt to clarify some of the ambiguities, I offer a running commentary. In doing so, I aim to play guide for the reader. As guide and commentator, I retain a first person point of view. As therapist, I move into the more distanced stance of the third person.

First Dialogue, Concerning the Therapist

The therapist brings into supervision the following scenario:

I recently returned from an extended vacation and met with Fay. I see her individually and in group. We had been working together for five years and this was the longest sustained time I had ever been inaccessible to her. She was very quiet and withdrawn. She told me a story about being passed over for a promotion at work and about how a new colleague has been behaving abusively toward her. Toward the end of the session, which was primarily verbal, she told me in a tearful way how much she missed me and how much it hurt to admit to this feeling. I felt it was important that Fay verbalized these difficult feelings and I told her so. I was full of feeling, myself. On the one hand I was bored by Fay's account of being victimized at work. I had heard dozens of similar stories from her and found myself turning off. On another level, when Fay spoke of missing me, I immediately saw myself as a love object and felt a mixture of guilt for abandoning her for so long and fear that I could not hold the ambivalence of the dual roles of therapist/lover. I shared none of this with her.

The session ended as I praised Fay for her openness and reminded her of our group meeting in several days. We ended with a hug, as is our custom following each session. The hug felt safe and containing to me.

During group, however, things went awry. Ruth, going through a confusing divorce, remained withdrawn. Jim, depressed and highly self-critical, went on a talking jag. It was difficult for anyone else to intercede. I felt a mixture of delight, in that Jim was working through some important material, and loss of control, in that I didn't know if I should or how I should shift the focus to others in the group. At some point, Fay shared a story about being ten and having to take care of her younger siblings all by herself while her mother was in the hospital giving birth. During this time, her father was home only long enough to criticize her for her shoddy care-taking. To make matters worse, the youngest baby was sick and there was no money in the house to buy proper food. All the tasks of caring for the baby and siblings, of shopping for and preparing food, of keeping the house clean and neat, fell upon ten-year-old Fay. She felt inadequate and angry, and having nowhere to go with these feelings, she keep them inside.

The group did not dwell upon Fay's story. In fact, without missing a beat, Jim continued his saga. At the end of the group, Fay was angry but could not express it. I could feel her anger but decided it was up to her to express her feelings. I was not going to rescue her. I would see her in several days privately and perhaps we could work with this particular issue.

When I meet her next, she was so quiet that I could hardly hear her.

Whatever she said made little sense to me. She spoke more about abuse from her work colleague, then said: "I really have nothing to say." I asked her to express her feelings non-verbally and she choose to draw a picture. She took a large piece of paper from my shelf, one she had drawn on before, and turned it over. She drew a large face in the center and began to construct colorful concentric circles all around the face. She spoke as she drew, accusing me of abandonment and caring for Jim much more than her. As she drew more and more circles, her accusations deepened. I became her abuser and she become flooded with feeling. I tried to hold on to the feelings of abuse and abandonment and to draw her attention back to the drawing, but she was far away, back to her abusive family of origin with little ability to return and little trust that I could ever be a worthy guide. I sat with her and felt the pain and the distance. I experienced my own fear of such accusations by intimates in my life. And I was also aware of a certain feeling of helplessness. There was nothing for me to do, I thought. I could neither reassure her nor could I take away her pain. All my skills as a creative arts therapist seemed lost. Yes, she was focused on the art work, but it took her too far away to an unreachable point and I could do nothing to get her back. All I could do was to sit there and wait. At the end of the session, she walked out. No hug, no goodbye.

During the next group session, Jim was unaware that Fay was angry at him. Ruth could feel Fay's anger and acknowledged it. In response, Fay told Jim she was not angry at him but at me. She verbally attacked Ruth who defended herself by saying: "I'm tired of taking care of people and I'm not going to take care of you." Jim expressed guilt and immediately thought he was the root of the problem. The session was rough and again I felt unable to contain all the anger and pain. At the end, Fay refused a hug or consoling word from anyone in the group.

Having listened attentively to this description, the supervisor asked: "What do you feel like doing?"

"I want her to leave me alone," the therapist cried. "I want her to break off our relationship. I need so much less anger in my life. I want easier, gentler, less wounded clients. I feel pushed to my limits, all the pieces of my peaceful vacation blowing up in my face."

"She seems very powerful," said the supervisor.

"Who?" asked the therapist.

"Fay. Your client."

"She is."

"Who is she?" questioned the supervisor.

"She's all the stuff on the other side of my peace. She's the demands, the threats, the double binds, the female."

Commentary

At this point, the therapist appeared to be as needy as the client. He needed to work through his countertransference. The supervisor pointed out that Fay serves an important purpose for the therapist. When he returns from vacation in a peaceful role, she is there to remind him to heed the other side. She is the counterrole, the one he tries so hard to push away. If he does not heed the part of himself that is wounded and demanding, the peace that he so greatly desires is truly threatened. If he cannot integrate the female part of himself that is so much a dark, demanding figure (see the essay, "In Search of the Muse," Landy, 1996b), he cannot find a way to play out the lighter quality of his male being.

"I know all this yin/yang stuff," the therapist told his supervisor, a woman.

She responded, "In your head, yes. You know how Fay plays out the counterrole and how you will predictably react by fantasizing that she will break off the therapeutic relationship. You know how this scenario has been played out many times in your life, particularly with wounded and abused women who demand too much of you. You are thrust in the role of victim who needs so desperately to escape, and she is your tormentor who can rip you apart like a mythological maenad. All this you know—your role, her counterrole. You even know of this struggle internally. But where is your helper? Where is the guide"

"I think you are my guide," said the therapist tentatively.

"You think?" she responded.

"Yes."

"But you are not sure?" asked the supervisor.

"I am not sure."

This dialogue continued for awhile until the supervisor asked the therapist: "What do you need in a guide?"

Even though the therapist recognized this as a question about qualities of roles, he tried to answer from his heart. "I need wisdom. Wisdom above all. But it has to go along with something else . . . . Care, I think, the ability to see the other person and to be there with him, to accept him uncritically. I need tolerance and patience and I need presence."

"Presence?" questioned the supervisor.

"The ability to be present with me, without distraction."

"Is there such a figure inside you?" she continued.

"There is a wise part of me to whom I can turn for understanding. And there is a caring part of me that is able to help others and to be there for them. Sometimes I even allow this part to care for me. But it is hard to integrate the two qualities into one guide."

"Is that what you'd like your guide to be—wise and caring?"

"Oh, yes, definitely," responded the therapist.

"How does the wise, caring guide go along with the other two roles—victim and tormentor?" she asked.

"The wise part of the guide understands that the wounded part of me brought me into the healing profession in the first place. When I work with wounded clients, that part of me is activated. The wise part also understands that I am my own tormentor, especially when I feel most wounded. This part, in its wisdom, could help me better understand the dynamics between the roles of victim and tormentor. But understanding isn't enough. That's where the caring part comes in. I understand my issues well enough. I now need to know what to do with that understanding. The caring guide, I think, helps transform the dynamic. Because I can learn to care for myself, I don't have to identify so deeply with my wounded clients. They are threats to themselves, not to me. If I can care more for myself, I will acknowledge the presence of the self-tormentor who loves to feed upon the wounded, vulnerable part of my psyche. But I will not allow it to cloud my sense of self-worth and power. I am powerful because I care for myself and trust that my clients can learn to take care of themselves. The caring guide leads me to that awareness just as the wise guide helps me understand the interplay of role and counterrole. When I can put the two qualities together, I have a guide that functions fully. As such, it helps me integrate and perhaps even transform the parts of me that seek peace and prevent that search from occurring."

Commentary

This dialogue addresses an application of the first part of the role model, that concerning role, counterrole, guide within the therapist. The therapist struggles to work through an internal process as it parallels the internal process of his client. The supervisor functions to help the therapist understand and perhaps transform his intrapsychic dynamics even as she points out the parallels with the dilemma of the client. As the therapist becomes stronger, he is able to better trust the strength of his client. It is not necessary for him to care for her, but to trust that she can care for herself. With this trust, she then becomes a mirror in which the therapist sees himself as strong, as capable to taking care of himself. Through this mirror, perhaps the therapist discovers a way to integrate the scary, out of control female part of his psyche.

Second Dialogue, Concerning the Client

The following dialogue addresses an application of the second part of the role model, that which pertains to an understanding of the client's internal dynamics of role, counterrole, guide.

"Tell me about Fay," said the supervisor.

"In which way?" asked the therapist.

"Subjectively. How is she like you?"

"Well, I think it has to do with trying to live with feelings of unworthiness and being afraid that the other side is not available."

"What is the other side?"

"It's what I said before—the side that feels worthy of love and care."

"Is that side available to her?"

"It is. I have worked long and hard with her to find that side. She has played it out expressively in dozens of ways—verbally, in movement, drawing. But she loses it so easily. The primary role of victim is so big."

"And you become the victimizer?"

"I do. I have to be very careful. There are predictable periods like when I go on vacation."

"Who do you then become for her?"

"Her tormentor. Her mother and father and siblings and all those who have humiliated her and robbed her of her self-respect and worth. I become the counterrole."

"Can you help her in the counterrole?"

"I had thought so. I thought I could play out some of the issues and help her hold on to and play out her role of worthy and lovable adult. I have even tried to do this in a more distanced way—through fictional stories, through sandplay and drawing. She enjoys drawing most of all. But often it doesn't work. She needs to stay on a more direct emotional level. She needs more of reality, less of fantasy. She gets confused when I take on the qualities of the counterrole. She needs me to be the guide, the same kind of guide that I need for myself—wise and caring. I would reverse the formula in her case—caring and wise."

"But can you always be the guide for her?"

"Not always, of course not. I get caught up in my own inabilities to guide myself through her cycles of pain and anger."

"What happens then?"

"I try to bring her back to her guide."

"Her inner guide?"

"It can be hard to get her there. When the wounded victim part of herself is very large and all possible helpers are seen as tormentors, that guide becomes quite small. I remind her about Mrs. Smith, the good mother in her childhood."

"Does that help?"

"It usually does. She is such a grounding figure. She is a reminder that a good mother can exist, has existed. It gives her hope. And it turns her inward, because she remembers that she can be kinder to herself. She can do for herself what Mrs. Smith had done for her."

"What did Mrs. Smith do for her?"

"It's not clear. Maybe when she was left alone with no money and a sick baby and the other children to care for when her mother was in the hospital and her father was out trying to scrape together a living, maybe she turned to Mrs. Smith. And maybe Mrs. Smith took her in or gave her some extra cash or said a kind word. Maybe when her mother beat her or humiliated her, Mrs. Smith would see her pain and bring her home in the afternoon and feed her cakes as she sat quietly in the living room. And maybe Mrs. Smith never actually did these things at all. But she was there as an antidote to the pain, somewhere across the street, treating her own children kindly. This, in itself, might have been enough."

"So you have come home from a long vacation, and Fay is angry at you. Her life is not going well. Her hurt and anger spills out not only on you, but also on members of her drama therapy group. You have the opportunity to help facilitate some action in group and in individual sessions. You are aware that her behavior affects your own sense of stability. What do you do?"

"I come to you."

"Am I the wise and caring guide?" asks the supervisor.

"I wish you were," I reply.

"Then I am not?" she asks.

"You are wise enough to not tell me what to do, and you are caring enough to believe that I can find the answer myself. I guess I have to do the same for her, right?"

"What do you mean?"

"I mean, not telling her what to do or interpreting what she is feeling, and caring enough to believe that she is capable of solving her own problem."

"Is she capable of this?"

"She knows the parts of herself that need to be put together–the wounded victim, the adult worthy of love and care, and the caring, loving guide. She loses the last two when she feels most abandoned. When I go away for more than a week, it must feel like a terrible abandonment. Maybe I just have to remind her that the good counterrole and the good guide are not lost at all. Even though I go away, even though the actual Mrs. Smith may had died years ago or may be more fantasy than reality, Fay still has internalized both figures of good therapist and good mother. I need to reinforce the idea that she is not one thing–a mass of pain and suffering, a tormented soul who has been abused and who will always be abused. She is also all the things on the other side, and she is someone capable of negotiating the voyage from one side to the other. She is capable of holding the three together."

Commentary

In the above dialogue, I have demonstrated some of the issues involved in helping the therapist view the intrapsychic dynamics of role, counterrole, guide within the client. In applying the role model, it should be noted that the therapist also becomes entangled in the interplay of roles and needs to draw upon his own internal cast of characters for guidance, even as he turns to an outside supervisor. Having looked at ways of conceiving the inner dynamics of the therapist and the client, we turn more specifically to their interpersonal relationship. Given that the therapist understands many of the intrapsychic dynamics, what should be his next steps?

Third Dialogue, Concerning the Relationship of Client and Therapist

The supervisor continues: "Let's get back to the group. The session has ended badly and you feel unable to contain the pain and anger. You feel like breaking off from Fay, but recognize that she has provoked many of your own issues. In reality, you will stay with the process and try to move it forward. You have not lost the ability to guide but fear that Fay has lost a positive and hopeful vision. What do you do?"

"I am worried about her. I call Fay on the phone, urging her to stay with her feelings, assuring her that I will not abandon her no matter how hard she pushes."

"And who do you become for her when you do this?"

"The good mother, maybe, or, in Winnicott's (1971) terms, the *good enough* guide."

"How does she respond?"

"In silence at first. I just let it be. We make another appointment. At the end of the conversation, she thanks me for calling."

"How do you explain her thanks?"

"Well, I have done something that her mother never would have done. She wants to believe me."

"Are you being honest?"

"With Fay?"

"And with yourself."

"Yes. I'm committed to her as long as it takes. And yes, I am also committed to making peace with the part of me that pushes away painful feelings."

"Can Fay help you discover that peace?"

"Yes. In that way she becomes my guide. It's complex. When she is in the role of the needy one, I become the helper, a counterrole. When she is in the role of the angry one, I sometimes take on the counterrole of victim and want the whole relationship to end. But as you suggest, her anger also guides me back to my own pain."

"It seems like your roles are dependent upon hers."

"To some extent, yes. But that's the nature of this relationship. We are dependent upon one another. We give each other another perspective, another side. Isn't this what you mean by role and counterrole?"

"Yes, but I am concerned about the dependency," said the supervisor.

"Why? I think it happens all the time in therapy. Fay is dependent upon my absence and presence, my holding and withholding, and when she touches on my issues, I become dependent upon her. I need her to find a way out of the cycle of pain and anger, of the victim role, so I can then be more of a guide for her."

"Or should it be the other way around?"

"What do you mean?"

"She needs you to find a way out of your own problems. She is the client. She pays you for your services. When a patient with an infection goes to the doctor, should she have to wait for the doctor to cure his own illness before prescribing effective medication?"

"I am not a doctor with magic pills."

"What are you?"

"A different kind of healer. I bear my own wounds and they sometimes get entangled in the treatment of others who have similar wounds. My treatment is not as clear as a doctor's. I have no pills. Just an expressive language and a repertory of roles, an ability to be many things in the service of my client and, I should add, in the service of myself."

"You serve two masters?"

"Maybe three."

"Who is the third?"

"You."

"Ah!"

Commentary

In the dynamics of client and supervisor, a certain dependency is noted. One's counterrole will depend upon another's taking on of a particular role. When the issues present are difficult for both client and therapist, that dependency will be strengthened. Absent from the above dialogue is a discussion of the appropriateness of the dependency. When client and therapist are working on a deep level, it may be that the dependency is unavoidable. In dramatic terms, every protagonist requires an antagonist. In most dramatic struggles, some form of conflict is present. And therapy is such a struggle. However, an effective psychotherapeutic process is noted by the shift from dependency to independence and finally, interdependence. In terms of the role model, there needs to be a point, after struggling with the role confusions of transference and countertransference, that the client and therapist recognize their independent qualities and are able to play them out in a balanced way. Beyond that is a further goal. Once both recognize their separateness, they can envision a connection based upon their difference. In their interdependence, the client and therapist create a meaningful dyad, a protagonist and antagonist, a role and counterrole.

To move from a state of dependence to independence to interdependence, the two role players require a guide. As we have seen in the above dialogue, each at times guides the other. Each, too, turns to an inner guide for the strength needed to move beyond a dependent relationship. The therapist has the option of seeking out a further guide in the person of the supervisor. In examining this relationship and connecting it back to the client, we move to the final piece of the role model.

Fourth Dialogue, Concerning the Relationship of Client, Therapist and Supervisor

The dialogue was interrupted at the point of viewing the therapist as the servant of three masters—his client, himself and his supervisor. To continue, the supervisor asks: "How do you serve me?"

"I come to you in humility and ignorance. You are strong and wise. I come to you with questions."

"But I am the one who has been asking the questions."

"Yes. So I serve the questioner."

"If I am the questioner, how do you serve me?"

"By taking on the counterrole and trying to answer your questions."

"Is that servile?"

"The kind of servant I play is not servile. It is more obedient."

"And what is it about me that you obey?"

"I obey your game of question and answer. I obey your power. You are a supervisor, one who has a superior kind of vision. I accept that."

"Do you?"

"Not always. Sometimes I see you as vulnerable as myself and as ignorant. Sometimes I see you as judgmental."

"How?"

"Like judging me for becoming so entangled with Fay, for not foreseeing her anger when I returned from vacation, for not containing her feelings better in a dramatic form, for calling her up on the phone and for a thousand other reasons."

"You don't tell me this."

"Right. Because sometimes I don't trust you enough to hold my negative feelings."

"You sound a bit like Fay."

"How do you mean?"

"Fay might say the same thing to you."

"Yes."

"When does she doubt your power of super vision?"

"When she feels most vulnerable, and I represent another of her tormentors."

"Yes. So who am I for you?"

"Many things. Not really a master. And as you are not a master, I am not a servant. You feel more like my therapist. Or when I question your care and suspect your judgment, you feel like my mother. But you are not really any of these things—master, mother, therapist. I guess guide would be the most accurate. Your questions guide me."

"Where do you need to be guided?"

"Back to my role as therapist. Back to my client who needs my guidance. Back to those parts of myself that can help a client and that can be helped by a supervisor."

The supervisor then added, uncharacteristically: "I think the guide is the key part. It is the piece that ultimately connects us all."

"How do you mean?" I questioned.

"On one level, I guide you and you guide your client."

"Who guides you?"

"Well, you do and even Fay does in a more distanced way."

"How?"

"You guide me into the messy territory of pain and anger which is hard to deal with for all of us—clients, therapists, supervisors."

"Isn't a guide supposed to help you out of the mess?"

"Before you can get out, I think you need to get in pretty deep. A guide also leads you to the muck. By bringing me rich material and being brave enough to look at your part in the drama, you lead me to invest a lot of myself. I get my hands dirty and when it all seems overwhelming to me, I speak to my own supervisor. Fay has become so vivid to me. In understanding her, I learn to serve you better."

"Then you are my servant?" I added.

"We all reverse roles. I serve you and you serve me and we serve Fay and Fay serves us."

"Role and counterrole and guide?"

"Yes. Client and therapist and supervisor playing all the parts of role, counterrole and guide. We are linked, held together by the pain and searching for a way to move beyond it, for a way to help one another even as we experience our own inability to help ourselves. I think we are all looking for the same thing–connection, integration, acceptance, the ability to hold contraries together–call them yin and yang, darkness and light, powerlessness and power, role and counterrole. And I think we are all in need of a guide to help us make that connection."

"The guide as supervisor," I added.

"Yes, one with super vision," responded the supervisor, a touch of irony in her voice.

"A god."

"Not a god. A person of this time and place, a vulnerable person. . . ."

"What about Mrs. Smith?" I asked.

". . . And a persona," added the supervisor, "one who is not necessarily flesh and blood, but who stands in for someone real and corrects the real person's painful ways. Mrs. Smith, as guide, gives Fay the corrective for growing up with an abusive mother. You give her the same. Maybe I give you some sort of corrective, too."

"I think our time is up," I said.

"Yes," said the supervisor, "for now our time is up."

"Thank you for allowing me to ask you some questions," I said. "I liked listening for a change to someone outside myself."

Conclusions

As therapist, I recognize that I need to listen to those persons outside and those personae inside that will help me better understand the dynamics of the healing process. In this paper, I have conceptualized the dynamics in terms of a model of role, counterrole, guide. As we have seen, this in an interactive model on two levels, interpersonal and intrapsychic. Within the process of supervision, each participant—client, therapist and supervisor—aims to integrate qualities of the others. And each participant does so by activating a particular part of the psyche, a role, discovering its other side, a counterrole, and locating a guide that can hold the two together in a meaningful way.

Although all participants in the supervisory process are defined by their specific qualities and functions, they engage often in role reversals. Their role definitions are both fixed and fluid. They are fixed in the sense that the client seeks help from a therapist who, in turn seeks help from a supervisor. They are fluid in the sense that all aim toward the interdependence of role, counterrole and guide, and any participant can assume the status of role, causing the others to regroup as counterrole and guide.

Supervision from a drama therapy role perspective, like supervision from a psychodynamic perspective, takes into consideration the many inevitabilities and consequences of transference and countertransferance. Transference and countertransference are therefore viewed as dramatic phenomena in that a person is as much defined by his personae as by his self. In untangling the complexity of perceptions and accepting the separate qualities and functions of each role, all are then able to move toward the goal of integrating the three. In the end, if the treatment has been successful, the client will see himself as the one who needed help and was willing to accept help from a guide. And he will see himself, finally, as one who can ultimately help himself even when his counter tendencies to feel helpless arise. In the end, the therapist will see himself as a helper who also needs help when he feels helpless. And in the end, the supervisor will see himself as a guide whose wisdom is based upon his ability to not know the answers, but to ask good enough questions that can lead all three role-players back to themselves. In the end, all three are separate but interconnected. That which has been transferred onto the other is taken back without diminishing the power of the other.

At the end of Shakespeare's play, Lear takes back the role of father to mourn the loss of his daughter, Cordelia. In giving her the love she deserved all along, he has, finally but tragically, undone the twisted transference. Over and above the physical destruction lies the spiritual power of redemption.

Few human beings in their lifetimes will play out the scope of a Shakespearian drama. But many will seek ways to make sense of their lives and discover the territory that lies on the other side of pain. The fortunate ones will do so with the help of a guide who will surely lack super vision but may well possess a modicum of wisdom and care.

Throughout this paper, I have offered an example of one searcher, Fay, whose journey required the help of several guides. Fay's story is emblematic of the tragic consequences of the human condition that once abused requires the skill of many to repair. Fay's story is still being told, although with the help of her guides, she is better able to integrate role and counterrole and proceed, however cautiously, with her life. As for the therapist and supervisor, their stories are endlessly unfinished. Like Pirandello's characters in search of an author, they await other clients to provide meaning. They await other guides.

Part Five

TERMINATION

Chapter 11

UNFINISHED BUSINESS–THE USE
OF STORIES IN CLOSURE

It was Spring and time to close with a two-year master's level training group at New York University. Many in the group were about to graduate and take up professional positions as drama therapists. The group consisted of ten women and two men. At the very beginning of the two-year experience, the group was larger by five. But some returned home or moved on or decided they needed more time to try their luck on Broadway.

As an educator and trainer with some 25 years experience, I tend to see each group differently. I liked this group as a unit very much and felt close to several individuals, yet I distanced myself too easily, even though in the training all had disclosed a great deal of personal material. In the first year of training, for example, all created autobiographical performances highlighting unresolved issues in their lives. Each performance was revelatory of deep and often painful issues involving sexual abuse, addiction, disability, abandonment, death and loss. All the performances touched me in the moment and drew me very close to the performers, but I could not fully sustain my attachment.

During these two years I was experiencing significant malaise apart from the group. Life in my family was difficult and I was struggling with my roles of husband and father. My son at six had a visual disability and my daughter at eight had a learning disability. With the more problematic temperament, my daughter was particularly challenging and our family was attempting to contain the chaos of life with two young children with special needs. At the same time, my mother was diagnosed with a terminal illness and I was thrust into another challenging and charged role, that of caretaker. Inspired by the research on terminally ill cancer patients by a former student, Joyce Sykes (1998), I tried to encourage my mother to take care of unfinished business. But within a family structure that embraced denial, I was unsuccessful.

In the midst of these personal issues, I found it easy to distance myself

191

from my students and indeed from the profession of drama therapy. I was not putting much effort into preparing for class. I was not writing much, nor was I feeling the excitement of sharing ideas and experiences with my students. To some extent I was projecting my feelings of chaos and powerlessness onto the group. It was the group that was rejecting drama therapy. This explained why so many left the program. It was the group that was fearful and confused, unable to understand and accept my reasonable teachings. It was the group's fault that I felt so out of control.

During the second year of training, it hit me that I was connected rather deeply to this group and it was time to withdraw the projections. My realization occurred late one night at a drama therapy conference. My students had decided to present a performance reflective of their training experience in the drama therapy program. Because there was little rehearsal time, the performance felt spontaneous, almost improvised. In very personal ways, all of the 12 presented their stories. Many were very painful but all were presented without apology or sentimentality. They were enacted in an aesthetically distanced style with puppets, masks, movement and song, full of feeling and reflective awareness. For a reason that was unclear to me, all wore red scarves.

At the center of the piece was a giant puppet draped in red fabric, a guide figure whose body contained all the actor/students. Taking it all in, feeling the tears well up, I realized that in many ways this performance was very much about the group's feelings of attachment to me. I was the guide. I had been the guide all along the way. My teaching held the group together, allowing the pain to surface, allowing those who needed to reject the group to go in peace, allowing those who so desperately needed to stay to search for ways to live with their ambivalent feelings.

At one point in the performance, Jim told a story about feeling betrayed by an important mentor in his life, this many years after experiencing sexual abuse. He recalled that at the beginning of our training I had asked the students to lead a warm-up exercise, and Jim proposed a trust fall where the group forms a tight circle and one member falls back into their arms and is passed around from person to person. I was the first to volunteer and as I floated from person to person, the group held me in their strong and gentle way, as they would have wanted to be held by me. Jim felt safe.

At the end of the performance, all members of the group removed their red scarves and attached them to others, forming a continuous circle. Although I watched from the audience, I felt very much on the line. This was not my family that was struggling for awareness, understanding and love. These were not voices from my past demanding that I take away their pain.

These were students taking responsibility for their own pain, acknowledging the power of their training and the love of their trainer.

After the tears, we all embraced and I returned home transformed, newly devoted to the students and the remaining six months of training. The next week I discovered, however, that following the performance the group took a fall. One member, with a history of trauma and addiction, regressed and acted out publicly in an aggressive and frightening way. Others, afraid that they could not contain the dark energy, blamed themselves for the intensity of the incident. Old anger and shame and blame surfaced and whipped through the group throughout the night and into the morning. After all the hugs and applause, the center caved in, the line dropped, the circle with all the brightly colored scarves knotted together broke.

When we resumed in class, we noted our task—to finish the unfinished business. We began slowly, verbalizing anger, regret, powerlessness, shame, fear and hope. We retraced our steps as a group seeking connection by engaging in enactments through movement and sound and various projective approaches in and out of role. We reincorporated the person who held the darkness for the group, a darkness born in abuse and neglect and loss, a darkness begging for attention that was acted out at the conference as a reminder that there is another side of love and acceptance that needs to be acknowledged.

As a later part of the process, after a long stretch of re-incorporation, I asked the group to write stories in the form of fairy tales around the theme of unfinished business. Consistent with our theoretical framework, I asked that the stories contain at least three characters representing the role or protagonist, the counterrole or antagonist and the guide figure, one who can help the protagonist complete her unfinished business and hold together the contradictory qualities of role and counterrole.

All were eager to begin and as a sign that I, too, was part of the group, they asked me to contribute my own story. For many, creating these stories about unfinished business was a critical step toward closure. For me, they were commentaries on the burden of closing an intense and powerful process of training to be a drama therapist. As commentaries, the stories operated on three simultaneous levels. The first and most concrete level is that of the here and now reality of the group. In our group, the direct line toward closure was interrupted by a crisis which we attempted to work through and resolve.

The second level is the transferential. A bit more abstract than the first, it refers to the past, the story of each student's family which is symbolically played out in the group and recreated in the fairy tales.

The third level is the fictional, the most abstract of all. The fictional level, in this case represented by fairy tales, transforms the actual past and present into a virtual time frame, noted by the phrase *once upon a time*. It also points toward the future when unfinished business can be resolved as the hero returns safely home from her journey into the dark woods.

The fictional level is the domain of archetypal figures that stand in for actual group or family members. The fictional level does not present an antithesis of reality but rather a heightened reality, characterized by symbolic figures and events. One of the most important archetypal figures is that of the guide, a fairy godmother or helper, who moves the hero into and out of the woods. Although guides exist in everyday life, in families and working groups of all kinds, they tend to appear larger than life within many types of stories, especially fairy tales.

I have chosen eight stories from the group, each of which can be read on all three levels. They are marvelous tales that tell the story of our group, of old family dynamics and of the exploits of fairies and other enchanted beings attempting to resolve significant dilemmas. Through these stories, the writers offer a vision of completion, connection and hope. Following each story, I will offer a brief statement of how the characters complete their unfinished business with the help of a guide. I will also share my thoughts on how the fictional story reflects the non-fiction of the group and helps it move toward closure.

Firen and Apoyo
By Erin Conner

Deep in the cool, damp Mossy Wood, there lived a fairy named Firen. She lived underneath the roots of an ancient, overturned cypress tree, where she would practice her Fairy Magic. It was cool in the middle of the hot summer sun, and offered protection at night, when the mosquitoes came out. The mosquitoes in her area of the woods were just dreadful! Mosquitoes, you see, are more than just an annoyance to fairies. Fairies are actually so allergic to mosquito venom that should they be bitten more than two or three times, the bites could prove to be lethal. But Firen had gone to great lengths to make this place her home. She had had the help of her froggy friend, Padre Fuerte, when she first obtained the old tree. He helped her pass gingko and jasmine leaves up between the roots, so the mosquitoes would not be able to get in. And if they did, he would gladly eat any leftover mosquitoes that might still have found a way through. But Padre Fuerte had grown tired of the taste of that particular variety of mosquito, so he moved on to seek more exciting adventures and tastier mosquitoes in Mossy Wood.

Once Padre Fuerte left, another froggy named Reprimir, came along and said he would live with Firen. Reprimir was not the trusted friend that Padre Fuerte proved to be, though. Reprimir would do nothing but sit around all day and night and sing froggy songs and wait for the mosquitoes to come out. There would then be more than his fill of mosquitoes flying around Firen's tree-home, and her Fairy Magic studies would constantly be interrupted by the buzzing of mosquitoes in her ear. He never helped her paste up new gingko and jasmine, once the old leaves had lost their mosquito-repellent scent. One day, Firen told him how she wished he would help her more, in return for letting him live with her. Reprimir just sort of croaked resentfully and hopped away, with no explanation or apology.

Firen began to get a little sad and scared. She missed Padre Fuerte and how he would do so much to help protect her from those wretched insects. After a fortnight of falling way behind in her Fairy Magic studies, and of having to constantly swat and bat at potentially lethal mosquitoes, Firen even started to miss Reprimir a little. Even though he only seemed interested in satisfying himself all the time, it still gave her the chance to do a little learning before another mosquito would inevitably come buzzing at her ear and nibble at her frail, fairy skin. She began to cry loud fairy sobs that, unbeknownst to her, seemed to echo through all of Mossy Wood.

About a snail-mile-and-a-half away, a froggy suffering from lockjaw syndrome hopped along and heard the harrowing sobs. Curiously, he traveled closer and began to realize it was the desperate cry of a fairy. After hours of hopping, the froggy came upon Firen's old cypress tree.

He knocked on her toadstool door, and startled, Firen stopped crying. Cautiously, so as not to let any more mosquitoes in, she opened the door. She didn't see anyone there.

"Hewwo! Down here!" the frog cried.

"Oh my goodness!" Firen said, with a bit of a start. "Who are you?"

"Yeah, could you just wet me in? The mosquitoes are weawwy bad out hewe, and if I'm not mistaken, Miss Faiwy, you'we awwergic to mosquito bites." And with that, he hopped into her home and began trying to catch some with his tongue, only his clamped jaw prevented him from catching a single one.

"That's very nice of you, little froggy," Firen said, as she shut the door. "But I don't even know your name. I don't know anything about you, and I don't just let anybody inside my cypress tree."

"My name is Apoyo," the froggy said.

"Mine is Firen," she said. "How do you do?"

"Weww, twuthfuwwy, I have been twavewwing for snaiw miwes and miwes–"

"Pardon me for being so forward, but why are you talking that way?" Firen queried.

"I have the worwd's worst case of WOCKJW! I'm so hungwy and tiwed, and I've exhausted evewy possibiwity of sowving my pwobwem."

"I'm so sorry, Apoyo. I wish I could help you," Firen said.

"Pawdon *me* fow being so forward, Miss Fairy, but why awe you cwying?"

"Oh, I'm missing my two froggy friends who used to live here and help me keep the mosquitoes away. They've since left me here to fight the mosquitoes off alone," she explained.

"Weww, why don't you just use some of youw Faiwy Magic to keep the mosquitoes away?"

"I don't know all the Fairy Magic yet. I'm only on the L's in the magic book. I just need a little more time to get to the M-O-S's before I can cast a fairy spell to keep them away from my home," she cried.

"It seems you'we in a bit of a pwedicament, too, my deaw! But I have an ideaw. You can wead in youw Faiwy Magic book to the pawt about cuwing wockjw, and once you cuwe me, I wiww gwadwy powish off any mosquitoes that come youw way. I can't repwace youw othew fwoggy fwiends, of couwse, but I would be happy to hewp you out fow a whiwe, if you hewp me."

"Just how long were you thinking of being of service to me, if I help you?" Firen asked him, still a little skeptical from the way Padre Fuerte and Reprimir had left so suddenly, when she needed them so desperately.

"I'ww stay hewe until you have weached the M-O-S's in youw Faiwy Magic book of spews. Then, you wiww have the powew and stwength to fight fow youwsewf again. How does that sound?"

Firen thought about his plan, and after a moment or two picked up her spell book and began reading. She read through the night until she came to "Lockjaw, The Infliction and Curing of. . . ." Picking up her magic wand, she spoke a few cryptic fairy words and zapped Apoyo's affliction away. Before he could thank her, he swallowed four mosquitoes with one foul swoop of his froggy tongue.

"Fank you!" said the froggy, his mouth still full of mosquito morsels.

Thank *you*!" Cried the grateful fairy.

And so, they lived together for a time, Firen continuing her Fairy Magic studies, and Apoyo keeping the house pasted with fresh jasmine and gingko leaves, and eating the stray mosquitoes that still seemed to sneak in their home. Their time was spent together in harmony, until, of course, Firen gained the knowledge and power to keep the mosquitoes and other threats away all by her fairy self. But they remain Frog and Fairy friends to this day, always remembering how the one helped the other just when they needed it.

In *Firen and Apoyo*, the fairy, Firen, struggles to overcome her fear of loneliness and death. With the help of her imperfect guide, the speech-impaired frog, Apoyo, she learns the language necessary to survive on her own. In closing, the challenge of our group was the same—to find a way to deal with its fear of dissolution and to allow its individuals the courage to survive on their own.

The Girl Who Shined As Bright As The Sun
By Susan Clayton

Once upon a time there lived a girl named Goldie. Her parents named her Goldie because she shined as bright as the sun. Even Goldie's parents were unable to look directly at the girl. Everyone in town knew when Goldie was coming as her golden light rays would shine brightly a mile before she arrived. The townspeople did not tease little Goldie though. In fact, they felt sorry for the little girl. She was so bright that no one could get very close to her. Goldie's light could actually burn! But because she was just a child, no one blamed her for being so bright. Therefore, everyone in town developed ways to prepare for her visits. Since they knew Goldie was coming from a mile away, they could make sure they were not too close, being careful to avoid being blinded or burned.

One day the parents were discussing what they could do. Goldie was seven years old and very bright. Goldie would only get bigger and brighter as she continued to grow.

They went to seek advice at the temple of the Moon God. They prayed to the Moon God and said: "Please help us. We love Goldie. She brightens our lives in many ways, but we wish to get closer to her without getting burned. She is just too bright!" As the mother shed tears that fell upon the Moon God's temple, she heard a voice:

> The love you have for your daughter is true
> As Goldie feels the same for you.
> Her brightness is a gift from above
> That shines as bright as her love.
>
> But even goodness can have a curse
> So listen carefully to this verse.
> Your daughter's brightness will only grow
> So she must learn what to carefully show.
> Though the sun is sometimes very hot
> Steady it is always not.
>
> This brightness is of great use
> But be careful of its abuse.
> For if the girl is too bright
> No one will truly see her light.
>
> So teach her to glow and shine so bright
> But to be clever with her light.
> For those who share their gifts with others
> Will find the world full of sisters and brothers.

The parents left the Moon God and rushed home to meet their daughter. As they approached Goldie to tell her what the Moon God had said they encountered a light brighter than ever before.

"Goldie", they called out, "You are so bright!"

"Yes," Goldie said. "I seem to be growing. But why do you stand so far from me?"

The parents relied, "Goldie, your light is wonderful but too bright for our eyes."

Goldie replied. "This is unfair. I don't mean to be so bright and I seem to get brighter everyday."

Following the Moon God's advice they said: "Goldie, don't be sad. Your brightness is a blessing."

Goldie replied, "But I am unable to get close to anyone, because I blind people and they get burned. The other kids can't even play with me."

The parents recited the Moon God's verse and Goldie tried to listen, but found herself mesmerized by the beautiful colors from the rays of light that emanated from her.

When Goldie's parents finished, Goldie went outside to play. As she wandered along the stream that ran from the house through town, her rays of light made the flowers bloom and the grass grow. Even the fish came up from the bottom of the stream to greet the light. Goldie saw a small frog that moved behind a rock as she approached. Goldie lifted the rock away and caught the frog in her hands. As Goldie became happier playing with the frog, she got brighter and brighter. As Goldie pulled the frog closer, the frog tried to squirm away. Goldie was having so much fun that she forgot about her brightness. But as she looked down, the frog burned and died in her hand. "Oh no!" cried Goldie, "what have I done? I'm so sorry little froggie. I did not mean to harm you. I don't mean to hurt anyone. Oh, I will never be able to have friends." As Goldie sat down in the grass and cried, she got brighter and brighter. The grass and flowers around her withered and died. Even the stream dried up near her.

Goldie thought to herself, "There must be a way for me to cover up some of this brightness." At that moment Goldie noticed a beam of light missing. Her arm was covered in mud obscuring a beam of light. This gave Goldie the idea of covering herself with the mud to prevent her light form shining through.

The mud felt cool on Goldie's arms and legs and face. Goldie liked this feeling, because it was something new. And when she had finished covering herself with the mud, Goldie could see that she was not even half as bright as before. She ran home to show her parents this new clever disguise. But Goldie's parents were nowhere to be found. So Goldie decided to go to town to find them.

On her way to town, Goldie was able to pet and play with the neighbor's dog and the sheep and cows along the way. Never before had she been able to get so close to the animals. As Goldie entered town, she saw lots of people walking and shopping. Goldie thought to herself, "I have never seen so many people in town before. And no one is running or covering their eyes from me."

Goldie went up to the baker's son and said hello. He did not run or turn away, but greeted Goldie with a smile. Goldie was so happy that she smiled really big, but this caused a bright light to appear. Fearing the baker's son would run away, Goldie closed her mouth quickly. But the baker's son had not noticed and asked Goldie to join a baseball game.

Goldie and the other kids played baseball for hours. Goldie ran so much and played so hard that the mud on her arms and legs began to slide off with the heat. As the day turned to night, the mud cracked and began to break off. This caused small light rays to shine through, and the light made it possible for the game to continue into the night. The kids commented on how bright the moon was and how much fun they were having with Goldie. But as the mud broke off in larger pieces, the kids went home to shield themselves from her light. Goldie was left alone in the field and again was sad.

Goldie began to walk home when she heard a cry. It was a little boy who was lost and could not find his way home. As Goldie approached the little boy, he shielded his eyes and begged for help.

Goldie said, "I can help you. Do you live in town, little boy?"

"Yes," said the boy. "But it is so dark and I can't find the path home."

"Let me help you," said Goldie. "I can light the way and we can find the path home together."

The little boy agreed and carefully uncovered his eyes. Upon Goldie's instructions he looked only straight ahead using her brightness to find the way. As they approached the little boy's home, he turned to Goldie to thank her and he did not need to shield his eyes. The little boy was able to see Goldie up close, for Goldie's light was bright but not too bright. As the parents came out to greet their son, they were also able to greet Goldie up close. Goldie was amazed. Never before had anyone been able to get this close to her. Goldie felt happy and her brightness grew a bit. And as Goldie looked down at herself and at her rays of light, she noticed that she was bright, but not too bright.

Goldie ran home to tell her parents. As she entered the house, her parents almost didn't recognize her. They did not have to shield their eyes, and for the first time in years, they were able to really see Goldie.

"Oh, Goldie, you are so beautiful! You have found your true brightness!" the parents cried.

"Yes, mother. I am not too bright anymore. I can see you better now, too."

And as the Moon God shone down upon Goldie and her parents, they knew there was no going back to the blinding light. Goldie's true light was found.

In *The Girl Who Shined as Bright as the Sun*, Goldie searches for a way to connect to people without hurting them. As she does so, she is able to discover a way to return home safely. Her guide is a lost boy who teaches her how to focus her brilliance and find balance. The group, like Goldie, searched for a balance at its close—a way to contain its intensity without losing the ability to shine.

Puppy-Dung
By Young Ah Kang

There was a puppy-dung living in a small village. He was a very shy and sensitive puppy-dung because he came from a shy and sensitive puppy family. One day, when he was taking a nap under the warm sunshine, a young lady wearing a red sweater saw him on her way to work.

"EE-k! What is this? So dirty!" With a wry face, she hurriedly went past the puppy-dung. The poor puppy-dung's face blushed with shame.

"Yes, I am such a dirty puppy-dung," he said.

After that, a tiny sparrow flew by and brought his beak to the puppy-dung. "Tsz. Tsz. Nothing to eat!" The heartless sparrow flew away into the blue sky. The puppy-dung was very sad. "Nobody likes me. I'm useless. I'm nothing." The poor puppy-dung felt like hiding himself from his neighbors.

At that moment, a soft voice like a spring wind reached the puppy-dung's ear. "Wow, the puppy-dung! It will be a good fertilizer for my garden." An old lady with a warm smile put the puppy-dung into her small bucket for her beautiful flowers. This made the puppy-dung very happy, because he knew that he was needed for something good.

In *Puppy-Dung*, the protagonist searches for a way to overcome shame and find a meaningful connection to the life cycle. With the help of an old lady he finds his purpose in creating new life. The theme of re-incorporation and resurrection was significant for the group as it worked through its crisis, metaphorically sowing the seeds of acceptance and love in a dark and shameful garden.

The Princess Whose Dress Changed Colors
By Junko Muraki

Once upon a time, in a world with no mirrors, there was a princess named Aurora.
The color of her dress changed colors. With the king, her father, her dress became
red. When she was with the Queen, her mother, the dress would turn pink. When
she was with her tutor, the dress would turn orange. When she was in a room full of
people, her dress would be a multiple of colors, a swirling marble of various colors.
The princess was unhappy with the way the dress changed colors. When she was
alone, the dress would be black. The princess spent most of the time alone, away
from people because she felt most comfortable in her black dress.

One day, the king's merchant came in with a beautiful blue cloak. This flowing blue
velvet cloak was long enough to cover her entire dress. All the people in the kingdom were mesmerized and said, "It would make anyone who wore it look handsome
and beautiful."

The princess thought, " If only I owned it, I would be able to cover my dress, and
I will be adored by all and live happy for the rest of my life."

The king, seeing that everyone wanted the cloak, said, "To be fair, I am going to have
a contest. To prove worthy to have this blue cloak, one must go on a journey and get
the treasure back from the dragon who lives in the cave."

Many set foot on the narrow and thorny path where the dragon lived. Some gave up
half way, and others, when they got to the dragon, were burnt by the dragon's
flames. The princess observed the killings, and decided to sneak in the cave at night
when it was dark. There were others who did the same, but the dragon, with its sensitive eyes, caught the reflection of the people's clothes, and burnt them. Since the
princess' dress remained black, she was able to sneak past the dragon undetected.
She found a beautiful wine red stone. As she tried to sneak back out of the cave, she
tripped over a gold chalice, and woke the dragon.

"Who's there?" the dragon roared in her deep, dark voice. The dragon's eyes were
like that of a full moon, shining brightly on the princess. In the dragon's eyes, the
princess saw her reflection for the first time. Although she could not recognize who
she was at first, the dress she had on told her the truth. But the dress looked white.

"Tell me one reason why I shouldn't burn you like the rest of them," the dragon said.
The princess took a deep breath and said: "If I don't win the blue cloak, I will be
forever alone and unhappy." And she went on to tell her about her dress, and how
it changed color.

"Come visit me and keep me company every time the moon shines in the sky," said
the dragon. "Then I will let you take the stone, and leave you unharmed. But if you
break your promise and fail to visit me, I will devour you and you shall remain pris-
oner in my stomach forever, alone."

The princess promised and went back to the castle. When she got back, she realized
that she no longer desired the blue cloak even though it looked just as beautiful and
precious as before.

The princess visited the dragon as she promised, and she kept the red wine stone.
One day, after many years, she told the dragon, "This, my friend, is my favorite
color," showing the red wine stone in her hand. As she spoke, she saw her dress turn
into the very same color. From then on, her dress remained red wine no matter who

she was with.

In *The Princess Whose Dress Changed Colors*, Aurora leaves her family and community feeling unacceptable in their eyes, only to discover her true colors with the aid, ironically, of a life-threatening dragon. In making peace with the dragon, Aurora finds a way to make peace with her own sense of unworthiness and shame. Like Aurora, the group took a journey into dangerous places and confronted their own demons time and again. All survived, individual and group, with a stronger sense of self-worth and connectedness.

Star Light, Star Bright
By Lisa Merrill

Once upon a time in a far away galaxy, a little star was born. Now you may not know that every star, like snowflakes, is different from every other star. They come in different sizes, shapes and colors, light and speed. Some shoot across the sky, trailing showers of light behind them. Others float gently, slowly across the universe, like dandelion wisps blown by a breeze. Stars flicker, twinkle, shimmer, sparkle, glimmer, glow and gleam. They radiate and flash, burning brightly like fires on a warm autumn night, or flaming in great conflagrations of color and emotion, white hot intensity and molten desire. After many millions of years, those that burn brightest are thought to be the luckiest, for they become suns and the center of their own very special universes. Stars die, too, just like us, pulsing with the glow of burning embers. Some, for reasons no one knows, die abruptly in great explosions of light, scattering across universes, or, worst of all, some simply disappear–there one moment and gone the next. No one can bear to talk about them.

Our little star, whose name is Gloria, was the daughter of a comet and a relatively obscure star in a minor constellation at the edge of the galaxy. She knew she was different–after all, comets and stars don't often get together, but was she special? She wanted desperately to be. She wished she were as important as a North Star, for then she would be a beacon for men to steer by. She wished her mother came from a greater constellation, but mostly she wanted to be a sun and have her own universe with many planets revolving around her and people on those planets worshiping her. And she would be a good sun. She wouldn't burn too brightly, burning people to a crisp, just brightly enough to be noticed. Yes, she would provide warmth and comfort and help flowers grow and snows melt, but the most important thing was she would be noticed.

Gloria lived and played with many other stars in her galaxy. The other starlets were beginning to twinkle and burn and shine and find their colors, but Gloria was mostly just a sort of pale pearl gray, shimmering slightly every now and then, but mostly feeling jumbled around inside and pretty drab on the outside. When the other stars talked about all the adventures they had and all the wonderful things they were beginning to feel, Gloria would always jump in and say, "Me, too! Me, too!" Even when a star who had been badly injured by a passing meteorite finally dared to tell the story (because stars feel great shame to admit they couldn't burn up a meteorite), Gloria said: "Look at me, I'm injured too. Well, maybe it wasn't a meteorite, maybe it was just an old broken down satellite, but it hurt just the same."

When the other starlets were by themselves, they just shook their points and said: "It really isn't fair, she always has to be the center of attention, she never gives anyone else a chance to shine."

Gloria felt very much alone. She felt like a moon, dull and pitted, only reflecting the light of a sun. So she pretended everything was fine. The day she heard a tiny voice wishing on the star right next to her was her moment of deepest despair. Would anyone, gazing at the billions of stars in the vastness of the universe, ever pick her out and wish upon her?

One day while she was floating around the galaxy feeling more than a little sorry for herself, she bumped right up against the Constellation of the Crone. Gloria was a little afraid, for the Constellation of the Crone was one of the oldest in the galaxy and had a reputation for burning hot and cold. It was said that some of her stars had blinked out, destroyed in hot flashes during the last several million years and, understandably, this made her a little prickly. Some stars thought they could ignore her because she was past her prime, but others knew she was a source of great star wisdom and dared to approach her.

The Crone looked down on Gloria that day and knew, deep in the bones of her stars, what it felt like to be dull and alone and ordinary. So she reached down and picked Gloria up by one of her points and held her in the palm of her hand. Gloria held her breath, quivering. "Oh my stars," she gasped, "I'm in the palm of the Crone, she'll surely blow me out like a candle flame and that will be the end of me."

And then the Crone spoke. "Gloria," she said, "Are you special?"

"Ye-es," said Gloria hesitantly.

"Gloria," said the Crone. "Do not lie to me. I ask you again. Do you believe, deep down in your star soul that you are a special star?"

Gloria felt herself enfolded by the voice of the Crone. She looked into her eyes and knew she could not lie. "No," Gloria admitted and wept bitter tears of shame.

"Gloria," said the Crone in a voice of great challenge. "Do you wish to shine with a light of your own and live fully in the glory of your name?" Gloria gazed into the bottomless depths of the eyes of the Crone and saw herself reflected there. It was almost unbearable. But in a clear, small voice she replied, "I wish to shine with a light of my own. I wish to live fully in the glory of my name."

"Then," said the Crone in a voice of deepest compassion, "you must journey the length and breadth of the universe. Dare to enter the void. Explore the black holes you find, for unless you do, you will never know what lies within them and you will always live in fear. When you meet others on their journey, give them what you most desire, allow them their moments to shine. You will weep unquenchable tears, but out of your tears new stars will be born. You will wish to give up many times. You must learn to bear being alone. And most importantly, you must dive into the universe of your own star soul and find the light that flickers there. And when you have found it, you must learn to fan it's flames, and as it grows you will find your true colors. Then you must discover whether you dare to wear them. Do you dare, Gloria? Do you really dare to shine?"

Gloria waited breathlessly as the Crone paused. Did she really want an answer right now? The Crone continued. "You must do this for millions of years, for once you begin along this path in your journey, it never ends, and there is no turning back. I will not promise you that you will become a sun. I will not promise that anyone will ever wish upon you. I will not even promise that you will become a rainbow constellation or a star of wonder or a beacon to steer by. But I do promise that if you choose to embark upon this journey, you go with the blessings and protection of the Constellation of the Crone, and one day, you will realize that you are, indeed, glorious."

The Crone heaved a great sigh for she knew what lay ahead. "Remember one thing, Gloria. The stars are always out, even when they do not appear to be." And with those words, the Crone waved her hand and Gloria floated gently away in a shower of stardust. She blinked and saw only blackness. She turned around, but the Constellation of the Crone had disappeared. With a deep breath, and a heart fluttering with anticipation, she moved slowly out into the blackness.

In *Star Light, Star Bright*, Gloria takes the journey into the unknown universe, fearful that she is unworthy and ordinary. With the help of the old Crone, another incarnation of the old lady in *Puppy-Dung*, she learns that she must be willing to take risks, to confront the empty spaces in the universe and in her heart in order to find her uniqueness. The story of the group is the same—each person feeling alone, fearing obscurity, all needing a nudge toward the void, the empty space where all is possible.

Welcome to the Enchanted Forrest
By Alan Pottinger

Once upon a time, there was a young boy named Asterion who lived in a large castle on a high rocky cliff surrounded on one side by an enchanted forest and on the other by a beautiful deep green sea. The castle was ancient, cold and dark except for the rooms where the boy's family lived. In those rooms at night the fires threw warm shadows on the old stone walls. The boy's father was a powerful king who had lived the violent life of a warrior and had many thrilling adventures. One day when the boy was young, the king his father disappeared. He was not seen actually going into the enchanted forest but it was said that he had sent his raven-black stallion back to the castle as he evaporated into the woods. The king was feared by all the townspeople and had been rumored to be connected with black magic. Some of the villagers swore that he was a werewolf.

The young boy was heartbroken about the sudden and complete absence of his father and climbed high to the tall battlements and looked into the forest day after day hoping to catch a glimpse of him. The queen his mother tried desperately to cheer the child up but after many years, even she concluded that the king was never to return.

One day without any preparation, the boy, much like his father, walked by the edge of the forest and made a conscious decision to become one with it. Asterion did not remember moving his feet or his body at all. He just had the thought and ran wildly through the thick woods.

At first, Asterion loved the life he had in the woods. He lived primitively and carved himself a shelter out of the side of a hill. He built huge bonfires and danced around them far into the night. He partook in all the food that the forest offered and was happy. One day a thought came that since his father was probably still in these woods somewhere, that it was Asterion's duty to go and find him. He searched for many days and became helplessly lost. He no longer saw the forest as a friendly place but as a sort of prison. As he lay down and began to fall asleep after a long day of futile hunting for his father, he heard the lonely chorus of wolves in the night.

When he awoke, he found himself under a bridge below a river that flowed inside the earth. He was surrounded by a host of horrible trolls who had found him sleeping and carried him off to their domain. He was bound and subjected to all manner of abuse and scorn and began to wonder why he had ever left the safety of his home. The trolls were seeking revenge, and told Asterion that he was the son of the wolf-king who had plundered all their treasure many years ago. Moreover, they told him that they would make him suffer for his father's crimes against them.

They decided to let him live but first Asterion had to endure a deep wound over his heart that would give him pain for the rest of his life. They also would affix a mask to his face by the power of the moon that would adhere forever, and if he tried to escape the people on the surface would see him as a hideous monster and forever scorn him.

The trolls took a blazing hot branding iron and burned Asterion's flesh just above his heart as they put on the horrible mask. The pain was so great that Asterion ran screaming out of the troll's lair and into the night where the moon struck the mask and attached it to his face forever.

All the animals of the forest that once were his friends growled at Asterion. The villagers who wandered through the wood pelted him with stones and mud because of the hideous mask on his face. Asterion was lonely beyond compare and spent most of his days hiding. At night on the cold ground, the only solace he had was the songs of the wolves. He thought: "My father is out there and he is safe, but I will never find him and I will never be saved."

One day when Asterion could bear no more pain he walked to the edge of a large pond and decided to drown himself and end his misery. He was about to plunge into the dark water when a giant snail slimy and thick appeared as if by magic and cried: "Stop! Before you end your life, I beg you to help me. The trolls destroyed my life also by turning me in to this horrible snail. The only thing that can break the spell is if I am kissed by a young man who is determined to end his own life."

Asterion looked at the creature and felt pity for its troubles. Since his own life meant nothing to him he asked: "What were you before?"

"I was the oldest, ugliest, foulest woman that ever walked the face of the earth," she replied.

"Did you love your life?" asked Asterion.

"Yes," she replied. "I loved my life very much."

With that, the boy listened to his heart and kissed her. "Then live," he said as he dove into the water. Just as he was sinking to the bottom a pair of strong hands grabbed him and pulled him back up to the surface and he found himself panting at his father's feet. Beside his father, the giant snail had been transformed into a beautiful maiden.

His father said, "I see the trolls have wounded you and that is good. Remove the mask for it will come off now. Because you have cared for the suffering of another at the hour of your death the spell is broken. This is the Lady of the Lake and because you eased her pain, she will guide you through the forest for the rest of your days. You have been spared death because there is much work for you to do. Show your wounds to those who suffer. Allow them to be touched but never allow them to heal completely for then you would be in danger of forgetting."

"But father! I came all this way to get you back! You must return with me!" the young man cried.

"That is not to be, my son, for I am a wolf and with the wolves I must run forever. But do not forget me and the suffering I endure for the sins of my life. Remember me in your prayers and know that I am proud of you."

And so Asterion, now a young man, took hold of the Lady of the Lake's hand, turned from his father for the last time, touched the wound that gave him pain and strode into the woods. The Lady of the Lake said: "Say good-bye now to your father and welcome to the enchanted forest."

Asterion's unfinished business in *Welcome to the Enchanted Forrest* is to find his father and to move on. The Lady of the Lake is his guide. Like Asterion, many in the group had revealed their wounds and masks, inherited from their less than perfect parents. As they were able to safely work through their dark roles and feel the healing touch of strong hands, they prepared to move on. Some, not ready to leave the enchanted forest of the training program, needed more time. Others, having confronted the wolves and trolls, were ready to return home to the everyday world of work and responsibility.

The Rattle
By James V. Tranchida

Once upon a time there lived an old blind woman whose years of life were more significant than her lack of sight. While she was often spoken about she did not speak, at least not in the common way, and she had not been spoken to for a time greater than the combined ages of the village elders. She was, by far, the oldest life in the kingdom and had been for millennia, a fact forgotten shortly before the invention of the written word. In essence, she was an unknown ancient. Had records been kept, the volumes devoted to containing her many names would stack knee-high. Yet no such records existed and none of her names remained in the vernacular of this generation or the one preceding it. So the people of this day referred to her as Cha-Nush, a title which meant Infant-Grandmother—infant for the rattle she clasped with both hands and held snugly to her chest as if to plug some hole, and grandmother for reasons obvious to any passerby.

Newcomers to the village commonly mistook her for one of two things, the first being a statue. Her lack of hair and splotchy beige-brown wrinkled flesh blended perfectly with her tattered garments, beads of wood, walking stick, and sandals; and it was difficult to discern where her form ended and the beige-brown rock, her sitting place, began.

If not a statue, those unaccustomed to seeing Cha-Nush would pause at first glance and think something akin to: "What a strange place for a dead woman, propped up on a rock in the center of the village baking in the sun." Yet, by our standards, she was far from dead. Though deeply furrowed, her flesh lacked decay, and though she sat motionless, one could, at times, catch a glimpse of a trembling in her lower lip which hinted of past words spoken, words which were too powerful for this day and age. Save for the deliberate tremblings of her lower lip, it was difficult to discern whether she was awake or asleep at any given moment. Only when her lip twitched could one be sure she was awake, but no one in the village knew this; nor did they know the sunrise would visit her dreams each morning, moments before it arrived on their horizon; nor did they know the danger of waking her during the dawn of her vision; nor did they know the significance of this particular day.

As Cha-Nush sat on her stone, facing East, with the afternoon sun directly over her knotted head, a child approached, a girl whose years were less than four, who had innocently wandered out of her mother's care by following footprints, or symbols that resembled footprints, in the sand. When the youth was but several feet from the Infant-Grandmother, she paused and took notice of the hunched beige-brown form stemming up from the rock, hands clasped upon a rattle, rattle held against the chest, lower lip gently trembling and eyes sealed. The child looked down and took note of the footprints that remained–three. Three steps put her at the base of the stone, where beige-brown sandals hung from gnarled feet.

As the young life looked up at the old, the sun hung in its place defying the known laws of time. The child stood as motionless as Cha-Nush sat, and their shared world soon filled with sound. From all directions the air vibrated as if all of the kingdom's citizens had taken to shaking rattles. The sounds were of stones inside wood, of seeds inside dried fruit, of heartbeats inside wombs, and at the very moment when this prattle became unbearable, it ceased.

In the pure stillness that followed, in a tomblike silence, the child knelt to examine her destiny. The contents of the ancient's rattle, nine stones, were at her feet; each smooth and each a different pale color. And as Cha-Nush once did far before the invention of the written word, the child selected a stone–pale green–and the sun resumed its path, and the remaining eight stones returned to their rattle; and the young girl's mother died unaware of her daughter's whereabouts; and the ancient's earthy-brown lips, the lower of which sometimes trembled, evolved into a smile.

The next day, prior to sunrise, the child, who had slept in her father's arms holding a pale green rock to her chest, dreamt of dawn. And the day came when the risk to remain tight in a bud hurt more than the risk to blossom.

In *The Rattle* we again find a powerful feminine figure, Cha-Nush, the infant-grandmother. But in this story it is she who needs a guide to complete the unfinished business of awakening. Her guide is a young girl. At the center of the story is a cataclysm, a transcendent vision of the collision of youth and age, life and death. Sometimes a group process ends in a bang not a whimper, the antithesis of T.S. Elliot's poetic image of closure in *The Love Song of J. Alfred Prufrock.*

The Rattle reminds our group that moving on and moving out, ending and closing are difficult and painful, but necessary. Change is the natural order of things-from bud to blossom, from fertilizer to flower, from uncontained brilliance to beacon, from father to son and mother to daughter and back again, repeating the cycle without end. In accepting the pain of the blossom, our group moved toward completing its business.

The Two Nests or Unfinished Business
By Robert J. Landy

A father lived all alone in the woods. His children had long ago gone to the city where they married and had children and built their lives. His wife had died suddenly several years ago and now he tended his garden and contemplated the changes of the seasons and sat down at his desk each morning to compose the small stories that came to him each day. He was well aware that he was near the end of his life. He could feel it in his sleep as he gasped for breath in the night.

His small stories came to him in dreams which he easily remembered from his restless sleep. Each night, dragged from bed by the urgency to urinate, he would scribble the odd images in a pad by his bed. After breakfast, he would decipher the scribbles and choose one to be the centerpiece of his small story.

On one particular day, a dreary October morning, he sat with an uncomfortable image. There were two trees, one much taller than the other. The shorter one was a tulip tree that grew wild on his land. It had shallow roots and bloomed once a year, its flowers the shape of tulips. It was the first kind of tree to fall in a storm. The taller tree was a cedar, with fragrant wood and dark green needles, a proud tree that weathered all storms.

There was a nest in each tree. In his dream, the nests didn't seem to be for birds but a larger animal, one too large for wings. But he could not recall an image of the nest creatures.

The nest in the cedar tree seemed complete. It had a lived-in feeling as if its occupants had gone off for a short sojourn and would soon return. The nest in the tulip tree felt cold as if no one had lived there or visited in a long time.

And so the old man sat down to write his small story which he called "The Two Nests." As he worked, the words poured forth from his dull pencil with ease. When he had finished his small story, he had the need to understand its meaning. He felt sad that he had no one to talk to and so he went out into the chilly October afternoon and approached the two trees.

First he stood by the tulip tree. He was dazzled by its beauty as it was in full blossom in late October, its leaves all gold and orange, red and crimson. He knew that in a week or so it would lose its magnificence. He knew that there was a chance that it would not survive a late autumn storm or a winter blizzard. Looking high up, he said: "My life has been like yours. I've had great moments of beauty and I have blossomed again and again. Sometimes I have questioned whether my blossoms were the real thing. And sometimes I have questioned whether I was rooted firmly enough in the earth. But I endured, building a home and family, even with the fear of exposure and the threat of death hanging over me. And now my nest is empty. There was nothing I could do stop the ones I loved the most from leaving home. I had to let go."

As he spoke, he was surprised to experience a lightness in his body. Something seemed to lift from his shoulders. And so he proceeded to the cedar standing tall just down the hill. He put his hand on the peeling bark and said: "You are so high above me and so far away. I have always aspired to be like you–mighty and steady and invulnerable. You have been a home for all those who left me. They preferred your steadiness and confidence and ease and clarity. I must admit I have hated you at times and envied you terribly. And here I am, also attracted to your marvelous smell, your magnificent skin, your promise of a safe, bustling home. Cedar, cedar, cedar. I am old like you and know that you will outlive me. You always win. And I want you to know that in the time I have left, I will try to find a way to appreciate your place on my land, even as I continue to envy you for all that I lack."

And so the old man returned to his house. He carefully placed his small story in a folder of small stories he left on the left side of his desk. On his way to the kitchen, he had a thought. The title of the small story was wrong. He went back to his desk and lifted the story from the folder. He took up his pencil and crossed out "The Two Nests." Above it he wrote: "Unfinished Business."

The Two Nests completes the theme of change and closure as the old man allows the young to leave the nests and learn to love the twin trees of brief and eternal beauty. In reflecting on the transferential level, I am at the stage in my life when all the elders are passing, some, like my mother, without acknowledging her demise and saying goodbye. In struggling to say goodbye to someone who thinks she is not leaving, I flounder and find it that much harder to finally leave the family nest. On the other side, however, I recognize the powerful connection to my roots, to an old matriarchal family structure that has provided a clear sense of identity and purpose.

Back to the fictional frame, I realize that in writing this story, I was guided by the willingness of the group to trust me as their guide. They are the ones who are leaving and it is my business to acknowledge the death of our process and let them go on their way.

When I finished writing *The Two Nests*, my daughter entered the room and asked me to read the story to her. She enjoyed the story and proceeded to draw two pictures (see Figures 12 and 13). I told her why I had written the story, and she offered to illustrate more. In our collaboration, it became clear to me that I would assemble a book of stories and present the book to my students. It would be called *Unfinished Business*, and it would be illustrated by my daughter (see Figures 14 and 15). It would hold together the three levels of group, family and fairy tale, of present, past and future. It would be a gift to me and from me, a holding on and letting go, an opening and closing. It would be about the greatest paradox of all–the pain of separation and the joy of connection.

Chapter 12

OPEN CABINETS

OPENERS AND CLOSERS

In her late 70s and otherwise a picture of health, my mother was diagnosed with a virulent and aggressive form of cancer. It happened suddenly in the midst of her orderly and predictable life. The most hopeful option seemed to be surgery, and my mother did not hesitate to jump in. Following the long surgical procedure, the doctor summoned the family to a room furnished in a comfortably nondescript fashion. He told us many technical details about the size and location of the tumor without directly revealing the answers to the only questions we cared about: "Was it successful? Would she live? Would she suffer? Would she be able to resume a normal life?" The most optimistic news was that he removed the tumor, but there was another side to his pronouncement. It seemed there was a cloudy image that appeared on the CT-scan, a shadow that he could not reach with his elegant, skilled fingers, a mass hidden behind a bend in the anatomy. Without answering any of the questions that we were afraid to ask, he left the room as mysteriously as he came. His final words were something like: "Let's wait and see the results of the pathology reports in a couple of days."

The pathology reports were not good, but options were presented by various doctors and my mother chose to avail herself of chemotherapy. Slowly and painfully, she proceeded to recover from the worst of the surgery and to diligently take her treatments and plentiful medications. She never complained and took great pains to keep her fears and feelings to herself. There were no tears of self-pity, no bouts of anger. But as the days and weeks passed, her stoicism took a toll. Progressively her hands shook and her mood turned inward. At times she became immobilized, clinging to her bed, unable to eat.

In response to my mother's symptoms, the doctors prescribed more pills. When it was time to invade her body again to determine the extent of the disease, my mother dressed carefully and appeared early at the hospital. After all the tests were in, the doctor called and told me that the cancer had progressed predictably, invading all major organs. She had just a few months left. He advised that my sister or I take her in and care for her. He asked me if I wanted to tell her the news myself. I said yes.

I can easily recall some of the most difficult conversations I have had over the years—reporting the death of my father, breaking up with a lover, expressing shameful feelings I had tried so hard to suppress. At the top of the list was calling my mother to tell her that she was dying. In the culture of our family, we did not speak openly to one another. In conversation around emotionally charged matters, there were often long moments of silence, especially on the part of my mother. As I considered how to present the news, I decided to just jump right in and be as direct as possible, risking the silences and condemnation for violating the rules.

My mother took the news quietly, asking a few perfunctory questions about the doctors and the treatment options. I wasn't sure if she heard me and was almost going to repeat the news, but then caught myself. It was too much to take in and she was not ready. Although all the signs of a recurrence had been present for some weeks, she needed to look the other way. After a few long seconds, I said: "Why don't you move up North and live with us? We'll take care of you." There was no verbal response. Because I could usually read her mind, a talent she taught me early on, I knew her silence signified a resounding "No." My mother chose to live her life as usual in her comfortable apartment within a gated retirement community in Florida, among her friends and few remaining relatives. For her, it was the right choice.

The first time I visited her since the phone call, I noticed significant changes. She had lost a lot of weight and her hands shook even more than before. She could barely contain her morning cup of coffee. It was difficult to get any food down although this reality did not diminish the incessant conversations about food. And one other thing. Every time I would enter the kitchen, I noticed that all the cabinets were open. After my mother would leave the room, I closed them all, feeling a great sense of relief as if I had just reinforced a barrier about to explode under the pressure of a floodtide. My relief would be temporary, because moments later when she again made her entrance for a cup or spoon, she would open the cabinets again.

The jutting edges and asymmetry disturbed me. The kitchen was small and the intrusive cabinet doors presented a minefield of sorts. Despite the dangers of a bruised head and hurt sense of proportion, I never had the heart to ask her to close what she had opened.

The doctor was wrong. My mother had two years left. Each time I visited her over these two years, we would enact the same drama of cabinets, never once deviating from the script, never once commenting upon our roles. She was the opener and I was the closer. This metaphor had a special significance to me because I was a baseball fan and it seemed that my mother would fall into crisis each October during the World Series, not incidentally around the time of my birthday in late October.

In baseball, the opener is the starting pitcher, arguably the most important figure on the team, responsible for making outs through a combination of control and intimidation. When the starting pitcher does well enough to last into the late innings of the game with a slim lead, the closer is called in. At that point, the starter has lost his freshness and is generally spent. It is the closer's job to save the game for the starter by making the final outs. Like the starter, the closer tends to win by a combination of finesse and intimidation, throwing blazing fastballs within an inch of the batter's life. The closer's job is highly specialized and comes with considerable anxiety. He generally only faces a few batters and with every pitch, the game is on the line.

Sometimes the closer is unable to hold a lead and allows the opposing team to score and win the game. When this happens, it is called a blown save. In my mother's house during three post-seasons of cancer and baseball, I tried desperately not to blow the saves.

I was never quite sure what I was trying to save. Death was the name of the game, and my mother was summoned to the Big Show. I couldn't stop the call, that was certain. I could only try to mediate between the physical reality and the spiritual inevitability. After all, I was a therapist by training, someone who knew something about care, about things seminal and terminal. But I was also the son, less skilled in the art of closing, intimidated by the pressure to save the women in my family.

Each time I would try to engage, to open the subject of taking care of unfinished business, of making decisions and sharing feelings, my mother would quickly close the door. And I would wonder—who is the closer? If it was me, I had blown another game. If it was she, she had prevailed, at least on the surface.

There were so many decisions to make, each a potential opening. Should she proceed with chemotherapy? For how long? How should she deal with her depression and loss of appetite? What kind of help should she have in the house? How often should her children be around? Should she engage with them in an emotional way, revealing her fears and her pain? Should she dare utter the lethal words related to her condition—cancer, hospice, death? How comfortable was she in the company of friends? Should she drive alone? Should she travel? Should she reveal the secrets of her will? Her living will? Should she consider the consequences of her will on those who must live with her legacy? Should she consider her legacy on the generations to come? And then, at the end, when all major systems began to fail, should she accept the care of the hospice program? Should she die at home or in the hospice? Who should be with her in her dying?

Over the course of two years, each decision was made silently. She never once articulated her desires. My sister, enmeshed with her, read her mind as always, and did what she wanted. My sister resented my attempts to be direct, feeling betrayed by my desire to speak the dreaded words and lobby for open dialogue and more care by trained professionals who were not blood relatives. On the level of team playing, I often blew save opportunities. In decision-making, it was my sister's will that generally prevailed and like Armando Benitez blowing a save against the Yankees in the 2000 World Series, I felt guilty and angry for letting my team down.

Lear's Legacy

Shakespeare's *King Lear* begins as Lear, the father, summons his three daughters before him to announce the conditions of his will. He is old and ready to retire from the business of being a king. His main asset is his real estate, vast tracks of land scattered throughout his kingdom. Before he divides his kingdom, he gives his daughters a rhetorical test, asking each to articulate the terms of their love for their father. The two daughters least capable of love are most eloquent. The third, Cordelia, sensing the absurdity of such a contest, remains silent. She knows that matters of the heart are best expressed in deeds and feelings. Because Cordelia cannot fulfill the needs of her wrong-headed father, he cuts her out of his will, banishing her from his kingdom. The missed opportunities of father and daughter to recognize the truth of their feelings and move into constructive action leads to tragic consequences. The most tragic of all is the sense of what might have been, a close bond of love between father and daughter, which in the play only occurs at the moment of Lear's awakening to the truth, a time when his daughter has died and he is dying.

Ultimately, Lear's legacy is an emotional and moral one that can be understood on two levels. On the one hand, he leaves an ego-driven sense of competition, pride and entitlement that easily finds its way into villainous acts. This is Lear's legacy of greed that his daughters, Regan and Goneril, inherit and play out to the end, with lethal consequences. On the other hand, Lear leaves the qualities of compassion and love that lie on the other side of greed and covetousness. Cordelia inherits this legacy from her father. After she dies, the Duke of Albany captures its spirit in the final speech of the play:

The weight of this sad time we must obey;
Speak what we feel, not what we ought to say.

It was the intent of Lear, the father, to divide his estate equally, but pride and confused feelings got in the way. When my father made out his will, he did not test the love of my sister and I. He made it clear that whatever he had left would be divided equally. My mother made her will at the same time, with the same stipulations. But over time, as my father died and my sister and I found our different ways in life, my mother changed her will secretly, leaving most to my sister. As she lay dying, I summoned up the courage to ask my mother for copies of her will and living will, assuming that they were the same that had been executed years before. She responded in silence. I knew something was wrong. When I pushed for more information she shamefully admitted the inequality. That was all she said. Up to the end, my mother never showed me any of the papers and never elaborated upon her wishes regarding her death and legacy. It was up to me to either read her mind, search for the papers myself or hope they turned up after she died.

A prominent estate lawyer once said: "Anyone who does not divide her estate equally among her children leaves a legacy of cancer." I experienced a toxic jolt when receiving my mother's news, and I knew that it would take more than chemotherapy and radiation to beat this disease. My mother came from a modest working class family that was exceptionally close with several generations living together and taking care of one another for many years. It was a large family, a matriarchy, led by strong, silent women. The family was everything to everybody. When one person fell down, others were sure to follow, like dominoes. The family was a world onto itself and outsiders were suspect at best. In their small city life, the family recapitulated the culture from which they came, that of shtetl existence in small town Poland during the pogroms preceding the Nazi holocaust.

As the younger ones married and moved to the suburbs and eventually, as the elders passed away, things changed. The death of the final elders, the only ones who ever managed to build up an estate, was marked by an odd will that unequally distributed the last of the family's wealth. A younger sister was favored over an older brother. Whole family units were passed over in favor of others. Some in the family spent months debating the betrayal of the elders, venting in anger, hiring a lawyer—all futile exercises. The will held and a seemingly new family legacy reared its ugly head. For the insecure, this was a statement about deserving and undeserving souls, about worth and unworthiness, about the chosen and the despised.

Having passed through this dark phase of my family history, it was particularly shocking to discover that my mother had done the same as her old aunt and uncle, the last remaining elders of a long line. When I finally confronted her with this fact, she shut down. There was no verbal response possible. The cognitive dissonance was too overwhelming. How could such a good and loving family, a good and loving mother divide her property so inequitably? There was no answer. It was not about love. It was not the quandary of Lear who needed assurance that his most beloved loved him equally. It was about confused feelings and the inability to articulate them.

In one burst of language, uncharacteristic of my mother, she said: "Who will take care of your sister? She needs the money more."

"Why?" I asked. "She has a secure job and has only herself to support." The only response I could get came to me in my head. It was Lear's voice and he said: "Reason not the need." "Don't I have needs, too?" I asked Lear, "all the years deferring to the needs of my sister, pretending I needed nothing!" Again in my mind, the wise king responded: "Nothing will come of nothing."

Lear was right. It was my time and I needed something, as unreasonable as that seemed. I was the closer. I was determined, if not to save the women, the starters, then to save myself. My goal was, paradoxically, to close and to remain open.

The Witness

How is it possible to stay open when you close, especially if the closure is a death? For years I had worked on developing distancing theory appropriate for drama therapy (Landy, 1983, 1994, 1996a), explaining the needs of clients and therapists alike to discover a balanced point between too much feeling and too much thought. I knew in this journey toward closing with my mother, I needed to find a point of balance so that I could effectively say goodbye without silencing my feelings, without raging against the silent demands that I could never satisfy. Freud posed a similar paradox—how is it possible to become aware of deeply repressed feelings if the reason you repress them is because they are too frightening to bring to awareness? In other words, how is it possible to be open to that which you have closed? In Freud's case, the answer lies in the transferential relationship, where the client treats the therapist as if he were the object of the repression. In drama therapy terms, the client works through more overt distance, taking on a role and projecting aspects of the repressed feelings onto the role. As she engages in role, she is aware that the role is part of her and that she is capable of disengaging and reflecting upon her actions in role. Thus, she becomes both actor and observer, me and not me, at the same time. With this dual consciousness, she is able to resolve the paradox of repression.

In looking for a way to resolve my dilemma of becoming the closer who is open, I searched for the appropriate distance. At some point, near the end, I discovered it through a role which I could only name much later. It is called the witness. It is a place of aesthetically balanced distance where one has the ability to clearly see what is happening and to see it dispassionately. And it is a place not only of clarity, but also of connection. When fully present as a witness, one is able, in the words of King Lear, to see feelingly. Thus the witness is dispassionate in the ability to perceive but compassionate in the ability to receive.

Shortly before my mother got sick, I visited her in Florida, without my family. I wanted to find a way to be with her in peace, without succumbing to the silences. As long as we had plans and kept on the move, we were fine. As long as we kept to the rituals of TV, food preparation and consumption, we were fine. As long as our conversation did not stray from the weather and the menus and the kids' health, we were fine. It felt good and safe to engage on this level, but whenever any subject arose that was difficult or foreign, silence reigned and I shut down, a beat behind my mother. When I returned home, I felt tense and irritable, as I always did whenever I returned from a visit to my parents in the past, with or without my significant others.

On the one hand, I was too distant, fearing an engagement that would entangle me in a web of guilt and shame for being unable to read my mother's pain and take it away. On the other hand, I was too close to an awareness of my mother's silent power and my dread of confronting it. And so I shut down even as I blamed myself for doing so. In the role of the closed one, I could not see clearly and I could not connect. I would easily lose my way. And so I didn't feel closed at all. In fact I felt too open and vulnerable, and I longed for balance. I needed a guide but on my mother's turf, especially in her final years in Florida, all those available seemed cut from the same cloth. They were the old men sitting around the pool debating for hours whether or not famous celebrities past and present were secretly Jewish. They were the women on the golf course and in the card room who filled each day of their lives with activities in a valiant attempt to stave off the fatal diseases that moved ever closer to their doors.

I went down to Florida the day of my mother's surgery. My sister had been there for several days, needing my mother's reassurance that all would be well. We all went to the hospital together, a very heavy trio. I remember my mother joking with the nurses and attendants, trying to lighten them up. They loved her. For a moment I saw her through the eyes of the witness. It was a revelation to watch her work the room. But then the sadness kicked in, left over from years of heaviness in the home. And just like that the witness was gone.

When I first saw my mother in the critical care unit, she was all hooked up, a gastro-nasal tube holding her insides together and blocking her ability to speak. She looked so old and sad in her immobility. I rarely ever touched my mother, but I followed my impulse and stroked her fingers and forehead. I told her that she did well, that the operation was successful, that she would get better. She looked up at me, struggling against the morphine and demerol in her blood to keep her eyes focused. For once I felt that she wanted to tell me something and I tried so hard to be a witness. Before she drifted off, her eyes grew watery as she fixed her gaze squarely on my face which might have been at peace.

Unfinished Business

At some point near the end, I ceased my attempts to close up everything. I had already gone through the files when my mother was asleep and found the important papers. I had already procured the service of around the clock home care workers. I had already logged in hundreds of hours on the phone with the doctors, soaking up any and all advice and options. I had already made arrangements for the funeral. The more I did, however, the more remained to be done, and I needed to let go.

Toward the end, there were many crises as my mother's body shut down, one system after another. There were more decisions to be made concerning her care and companionship. My birthday was coming up and I decided to celebrate at home, with my family. I would go down to be with my mother early in October this time, just before the most austere holy day in the Jewish calendar, Yom Kippur, the Day of Atonement. When I arrived, she was very weak. The doctor saw no reason to continue the chemotherapy. She could no longer eat and just wanted to sleep all day. I managed to bring her to the emergency room of the hospital one last time and they hydrated her intravenously. I sat with her in the treatment room as she attempted to lighten up the dour doctor palpating her abdomen.

"It's funny," she said. "I always fasted on Yom Kippur and here you are giving me supper." But she was too weak to pull off the punch line and he was too busy to respond. I took it all in, witnessing everything. Time passed very slowly that day, as it always does in hospitals. Oddly, a line from a poem by John Milton passed through my mind: "They also serve who only stand and wait."

The hospital staff eventually admitted my mother and she shared a room with a young woman who had trouble bringing her pregnancy to full term.

She had many visitors and my mother had me. I watched the end of the last playoff game between the Mets and the Giants. My mother slept soundly, nourished by her IV fluid.

When I left the room, my mother was still asleep. It was warm and breezy in early October. The ocean was across the street from the hospital and I took a long walk on the path as the sky grew dark. All was very still until I came upon a synagogue, bustling with congregants. Suddenly I remembered that it was the end of the Day of Atonement and the worshippers were concluding their long day of prayers, preparing to return home to break the fast of 24 hours. When I was young, my mother always prepared a traditional meal on this night of pickled herring, scrambled eggs and boiled potatoes. She would break the fast with a shot of scotch, I with a glass of orange juice. Since my father was disinterested in the Jewish rituals, my mother and I shared a deep connection on the holidays which was more familial and sentimental than spiritual. We believed, as my grandfather told us, that on Yom Kippur God would seal the fate of all human beings. On this day, it would be determined who would live and who would die.

The next day I brought my mother home. She did not want to stay in the hospital and there was nothing more they could do for her. She was exhausted and stayed in bed most of the day. In the evening we watched a little TV together. The IV fluids did little to affect her energy or her appetite. She watched me eat my take-out dinner and no longer pretended to sample the food. We spoke very little. Finally, she announced that it was time for bed, and I reminded her that I was leaving very early the next morning. She asked me to wake her to say goodbye. I told her I would.

As my mother settled into bed, I wandered into the kitchen. All the cabinet doors were closed. They had been closed as long as I was with her.

The taxi arrived early to pick me up the next morning. I slept very poorly. Before I left, I tiptoed into my mother's room. She was curled up like a kitten, sound asleep. I bent over and kissed her and said goodbye. I told her I loved her, words I had only recently learned to say to my mother. She didn't respond at all. She slept peacefully through my leaving.

When I returned home, I was well aware that the next shift of relatives and health care workers would be the ones to shepherd my mother to the other side. And I felt at peace, somehow, the kind of peace that comes from taking care of unfinished business. The cabinets were closed and I was not the closer. There were no more saves to blow.

Termination

Goodbyes in my family lasted forever. After a holiday dinner I can recall

10 minute goodbyes, 20 minutes, even half hour goodbyes when we would all stand in the doorway of my grandmother's second floor apartment and begin conversations we should have had hours ago when we had plenty of time. But then again, they were often conversations like all others, about nothing really, or they were conversations the adults never really wanted to have at all. My father would pace and eventually excuse himself to smoke a cigarette in the fresh air. My stomach would churn and I would feel trapped. Why can't these people talk? I screamed inside. I want to go home!

Then, when we all got into our car and my father quickly jammed the key into the ignition, my mother would make him shut down the engine, and we would all look up to the second story window and wave to all the relatives behind the dusty windows, looking after us. And then, finally, waved out, we would fight the holiday traffic home. Once there, feeling safe, the phone would always ring, as if the elders could see us arriving from their windows across the river, far, far away. And in the last family ritual of the day, my mother would speak to her mother for what seemed to me like hours in sounds rather than words about nothing.

One way of looking at growing up is as a loss. A very powerful one to me was the loss of the women—my great-grandmother, my grandmother, her two twin sisters, my mother. Each one was a rent in the family fabric. Each one felt monumental to those who remained. And yet the others picked up and went about their business, even though they never said goodbye and they never let go. My grandmother told me that she continued to speak to her mother, and after the death of my grandmother, my mother told me the same. Maybe this was like the moments of non-conversation at the door when we attempted to leave after the Passover seder, or like the long phone calls when arriving home, both of which, to the uninitiated listener, seemed to be about nothing. What did they speak about, these women, standing at the door, on the phone, at the grave? In my memory, it was always about the traffic, the weather, the kids, the recipes, the small rheumatic aches of the body, the phone calls made and received, the price of coffee. Didn't they know my father was pacing the street, chain-smoking, that my stomach was churning? Didn't they know people were dying and important matters needed to be discussed? Didn't they know that God was sitting up in heaven with his Book of Life, judging, witnessing all? Where was the will? Where was the love? The care? Where was the important conversation, the words that would tip the scales of love and fortune? Why couldn't they heed the weight of this sad time? Why couldn't they speak what they feel, not what they ought to say? Didn't they know that nothing will come of nothing?

My mother was part of a long line of women who had no use for existential questions. They were too busy taking care of the details of existence. They were strong, stoic, solid. Death was another episode that called for action, not contemplation. They had no interest in saying goodbye. Each day was pretty much the same as the one before. Where were they going?

When I went down to Florida during the last months of my mother's life, people would ask me whether I had said goodbye. I would answer, "How can you say goodbye to someone who is not leaving?" But I knew I was being disingenuous. She knew she was dying, despite the fact that in the last week of her life, too weak to sign her name, she had her helper sign a check for a yearly membership in a golf club. She knew she was dying, even though she would tell her friends that she would soon return to the Wednesday afternoon card games. She knew she was dying, even though she couldn't say goodbye to her children. Why should her dying be different from her living? She could never say goodbye. She had no need for a closure, a termination. For my mother, like her mother and grandmother before her, life was an open cabinet that no one had the right to close.

My sister remained with my mother for the last weeks of her life. She pleaded with me to come down and see her before she died. I was adamant about staying home. I had the fantasy of the women taking care of the final passage. And in my stomach, I held the anger and guilt of the men who felt forced to take care of the women in silence, to tend to all of the external details, to take away their pain even as they denied that they were in pain. I didn't want the anger any more. I wanted to feel that I was a good and loving son, that the goodbye I had experienced on Yom Kippur was real and was enough. And so I resisted my sister's intense pain and pressure.

At the very end, however, something opened in me. My phone conversations with my mother were very brief. Her ability to focus was severely impaired, but she would hear my voice and perk up, waiting for the punch line, the one that would always come from me: "I love you." The tension I had been holding in my body began to ease. My mother was in the hospice, finally. It was the last stop. Agitated one morning, I called the hospice and spoke to the doctor. I changed my mind. I would come down once more. It wasn't exactly a save opportunity. It felt more like another opening. The doctor told me her passing was imminent and I raced down.

The hospice was an oasis in a depressed neighborhood. It was late at night. My plane was delayed. I had to sign in at the desk and I was ushered to a corner room. As I entered the open door, I noticed that the lights were all on and that two women were at the head of the bed, absorbed in their work. At first I thought they were changing my mother's gown or helping her shift her position in the bed. Maybe she was trying to tell them a funny story, to ease their discomfort. They looked startled at my sudden appearance so late at night. I wanted to apologize for my intrusion, but before I could do so, they both stared at me, silently, communicating the news before the words emerged: "She just passed. Five minutes ago." They asked me if I wanted to stay with her in the room alone. I said yes. They told me to take my time.

My mother looked younger somehow, frailer than she was when I last saw her. Her eyes were opened. My sister had told me that since she arrived at the hospice, she would sleep with her eyes open, afraid that if she closed them, she would disappear. I held her hand for a moment and then just sat there alongside the bed. I thought: What if the plane came in on time and I had arrived five minutes before she died and could have held her hand as the blood circulated in her veins and could have let her know that I was present? Would it have mattered to her? to me? Would I have been a better son? Would I have felt more closed with her? I let these thoughts pass through and they were quickly gone. I sat for a while, sometimes looking at my mother, sometimes averting my glance. My mother passed. There was nothing much to say. I stayed present and then I left. There was work to be done.

Throughout our lives together, my mother and I spoke in the language of the family–through images of events and details with few attempts to penetrate the surface or revert to a language of feeling. At the funeral, many people praised my mother for her courage, her strength, her dedication and love for her family and friends. My sister was most effusive in her heartfelt words of adulation, of deep attachment and painful loss. I thought long and hard about my speech. I wanted it to be in the language that was hers and ours together, and yet I wanted it to be in my voice as well, separate from her.

My eulogy was not spontaneous. I rehearsed it several times in my mind, watching myself speaking the speech to the small crowd huddled around the open grave. But at the end, I spoke to my mother directly. I told her at the graveside that I had eaten a good breakfast. I enumerated the food I had consumed. I told her my children were well and that the weather was much too cold for this time of year. And I spoke the words I had learned to say all by myself in the last months of my mother's life. They were underneath the surface all the time and I just didn't get it. They were the magic words that needed to be spoken if a closer really wanted to close in a way that felt open. They were the words that Cordelia couldn't say directly to her father. They were the words that if spoken from the heart in the end point to endless beginnings. "I love you," I said to my mother at her funeral. It was a goodbye and it was a hello.

REFERENCES

Artaud, A. *The Theatre and Its Double.* New York: Grove, 1958.

Berger, J., et. al. *Ways of Seeing.* London: BBC and Viking Penguin, 1973.

Blatner, A. Pyschodrama—The state of the art, *The Arts in Psychotherapy, 24:* 23–30, 1997.

Blofeld, J. *Taoism, The Road to Immortality.* Boston: Shambhala, 1985.

Bloom, B, et. al. *Taxonomy of Educational Objectives, Handbook I: Cognitive Domain.* New York: David McKay, 1956.

Boal, A. *The Rainbow of Desire.* London and New York: Routledge, 1995.

Brecht, S. *The Bread and Puppet Theatre,* 2 volumes, New York: Routledge, 1988.

Brissett, D. and Edgley, C., Eds. *Life as Theatre: A dramaturgical sourcebook.* Chicago: Aldine, 1975.

Brokett, O. *The Essential Theatre,* 5th ed., New York: Harcourt Brace Jovanovich, 1992.

Brook, P. *The Empty Space.* New York: Macmillan, 1978.

Campbell, J. *The Hero with a Thousand Faces.* New York: Pantheon Books, 1949.

Capra, F. *The Tao of Physics.* Boston: Shambhala, 1975.

Casson, J. Archetypal splitting: Drama therapy and psychodrama. *The Arts in Psychotherapy, 23,* 307–310, 1996.

Cattanach, A. *Playtherapy with Abused Children.* London: Jessica Kingsley, 1993.

Cattanach, A. *Playtherapy—Where the sky meets the underworld.* London: Jessica Kingsley, 1994.

Cattanach, A. *Children's Stories in Playtherapy.* London: Jessica Kingsley, 1997.

Chung, M. *Mending the Sky: The Bread and Puppet Theatre in Taiwan.* Taipei: Executive Yuan, 1995.

Cole, D. *The Theatrical Event.* Middletown, CT: Wesleyan University Press, 1975.

Cooley, C. *Human Nature and Social Order.* New York: Scribner's, 1922.

Courtney, R. Islands of remorse: Amerindian education in the contemporary world, *Curriculum Inquiry, 16,* 43–64, 1986.

Cox, M., and Theilgaard, A. *Shakespeare as Prompter—The amending imagination and the therapeutic process.* London: Jessica Kingsley, 1994.

Cox, M., Ed. *Shakespeare Comes to Broadmoor.* London: Jessica Kingsley, 1992.

Dokter, D., Ed. *Arts Therapies and Clients with Eating Disorders: Fragile board.* London: Jessica Kingsley, 1994.

Dunne, P. *The Narrative Therapist and the Arts.* Los Angeles: Possibilities Press, 1992.

Eliaz, E. *Transference in Drama Therapy,* Ph.D. dissertation, New York University, 1988.

Emunah, R. *Acting for Real—Drama therapy process, technique, and performance.* New York: Brunner/Mazel, 1994.

Evans, B. *Shakespeare's Comedies.* London: Oxford University Press, 1967.

Evreinov, N. *The Theatre of Life.* New York: Harrap, 1927.

Fistos, J. *Role Call: The development of a card sort assessment based on the role method of drama therapy,* MA thesis, New York University, 1996.

Forrester, A. Role-playing and dramatic improvisation as an assessment tool. *The Arts in Psychotherapy, 27,* 235–243, 2000.

Fox, J. *Acts of Service—Spontaneity, commitment, tradition in the nonscripted theatre.* New York: Tusitala Publishing, 1994.

Fox, J. A step in the right direction. *The Arts in Psychotherapy, 23,* 197–198, 1996.

Fox, J., Ed. *The Essential Moreno*, New York , Springer, 1987.

Gersie, A. *Storymaking in Bereavement.* London: Jessica Kingsley, 1991.

Gersie, A. *Earth Tales.* London: Green Press, 1992.

Gersie, A. *Reflections on Therapeutic Storymaking.* London: Jessica Kingsley, 1997.

Gersie, A. and King, N. *Storymaking in Education and Therapy.* London: Jessica Kingsley, 1990.

Goffman, E. *The Presentation of Self in Everyday Life.* Garden City, New York: Doubleday, 1959.

Grainger, R. *Drama and Healing: The roots of dramatherapy.* London: Jessica Kingsley, 1990.

Grainger, R. *The Glass of Heaven–The faith of the dramatherapist.* London: Jessica Kingsley, 1995.

Grotowski, J. *Towards a Poor Theatre.* New York: Simon and Schuster, 1968.

Heider, J. *The Tao of Leadership.* New York: Bantam, 1986.

Hillman, J. *Healing Fiction.* Barrytown, New York: Station Hill, 1983.

Hug, E. Current trends in psychodrama–Eclectic and analytic dimensions, *The Arts in Psychotherapy, 24,* 31–35, 1997.

Irwin, E. Puppets in therapy: An assessment procedure, *American Journal of Psychotherapy, 39,* 389–400, 1985.

Irwin, E., Levy, P., and Shapiro, M. Assessment of drama therapy in a child guidance center. *Group Psychotherapy and Psychodrama, 25,* 105–116, 1972.

Jackins, H. *The Human Side of Human Beings.* Seattle: Rational Island, 1965.

James, W. *The Principles of Psychology.* New York: Dover, 1890/1950.

Jennings, S. *Remedial Drama.* London: Pitman, 1973.

Jennings, S., Ed. *Dramatherapy, Theory and Practice for Teachers and Clinicians,* Vol. 1. London: Routledge, 1987.

Jennings, S., Ed. *Dramatherapy with Children and Adolescents.* London: Routledge, 1995.

Jennings, S. *Theatre, Ritual and Transformation: The Temiar experience.* London: Routledge, 1995a.

Johnson, D.R. Principles and techniques of drama therapy. *The Arts in Psychotherapy, 9,* 83–90, 1982.

Johnson, D.R. The diagnostic role-playing test. *The Arts in Psychotherapy, 15,* 23–36, 1988.

Johnson, D.R. The theory and technique of transformations in drama therapy. *The Arts in Psychotherapy, 18,* 285–300. 1991.

Johnson, D.R. and Quinlan, D. Representational boundaries in role portrayals among paranoid and nonparanoid schizophrenic patients. *Journal of Abnormal Psychology, 94,* 498–506, 1985.

Johnson, D.R., Forrester, A., Dintino, C., James, M. Towards a poor drama therapy. *The Arts in Psychotherapy, 23,* 293–306. 1996.

Jones, P. *Drama as Therapy, Theatre as living.* London: Routledge, 1996.

Jung, C.G. *Man and His Symbols.* Garden City, New York: Doubleday, 1964.

Jung, C.G. *Psychological Types.* Princeton: Princeton University Press, 1971.

Junge, M., and Linesch, D. Our own voices: New paradigms for art therapy research, *The Arts in Psychotherapy, 20,* 61–67, 1993.

Kedem-Tahar, E., and Felix-Kellermann, P. Psychodrama and drama therapy: A comparison. *The Arts in Psychotherapy, 23,* 27–36, 1996.

Kelly, G.A. *The Psychology of Personal Constructs.* Vol. I. New York: Norton, 1955.

Kirby, E.T. *Ur-drama: The origins of theatre.* New York: New York University Press, 1975.

Landy, R. Training the drama therapist–A four-part model. *The Arts in Psychotherapy, 9,* 91–99, 1982.

Landy, R. *Handbook of Educational Drama and Theatre.* Westport, CT: Greenwood, 1982a.

Landy, R. The use of distancing in drama therapy. *The Arts in Psychotherapy, 10,* 175–185, 1983.

Landy, R. Conceptual and methodological issues of research in drama therapy. *The Arts in Psychotherapy, 11,* 89–100, 1984.

Landy, R. *Persona and Performance–The meaning of role in drama, therapy and everyday life.* New York: Guilford, 1993.

Landy, R. *Drama Therapy: Concepts, theories and practices,* 2nd edition. Springfield, IL: Charles C. Thomas, 1994.

Landy, R. Three scenarios on the future of drama therapy, *The Arts in Psychotherapy, 21,* 179–184. 1994a.

Landy, R. *Essays in Drama Therapy: The double life.* London: Jessica Kingsley, 1996.

Landy, R. Drama therapy and distancing: reflections on theory and clinical application. *The Arts in Psychotherapy 23*, 367–373, 1996a.

Landy, R. *In search of the muse*, In *Essays in Drama Therapy: The double life*. London: Jessica Kingsley, 1996b.

Landy, R. Drama therapy–The state of the art, *The Arts in Psychotherapy, 24*, 5–15. 1997.

Landy, R. Role Profiles, unpublished assessment instrument, 1997, 1998, 2000.

Landy, R. Tell-A-Story, unpublished assessment instrument, 1998a.

Landy, R. The role model of supervision. In Tselikas-Portmann, E., Ed. *Supervision and Dramatherapy*. London: Jessica Kingsley, 1999.

Landy, R. Role theory and the role method of drama therapy. In Lewis, P. and Johnson, D.R., Eds. *Current Approaches in Drama Therapy*. Springfield, IL: Charles C. Thomas, 2000.

Landy, R. *How We See God and Why It Matters*. Springfield, IL: Charles C Thomas, 2001.

Landy, R. *God Lives in Glass*. Boston: SkyLight Paths, 2001.

Langley, D. The relationship between psychodrama and dramatherapy, in Jones, P., Ed. *Dramatherapy: State of the Art*. St. Albans: Hertforshire College of Art and Design, 1989.

Lewis, P. and Johnson, D.R., Eds. *Current approaches in drama therapy*. Springfield, IL: Charles C Thomas, 2000.

Lynn, R., trans. *The Classic of Changes*. New York: Columbia University Press, 1994.

Mead, G.H. *Mind, Self and Society*. Chicago: University of Chicago Press, 1934.

Mitchell, S. *Tao Te Ching*. New York: HarperCollins, 1988.

Mitchell, S., Ed. *Dramatherapy–Clinical studies*. London: Jessica Kingsley, 1996.

Moffett, J. *Teaching the Universe of Discourse*. New York: Houghton Mifflin, 1968.

Mooney, P. *Taiwan–Treasure Island*. Lincolnwood, IL: Passport Books, 1993.

Moreno, J.L. *Psychodrama*. Beacon, New York: Beacon House, 1946.

Moreno, J.L. *The Theatre of Spontaneity*. Beacon, New York: Beacon House, 1947.

Moreno, J.L., Ed. *The Sociometry Reader*. Glencoe, IL: The Free Press, 1960.

Murray, H. *Explorations in Personality*. New York: Oxford, 1938.

Pearson, C. *The Hero Within*. New York: HarperCollins, 1989.

Pearson, J., Ed. *Discovering the Self through Drama and Movement*. London: Jessica Kingsley, 1996.

Petzold, H. *Gestalttherapie und Psychodrama*. Nicol: Kassel, 1973.

Portine, A. *The Process of Creating and Refining a Projective Role Assessment Test in Drama Therapy*, MA thesis, New York University, 1998.

Raz, S. *Psychological Type and Changing Acting Personas–A hypothetical model of role theory in role acquisition among performing artists*. Ph.D. dissertation, Miami Institute of Psychology, 1997.

Riso, D. *Personality Types*. Boston: Houghton Mifflin, 1987.

Rosenberg, Y. *Role Theory and Self Concept*, MA thesis, Lesley College, Israel, 1999.

Roth, P. *Operation Shylock*. New York: Simon and Schuster, 1993.

Salas, J. *Improvising Real Life–Personal story in playback theatre*. Dubuque, IA: Kendall/Hunt, 1993.

Sarbin, T. and V. Allen. Role theory, In Lindzey, G. and E. Aronson, Eds. *The Handbook of Social Psychology*, 2nd ed. Reading, MA: Addison-Wesley, 1968.

Schechner, R. *Between Theatre and Anthropology*. Philadelphia: University of Pennsylvania Press, 1985.

Scheff, T. *Catharsis in Healing, Ritual and Drama*. Berkeley: University of California, 1979.

Scheff, T. The distancing of emotion in psychotherapy. *Psychotherapy: Theory, research and practice, 18*, 46–53, 1981.

Scheiffele, E. *The Theatre of Truth*. Ph.D. dissertation, University of California, Berkeley: 1995.

Schnee, G. Drama therapy in the treatment of the homeless mentally ill. *The Arts in Psychotherapy, 23*, 53–60, 1996.

Schutzman, M. and Cohen-Cruz, J., Eds. *Playing Boal: Theatre, therapy, activism*. New York: Routledge, 1994.

Seitz, P. *Drama Therapy Storytelling Assessment: A comparison of mentally ill and normal neurotic stories*. MA thesis, New York University, 2000.

Serafica, F. *Social-Cognitive Development in Context*. New York: Guilford Press, 1982.

Slade, P. *Child Drama.* London: University Press, 1954.

Slade, P. *Dramatherapy as an Aid to Becoming a Person.* London: Guild of Pastoral Psychology, 1959.

Smith, H. *The Religions of Man.* New York: Mentor Books, 1962.

Snow, S. Fruit of the same tree: A response to Kedem-Tahar and Kellermann's comparison of psychodrama and drama therapy. *The Arts in Psychotherapy, 23,* 199–206, 1996.

Solomon, A. On each palette, a choice of political colors. *The New York Times, 29,* August 4, 1996.

Stanislavski, C. *An Actor Prepares.* New York: Theatre Arts, 1936.

Sternberg, P. And Garcia, A. *Sociodrama–Who's in your shoes?* Westport, CT: Praeger, 1989.

Sussman, F. *Application of Role Theory and Myth to Adult Schizophrenics in a Continuing Day Treatment Program,* MA thesis, New York University, 1998.

Tangorra, J. *Many Masks of Pedophilia: Drama therapeutic assessment of the pedophile,* MA thesis, New York University, 1997.

Wilder, R. and Weisberg, N. *Creative Arts with Older Adults: A sourcebook.* Norwell, MA: Kluwer Academic, 1984.

Willett, J., Ed. *Brecht on Theatre.* New York: Hill and Wang, 1964.

Winnicott, D.W. *Playing and Reality.* London: Tavistock, 1971.

AUTHOR INDEX

225

Kendall, 130
King, A., 7
Kirby, E. T., 5

L

Landy, R., viiii, ix, 10–12, 15–17, 36, 41, 43, 44,
    47, 57, 66, 75, 130, 136, 172, 177, 214
Langley, D., 8
Lewis, P., viii
Lindkvist, M., 7
Linesch, D., 10
Linton, R., 29

M

McReynolds, 130
Mead, G. H., 29
Mitchell, S., 10, 11, 13, 80, 84, 89
Moffett, J., 32
Moreno, J. L., 6, 24, 29, 58, 130

P

Pearson, C., 7
Petzold, H., 6
Portine, A., 144

Q

Quinlan, D., 10

R

Raz, S., 16, 39, 144
Rosenberg, Y., 39
Roth, P., 23

S

Salas, J., 69
Sarbin, T., 29
Schechner, R., 24, 59
Scheff, T., 57, 58
Schieffele, E., 6
Schnee, G., 10
Schutzman, M., 69
Seitz, P., 130
Serafica, F., 47
Slade, P., 7
Smith, H., 72
Snow, S., 15
Solomon, A., 73
Stanislavski, C., 24
Sternberg, P., 9
Sussman, F., 46
Sykes, J., 191

T

Tangorra, J., 39, 144, 147
Theilgaard, 11

W

Weisberg, N., 9
Wilder, R., 9
Willett, J., 24, 59, 81
Winnicott, D. W., 92, 181

SUBJECT INDEX